Decision Intelligence

by Pam Baker

for
dummies®
A Wiley Brand

Decision Intelligence For Dummies®

Published by: **John Wiley & Sons, Inc.**, 111 River Street, Hoboken, NJ 07030-5774, www.wiley.com

Copyright © 2022 by John Wiley & Sons, Inc., Hoboken, New Jersey

Published simultaneously in Canada

For general information on our other products and services, please contact our Customer Care Department within the U.S. at 877-762-2974, outside the U.S. at 317-572-3993, or fax 317-572-4002. For technical support, please visit https://hub.wiley.com/community/support/dummies.

Wiley publishes in a variety of print and electronic formats and by print-on-demand. Some material included with standard print versions of this book may not be included in e-books or in print-on-demand. If this book refers to media such as a CD or DVD that is not included in the version you purchased, you may download this material at http://booksupport.wiley.com. For more information about Wiley products, visit www.wiley.com.

Library of Congress Control Number: 2021952522

ISBN: 978-1-119-82484-8 (pbk); 978-1-119-82485-5 (ebk); 978-1-119-82486-2 (ebk)

SKY10032207_122921

Contents at a Glance

Table of Contents

Introduction

Ready for a mind-blowing reveal on how to make great decisions, whether you're using your own brain or some supercharged artificial intelligence application? *Decision intelligence,* a methodology for forming a decision aimed at achieving a specific outcome, is here, and it's on track to change forever how businesses plan for their future.

Everybody would agree that the goal in all decision-making is to reap the best possible outcome. Decision intelligence helps you achieve that goal by requiring that you decide that outcome first and then work backward from there to identify the processes and information you'll need to make it happen!

Decision intelligence is built on science — several sciences, actually — but some of those scientific formulas can be grasped intuitively. The decision intelligence process is designed to improve your professional performance by a) ensuring that every business decision delivers the best possible outcome, b) pointing you toward innovations that are profitable, c) helping you become an industry mover by becoming a creative disruptor, and d) enabling you to flip failed AI projects into successful endeavors. What's more, decision intelligence can also be used to improve your private life via better decision-making, and you can often do it in your own head or on the back of a napkin or by using a simple table or spreadsheet.

The secret to success in decision intelligence lies in changing how you think about problem-solving and reordering your steps when it comes to the decision-making process. Ask yourself how much money, time, and effort your organization is willing to waste on yet another bad business decision or one more failed AI project, and then ask yourself whether you can afford to ignore a better way to make decisions — especially when you already have on hand much of what you'll need to take advantage of a decision intelligence approach. It's not often that you can turn your business around at little or no additional cost to you.

About This Book

The book you're holding in your hands is a guide primarily for you if you're a business or finance leader. The book aims to fill you in on decision intelligence, a new framework for making better, more profitable business decisions. It also serves as an introduction for artificial intelligence (AI) and digital decisioning practitioners to take a different approach aimed at making automated decision processes deliver desirable business outcomes. To top it all off, this guide shows you that decision intelligence is not merely a business approach — it's equally useful when making decisions about your personal life.

This book takes a studied approach to having you reimagine the decision-making, by focusing on a set of discrete tasks you need to accomplish. Here are those tasks, in no particular order:

>> **Flip the data mining model from data first to data last.** You start with a decision aimed at the best possible business outcome and end with the data and the processes you need to bring about that outcome in the real world.

>> **Rebalance human and machine roles.** Decision intelligence calls for a redirection from a data driven to a decision driven organization. This framework clearly casts humans as decision-makers, where AI acts as sidekick, and where data is relegated to a supporting actor.

>> **Map changes caused by putting the decision first in terms of**

- *Business impact*
- *Processes*
- *Tools*
- *Business and Ethical Principles*
- *Teams*

>> **Learn decision theory and a multidisciplinary approach to decision-making:** You learn which steps you must take in order to succeed with decision intelligence, from new perspectives on

- *Business impact*
- *AI projects*
- *Upstream and downstream decisioning*
- *Disruptive innovation*
- *Job roles*

This book answers your questions about what decision intelligence is, which conditions must be created at your company in order for it to succeed, how you can plan a project, and how to implement it successfully. I've also made an effort to ensure that this book can be used in myriad ways and by anyone, from individuals to powerful leaders of huge organizations. As such, it offers these benefits:

>> An overview of the steps involved in putting the decision before the data in the decision-making process

>> A guidebook with practical suggestions for the various options, overall flexibility, and choices of implementations of a decision intelligence strategy

>> A reference book divided into parts, chapters, and sections so that you can quickly find the content you're looking for when you need it

This book — designed so that you can swiftly get a grasp on everything — features many examples, instructions, checklists, illustrations, and tables. It's also structured systematically according to the decision intelligence framework and its many moving parts.

Conventions Used in This Book

This book doesn't have many rules. The entire book is structured so that you can quickly find everything you need and get a grasp on the content. The detailed table of contents helps you jump right to the information you need, and each chapter begins with a brief and succinct description of the chapter's main topics. Whenever topics overlap or other chapters are mentioned, cross-references help you conveniently jump back-and-forth between the chapters. If you're interested in a particular term, you can look it up in the index.

Foolish Assumptions

This book is not (only) for decision-makers in business or finance. Decision intelligence is too crucial for improving business outcomes to be contained only to the C-suite and data scientist levels. In organizations that practice or seek data- and AI-democratization, decision intelligence should be practiced at every level of decision-making throughout the organization, even at the microdecision and mundane-decision levels. Whether you work at a company, an educational institution, a research institute, a public agency, or a nonprofit organization, you can benefit from the decision-driven approach that is at the heart of decision intelligence. Whether you have an education in the technical, economic, management science, or social science fields, this creative approach gives you new ideas on how to use what you know (and what you have to decide) more productively.

On an individual level, the following assumptions are made in this book about readers who will most likely gain the most from the information in this book:

>> You're in charge of an organization or department and you want to be decision driven instead of data driven so that every decision is productive and profitable.

>> You're trying to accelerate your career plans and you want to shine by making important decisions so that the best possible outcome is realized.

>> You are applying, or you are planning to apply, AI or machine learning at your organization, and you need to know how to make projects succeed in terms of measurable business impacts.

>> Your company is already working with data-driven methods and falling well short of your organization's goals and expectations. You want to enhance or replace your previous work with new methods, tips, and tricks for improving its implementation, and you want a guide on how to make it work and perform consistently well over time.

You don't need to have any specific skills for this book — you only have to be curious and intent on making good decisions — every time.

What You Don't Have to Read

It's worth your time to read the entire book. You can find important tips everywhere in it. Even if you can use only a few of its suggestions, the time and money you invest will be worth it. I guarantee that you'll be able to use more than just a few elements of this information in your private life, your career, and your organization — regardless of your job role or your experience in decision-making. Some of the text in this book appears in a gray box, in order to highlight background information. You don't absolutely need this info, but it's always helpful.

How This Book Is Organized

This book is organized into six distinct parts, as described in this section. The design is intended to help you break free of any brain ruts and consider new ways of thinking about making decisions based on a variety of perspectives.

Part 1: Getting Started with Decision Intelligence

This section gives you an overview of the principles and methods in the decision intelligence framework. You can find out why being decision driven outperforms being data driven. You can also learn how to create the necessary conditions for decision intelligence projects to succeed at your organization, how to plan a project, and how to reinvent what it means to have an actionable outcome.

Part 2: Reaching the Best Possible Decision

The first phase of the decision intelligence process is all about making the decision from which you build the steps and then choosing the tools and data to realize the result of that decision in the real world. Shaping the decision, mapping a path, and choosing the right tools are essential to creating the best possible outcome. At the conclusion of deciding the impact you seek lies the beginning of the questions to be answered.

Part 3: Establishing Reality Checks

In the decision intelligence framework, you need to start with a decision, but that decision must be rooted in reality, and it must be attainable. In other words, this isn't the place for pipedreams, even if profoundly creative disruption is your goal. To keep things grounded, you simply have to take the measure of job roles and team skill diversification, play to both human and machine strengths, ensure that decisions you intend to automate at large scales actually work at scale, among other reality checks. You can't manage — or make a reality — that which you can't measure. Be sure to measure the important things and skip the unimportant to ensure your decision (as well as its expected impact) is solid.

Part 4: Proposing a New Directive

Decision intelligence has many uses and is heavily based on ideas tied directly to favorable outcomes. As such, it plays a significant role in the Idea Economy, in impacts on entire industries, and in building competitive advantage for organizations, governments, and economies. In short, disruption is the point, change is constant, and you can use decision intelligence to command or at least direct both.

Last but not least, the use of decision intelligence can also quickly build and accelerate career paths and turn decision masters into highly influential power brokers. All of these grand rewards come with varying degrees of risks, however.

Part 5: The Part of Tens

No *For Dummies* book exists without The Part of Tens. In this part, you can read about ten (or so) steps to set up a smart decision and ten (or so) pitfalls to avoid in implementing decision intelligence projects.

Icons Used in This Book

Now and then, you find symbols in in the margins of this book. Their purpose is to make you aware of important information, as described here.

This icon points to tips and tricks that should be helpful when you apply and implement an idea. They show you how you can improve your project.

The Remember icon is used to highlight information that's particularly important to know or that can help clear up possible confusion later.

This icon makes you aware of potential stumbling blocks and warns you when to *not* do something. If you avoid errors that others have made before you, you'll save time, money, and effort.

Beyond the Book

In addition to the text you're reading right now, this publication comes with a free, access-anywhere Cheat Sheet that offers a number of tips, techniques, and resources related to data science. To view this Cheat Sheet, visit www.dummies.com and type **decision intelligence for dummies cheat sheet** in the Search box.

Where to Go from Here

You can start immediately by choosing one of these two strategies:

» Read the book straight through, from cover to cover.

» Find individual chapters that you want to read first. (Each chapter covers an entire subject area so that you can read and understand it independently of the other chapters.) If you have no experience with decision intelligence yet, I recommend starting with Chapter 1, which offers a crash course introduction to the concept.

My advice to you: Be aware that decision intelligence, though it has a firm definition, is used more loosely by several groups. For example, people working in AI most typically use it to mean putting the decision first in programming automation or training machine learning to make better automated decisions at scale. That's an application rather than a definition, but its common use as such can cause some confusion over the meaning of the term in general reading. For the purposes of this book, decision intelligence is meant by its broader definition and not a single application. However, given its prevalence in AI, the applications there are covered in more detail than other forms of decision implementation. Therefore, I recommend that you read the Parts 1 and 2 first to ensure that you have a good grasp of the framework overall before touching on related topics in other parts or chapters.

Otherwise, experiment with the reading strategy that works best for you. Jump to different sections while you read this book, if that makes sense to you. If necessary, reread a chapter multiple times or look up individual terms in the index. The idea here is for you to come up with your own way to read this book effectively. And don't forget to keep it nearby for quick-and-easy reference as needed while you work through your first few decision intelligence projects.

1

Getting Started with Decision Intelligence

Chapter **1**

Short Takes on Decision Intelligence

D o you find yourself looking at a spreadsheet or viewing charts or gazing glassy-eyed at a fancy visualization that some bit of artificial intelligence magic has produced for you and wondering what you should do next? You're not alone. Millions of other business and finance people are doing the same thing. So are legions of leaders and decision-makers in other industries.

While you're trying to puzzle out which parts of those "actionable insights" being handed to you *are* in fact actionable and, if so, what action would apply, you've likely wished for something a bit more cut-and dried when it comes to determining what your organization would implement — and you certainly wouldn't mind being considerably more certain about what's going to happen post-implementation.

Would your best bet in such a situation involve letting the miracle of artificial intelligence (AI, for short) make your decisions for you? Well, it turns out that AI isn't so miraculous. In fact, an estimated 80 percent of all AI projects fail, where *failure* here is defined in terms of failing to deliver a measurable business value. That means most AI projects end up on the trash heap for leaning too heavily on the experimental side and being useless on the applied side.

It is painfully (and expensively) obvious that this strategy isn't quite working out the way everyone hoped. An alternative approach is needed to make data more helpful and better aligned with consistently delivering business value. One such approach flips the model from data driven processes to decision driven processes. Known as decision intelligence, human and machine decision-making skills are combined with decision theory, decision sciences, and data sciences in a customizable mix that pins decisions to a precise and expected business value.

The concept isn't entirely new — one of its oldest published mentions cropped up in 2002 in Uwe Hanning's scholarly paper "Knowledge Management + Business Intelligence = Decision Intelligence" — but it has evolved over time, incorporating long-accepted scientific formulas from several well-established sciences. This means its inner workings are well known and tested. Switching over to a decision intelligence approach is therefore no gamble — it's simply a supremely logical way for you to achieve the business outcomes you desire. Decision intelligence leaves little to chance, in either its own construct or the value it consistently delivers.

What differentiates one decision intelligence project from another is the talent and acumen of the decision makers at the helm. They make the recipe that cooks the business value into the process. And they decide when and whether to invite data and machines to the planning table.

Decision intelligence is highly agile and versatile. Decision makers can use it to make decisions either on the back of a napkin or with the help of the most sophisticated AI on the planet.

The Tale of Two Decision Trails

The business world has long been madly in love with the notion of being a data-driven enterprise, but it's also beginning to feel the pain of being in a bad relationship. Few actually want to break off their relationship with data entirely, mainly because most are loathe to ditch their significant investments in data, analytics, and related technologies. Add to this the fact that, for many, it would feel like a colossal failure and a huge embarrassment to fall short of becoming the data driven enterprise that all investors and stockholders expect these days.

Looking for a way forward, many started to ask themselves this question: "What can we do with all the data investments we've already made and already own in order to make better decisions?" In other words, folks realized that a *rethink* was needed rather than a *redo*. And many of those same folks decided that re-strategizing and restructuring how these same investments are used and aligning them with specific business impacts was the answer to the questions that had been plaguing them.

REMEMBER

A decision intelligence approach doesn't mean that there's no place for more traditional data mining tactics. Most organizations are using a combination of both, and it's already proving to be a winning play for many of them.

Pointing out the way

AI and data analytics no doubt deliver real business value in some use cases. They're helpful when it comes to recognizing patterns in massive amounts of data and spitting out equations, scores, predictions, and estimates. The point is that such facts *point to* possible decisions but suggest none. (That's why I refer to the outputs from such tools as *pointers* in this section.)

These tools are also capable of automating certain decisions based on business rules that are determined and set by you or your organization. At its core, AI is automated decisions at scale. Traditional analytics must be integrated with automation software to cause an action to occur.

But before the various software — analytics, AI, and various forms of automation — begin their work in producing insights and automating your decisions, someone has to either program the analytics and automation software, and/ or train the AI. This group of data professionals often provide the interpretations of the outputs as well (usually as visualizations and/or automated AI-generated narratives).

In other words, people in specific job roles who do these tasks typically determine which insights — pointers, in other words — are accessible to other people in the organization who either use the software in a much more limited way or only view the results on dashboards to consume the information. Given the high degree of data illiteracy throughout organizations and across countries and industries, this process is both logical and necessary.

The downside here is that it is also limiting what information end-users can access when it comes to their own decision-making processes and what prompts the direction their thinking takes. This is why data democratization and AI democratization — decentralization so that more people in the organization can use the tools — is so critical to businesses. By making these tools far more user-friendly, professionals in other disciplines and employees at all levels of the business can make better use of these resources.

However, both data and AI democratization still require data professionals to develop more intuitive and highly automated software to remove barriers before non-data professionals can use the tools in ways that bring their own talents and skill sets to bear. Think of this as very similar to the path other software has taken. For example, Microsoft Office enables people to create documents, notes, spreadsheets, and PowerPoint presentations without knowing how to write code, what keyboard commands to give, or anything at all about how the software works. This is the path analytics and AI software are headed down now.

So, who are these data professionals who are making and/or using analytics and AI to provide you with the pointers you're currently getting from various analytics software?

Typical job roles in data mining and analytics are data scientist, business analyst, data mining specialist, and data mining engineer (and variations of the same) to reflect a specific industry such as healthcare data analyst and risk-mining data scientist.

In AI, job roles include AI scientist, AI researcher, business intelligence developer, robotic scientist, software architect, data scientist, and data engineer, among others.

All these jobs will continue to be important positions in many organizations, and the demand for people with these skills will remain high for the foreseeable future.

However, much of their work is also being automated as part of the data and AI democratization movements.

As to specific examples of the work that these professionals collectively and individually produce for use in several business areas, below are some of the more common use cases for traditional data analytics and/or AI automated decision making:

>> **Anomaly detection,** also known as outlier analysis, is a step in data mining (which can be aided by AI/ML or not) that finds deviations in the data from the norm, such as events (purchases on a charge or debit card in another country from where the cardholder is known to live or be, for example), and data point changes (attempts to change a social media account's password via a device or browser that the true account holder is not known to use before, for example).

- **Pattern recognition is** the automated recognition of patterns discovered in the regularities in data. One example would be finding earlier signs of cancer in patient data than doctors and diagnosticians previously knew existed.

- **Predictive modeling,** also known as predictive analytics, analyzes historical patterns in the data using a mathematical process to predict future events or outcomes. One example would involve predicting when a machine part will need repair or replacement based upon its past usage compared to how long identical parts lasted under the same conditions.

- **Recommendation engines** analyze data to make recommendations or suggestions based on users' past behaviors. Examples include analyzing your purchasing patterns in order to offer you a coupon for a grocery item you should be ready to buy again soon, or to recommend a movie based on movies you watched and rated earlier.

- **Personalization systems** use data analysis to customize a service, product, or automated communication. Examples include marketing emails sent to large numbers of customers, each personalized with the customer's name and a custom discount offer for a favorite product or service.

- **Classification and categorization systems** automate the organization of vast amounts of data. Examples include sorting data files and data sets according to importance, topic, secrecy level, or other identifier; legal requirements governing the handling of specific data points (think of laws like General Data Protection Regulation (EU GDPR) which limit where personal data can be stored); and the nature of the data (such as structured machine data or unstructured Twitter posts). Data must be correctly classified and categorized for analytics or AI to work correctly. Automation is the ticket here because there's so much data that it's impossible to do it manually.

- **Sentiment and behavioral analysis** is contextual data mining to discover and analyze the subjective expressed responses (sentiments or feelings) about a brand, product, service, idea, political candidate, and so on in online conversations or customer channels (conversations and customer ratings found in texts, on websites and blogs, in voice recordings or streams during phone calls, and app rating systems. Did you rate that Door Dash driver's service in the app? Yeah, that sort of thing!) Behavioral analysis can extend beyond sentiment analysis to include things like how long you spent reading a news article on your phone and how many times you return to a website, to what time of day and what device you normally use to post on Facebook.

- **Chatbots and conversational systems** frequently appear as a popup sales or customer service chat box on websites where you can ask questions about a product or service or your account and get an automated answer from the resident AI-powered chatbot. Some of these are so good it's hard to tell they aren't human customer service agents. Data on the user and on the stated problem is collected and analyzed to rapidly respond with answers the user needs. Examples of other conversational systems include every digital assistant you've ever heard of: Alexa, Siri, Google Assistant, Bixby, and Cortana. Each is a data king, with Alexa and Google Assistant reigning over two of the largest kingdoms in terms of technical and market prowess.

>> **Autonomous systems** are actually a network or a collection of networks that are all managed by a single entity or organization. Data is live streamed and typically analyzed at the sensor or gateway level, although some data is often sent to a data center for additional analyses later. Think the Internet of Things, such as self-driving cars, robotic systems in manufacturing, and smart cities that use information and communication technologies (ICT) to increase operational efficiency, share information with other systems (such as self-driving cars), and promote sustainable development.

There's no question that the above list is populated with wonderous achievements that would not be possible (or at least not at such huge scales and fast speeds) without data, analytics, and AI. Nevertheless, the promised "actionable insights" produced by analytics and presented in many of today's fancy visualizations and dashboards to business users are often merely pointers. They point to something you might want to use as a key factor in your decision, but they aren't in a position to make that decision for you. You have to conjure some mad data interpretation skills and do some creative problem-solving on your part to figure that one out on your own.

Making a decision

Pointers (also known as *actionable insights*) are typically useful in so far as they go. The trouble is that they point to possible decisions but don't suggest any. Users are often unsure about what action to take, or which option would produce greater value for the business. By contrast, the decision is the be-all-and-end-all of decision intelligence, and everything else in the process supports that decision.

REMEMBER

Whether data driven or decision driven, in both cases humans are the decision makers in this context. It's just that they decide at the tail end of the process in traditional analytics, whereas they decide in the lead position of the decision intelligence process. The starting point for the decision maker matters in terms of the level of control a person has over the impact and value. It's hard to exert much control from the rear.

A history lesson

Disgruntlement with the limitations of traditional data mining is growing. Increasing frustration often leads to both the business side and the AI and IT sides starting to wonder aloud: "What's the point?" But as geeks and businesspeople are wont to do, they realized that there is a point — they just hadn't arrived at it yet.

Eventually, the data driven model was flipped into a decision driven model as people experimented with making the point first and working their way back to the start from there. Decision intelligence is the name of the game where the gamers can all be winners. Now every move made has a point — a point that has value. That's because the point is based on a decision aimed at creating a specific business impact.

The current turn to decision intelligence

Several leading AI luminaries and tech giants have been pioneers in, and first adopters of, decision intelligence. They've already added the title of chief decision scientist to their leadership ranks. One example is Google's eminent chief decision scientist, Cassie Kozyrkov, who spends her days at Google democratizing decision intelligence and developing a more reliable AI approach. She also teaches it to others via conference speeches, YouTube videos, and writings in many online publications.

Kozyrkov appears to embody decision intelligence, partly because of her formal training in economics, mathematical statistics, psychology, and neuroscience. Decision intelligence incorporates all these disciplines — and then some. Although not all who share her title possess the same skill mix, they nevertheless do share strong critical thinking skills as well as a thorough understanding of creative problem-solving strategies, decision theory, and decision science approaches. (For those not familiar with the term, *decision science* focuses on decisions as the unit of analysis; it is the interdisciplinary application of business, math, technology, design thinking, and behavioral sciences to the decision-making process.)

Every day, more leaders are stepping forward to endorse the decision intelligence framework and explain its workings. Many of them work in AI, but others hail from disciplines collectively known as the decision sciences. Business leaders outside the technical domain are also catching on and reveling in their official return to the helm, as opposed to following data's lead (which most never did anyway), and armed with a better strategy. They're also happy about being able to keep their traditional analytics and tools. You don't win battles by limiting your options or abandoning your investments.

Deputizing AI as Your Faithful Sidekick

At its essence, AI automates decisions that are executed rapidly in an exceedingly large number of instances, often simultaneously. You train it by having it work with task-related data sets so that it can recognize what it's looking at in other data sets and learn from the patterns it finds there. Then it makes decisions based on well-defined business rules. (The reality is a good bit more complicated than that, but that's pretty much the gist of it.)

For example, banking institutions use AI to automatically decide which loan applications to approve and which to reject. This is how you can get an answer on your loan application within seconds, no matter how many other people are applying for loans at the same time you are. AI makes these decisions based on the rules it has been given, such as a range of acceptable credit scores, length and types of employment history, items of public record, and other such risk weighting values. AI is able to make such decisions on each individual application, yet at enormous scale and all of it within seconds or minutes. Therefore, borrowers can receive immediate responses to their applications, and lenders can secure more loan deals in minutes than they previously were able to secure over a period of months and at the larger payroll cost of many manhours.

AI is set to continue to serve in this and other automated roles for the foreseeable future. As a technology, it will continue to improve as all technologies do, but placing it within a decision intelligence framework means that its performance will improve exponentially because it is given not only rules to follow but also a target to aim at. Its tasks will be set upon a path of specific actions necessary for creating a specific business impact, and it will faithfully pound away at these tasks until its model decays or someone makes a new model to create another path leading to another targeted impact.

REMEMBER

Other technologies, such as robotic process automation (RPA) and application programming interfaces (APIs), integrate processes. (RPAs are now called virtual workers because they mimic how human workers work, including interacting with user interfaces in the same way.) As RPAs continue to automate processes that were previously difficult to automate, AI can be added to make some automated decisions affecting these processes as well. In other words, the whole of technology engaged in decision making is getting smarter and better and more able to work together.

All this might sound like a setup for a dystopian science fiction movie, but in reality, these developments are nothing to fear. In decision intelligence, whichever technologies you end up using are chosen specifically to augment human soft skills, like creative problem solving, critical thinking, empathy, emotional intelligence, creative design, creative disruption, intuitive intelligence, and intuitive decision making — skills considered nearly impossible to mimic and automate. Even gut instinct can be considered a soft skill, and it too is well out of AI's reach. What ends up happening in decision intelligence is that all human strengths attributable to good judgment and smart decisions are by necessity added to the mix.

REMEMBER

AI is better cast in the role of sidekick, where it augments human decisions rather than dictates or directs them. The same is true of analytics tied to other automated processes as well.

Much of the decision intelligence revolution is happening out of the end user's line of sight, but there's one place where anyone can see the changes unfolding: AI digital assistants such as Google Assistant, Alexa, and Siri. Watch closely as they move from giving you facts in response to your questions to making unprompted recommendations based on your behavior and moods.

Fact reporting such as, "Here are pharmacies near you" or "The name of that song is ABC" will begin to shift to customized and unprompted recommendations. They may look and sound something like this: "XYZ Restaurant has added one of your favorite dishes to its menu. Would you like for me to book the opening in the reservation schedule on Thursday at 7pm and put it on your calendar?" Or, it may say something like this: "Would you like for me to place your favorite coffee order for the pickup window? The one a block from your meeting place has less than a 10 minute wait."

The AI assistant will also produce files for meetings and other handy actions as the user moves through their day. As sidekicks in a user's personal and professional life, the augmented activities will be far more productive than had the human personally tended to all the details and micro decisions.

In digital decision-making, AI will improve at everything it now does — and then some. For example, it will improve at writing algorithms to rapidly meet an organization's or researcher's desired outcomes. That means that, for today and far into the future, AI will be in a position to continue its role as sidekick, producing everything you need to win the day. It's unimaginable that AI won't have some role, small or large, in most Decision Intelligence processes.

Seeing How Decision Intelligence Looks on Paper

Though the decision intelligence framework is perfect for guiding AI to consistently produce business value for you, the methodology can be used with no digital data or machines. For example, you can use AI to make decisions on a spreadsheet, on the back of a napkin, on a single sheet of paper, or even on a wall (using a crayon, of course). That's because the process you use is up to the decision-maker to choose. The Decision Intelligence process itself can be quick and short, or it can be quite complex and take some time to complete. You may want to start with a SWOT table listing the *Strengths*, *Weaknesses*, *Opportunities*, and *Threats* when making your initial decision. From there, you can determine the steps you need to take to make your decision render a desired impact in the real world.

The process is similar to determining a destination and then mapping out the best route between where you are and where you want to be. It's the impact you desire, however, that will define which route is best. Need to be there fast? The direct route is best. Want to see more along the way or stop at tourist attractions? Then a scenic route is the best way. Want to use your hotel rewards points or your gas rewards card on the trip? Then mapping a route based on the location of certain hotel and gas brands is the best route.

REMEMBER

In decision intelligence, the impact always matters most, for it is the manifestation of your decision.

Working within a decision intelligence framework forces you to become more aware of how the decision-making process works. For example, many of the mental processes you use are intuitive — that's what makes it possible for you to come to conclusions quickly. But make no mistake: Whether you realize it or not, your brain is calculating the same mathematical formulas as a machine would use to help you reach the same conclusions. There's a simple reason for that: Machines copy how people think. As such, machines are definitely the sidekicks in decision intelligence processes, there to assist and augment your efforts.

REMEMBER

Superheroes don't always need a sidekick, and you won't either. Choose the processes, tools, and information according to the needs in executing your decision. Don't default to the technologies and queries with which you're most familiar. The point is not to repeat the same acts, but rather to produce consistent value in personal, professional, or digital decisions.

Tracking the Inverted V

You may be wondering how the processes in decision intelligence differ from those used in data analytics. After all, it's obvious that decisions are also made first when using data analytics in the usual way. For example, someone decides what the business rules are before they apply them to data analytics or AI. Someone also decides what data to use, what data sources to join, and what queries to make. Further, someone decides what projects to launch and whether to send them to production. And so on.

With all these decisions upfront, what does "Put the decision first" in decision intelligence mean? And how does it change anything? It helps to remember that the process in machine-based decision-making is linear, meaning that it moves consecutively from data preparation and selection to algorithm inputs and, finally, to an output. The output is typically an insight or a recommendation delivered as a visualization, as narrative text, or as both, from which a human can decide what action to take. Sometimes, the output is connected to an automated process that then takes an action as directed by the output.

In any case, the path is a straight line.

Now tilt that line upward so that it's the first leg of an inverted V. At the bottom is the starting point, which is the data to be analyzed. At the top is the decision to be made based on the analyses. That's your path upward.

Ignore that path and work your way back down from the decision to the data. Rarely will you follow the same path down. Instead, you'll create a different path that will be more specifically tied to the decision. The two paths together resemble an inverted V.

The first leg of the inverted V begins with mining the data, and then an analysis follows. If you think about it, this process is now defining the decisions you can make. By contrast, in the V's second leg, the decision is defining the data, tools, and queries.

The first leg is a discovery mission. The second is a mission with a purpose.

Which leg do you think will consistently deliver a payload?

And that, my friend, is why and how you put the decision first.

Estimating How Much Decision Intelligence Will Cost You

Ah, yes, the bottom-line question on everyone's lips is cost. Certainly, cost is a major consideration in nearly every business decision. This time, however, it isn't much of an issue. Because decision intelligence is a rethink and not a redo, you likely already have in place many of the technologies and tools you need. (Think of it as leveraging those items to produce a higher return on investment, or ROI, on what you already have.) Of the tools you may not have, many of the products you need offer free versions or at least free trials so that you can see how they work and whether they're a fit for your organization.

That may leave a few tools to buy, depending on your current mix of technologies. All told, it's rarely a huge expense to switch from data mining tactics to decision intelligence.

The following checklist can help you form an idea of some of the technologies commonly used in decision intelligence. That way, you can quickly see what you may need to put on your shopping list — or which functions you might want to hire a third-party who has these things and the experience to use them to do some of this for you.

>> **Decision modeling software** is a part of decision management systems that represents business decisions via a standardized notation — often the Business Process Model and Notation (BPMN) standard — that is used by business analysts and subject matter experts (SMEs), rather than developers. Examples include ACTICO Platform, Red Hat Decision Manager, and FICO Decision Management Platform.

>> **Business rule management software** to manage the business rules in decision-making. Sometimes these are standalone software products and sometimes they are part of a decision management system as well. Examples include VisiRule, Red Hat Decision Manager, SAS Business Rules Manager, InRule, and DecisionRules.

>> **An AutoML stack** *or* another collection of software capable of automating all or part of the building of ML models. AutoML simplifies the machine learning model developer process by automating many of the more laborious steps, such as feature engineering, hyperparameter optimization, and creating the layers in the neural architecture. Don't worry if you don't quite grasp what these automated activities entail because the point in having AutoML is to do all that complicated and time intensive stuff for you. The cool thing is that

while AutoML is a useful tool for data scientists, it's just as useful in democratizing AI. Yes, you too will one day make the AI you want to use in your DI process — by telling AI to make it for you. See, not as hard a concept as you thought. Examples of AutoML vendors include DataRobot, H2O.ai, and Google Cloud AutoML.

>> **A good data platform** which is a technology that bundles several big data applications and tools in a single package. Preferably get one that supports both the creation of algorithms and the delivery of transactional data in real-time. Examples include Google Cloud AI platform, RStudio, TensorFlow, and Microsoft Azure.

>> **A BI app** with natural language processing, AI assistance, and a built-in visualization tool. Examples include Qlik Sense, Domo, Microsoft Power BI, Yellowfin, Sisense Fusion, Zoho Analytics, and Google Analytics.

Members of your data science team will spend most of their time and effort (at least at first) learning how to capture your newly made decision's requirements using decision model and notation standards such as the Business Process Model and Notation (BPMN), Case Management Model and Notation (CMMN), and/or Decision Model and Notation (DMN) standards.

For decisions where digital data has less of a role or no role, look to the standard tried-and-true array of decisioning tools, like the ones described in this list — and others:

>> **Mind mapping tools** are used to create diagrams to visually organize information, typically from brainstorming sessions or collaboration sessions. Examples of mind mapping tools include Coggle, Mindly, MindMup, MindMeister, Scapple, and Stormboard.

>> **SWOT tables** consist of four quadrants labeled *S*trengths, *W*eaknesses, *O*pportunities, and *T*hreats. Users list line items in each quadrant to clarify considerations (and what might be at stake). SWOT tables can be simple or very complex. There are numerous templates available online if you want to use one.

>> **Comparison tables** are also known as comparison charts. These are typically line charts, bar charts, pie charts, or other types of charts used to compare or contrast data about any number of things such as data fields (expense categories, for example), competitors, or any other item needing a comparative analysis. Examples of these are everywhere online and off and templates and tools to make such charts are available in visualization and BI tools like Microsoft Power BI, Google Charts, Tableau, Chartist. js, FusionCharts, Datawrapper, Infogram, Canva, and ChartBlocks.

>> **Decision trees** depict cascading questions where the answer to one question leads to the formation of the next question. Decision trees are particularly effective in making very complex decisions. They can be simple or very involved depictions, depending on the level of complexity of the problem to be solved. Templates are plentiful online, but there are also tools that will help you make and use them. Examples include Smartdraw's Decision Tree Maker, Lucidchart's Decision Tree Maker, and Creately.

>> **Spreadsheets** are those all-too-familiar tools that exist in paper and digital forms, such as Excel and Google Sheets.

>> **Paper and pencil** are the tried-and-true standbys. A simple list of pros versus cons on the back of a cocktail napkin has solved many decision dilemmas and they still work today in some instances.

For smaller organizations and start-ups looking to leverage technology in their decision intelligence processes without investing much money, try starting out with a cloud- or browser-based business intelligence app, or one that's embedded in software you already have and use, like Microsoft Power BI, which is embedded in Excel in the Microsoft Office suite. You can find many BI apps with free versions as well. If that's more firepower than you need, check out one or more of the online visualization tools listed above (some are even free!).

REMEMBER

One important caveat: Business intelligence (a BI app that produces reports on current and predicted performance of various aspects of the business based on business data analysis) is *not* the same as a Decision Intelligence process, though BI apps can be used as part of the DI process. A good BI app is simply a quick and reliable way to analyze the data that supports your decision.

The bottom line here is that monetary costs should be relatively small. You may need to spend more on training, however, because your tech people may need additional training on decision theory and the decision sciences — as well as on decision intelligence tactics. Conversely, your business leaders may need that training, too, as well as some training on BI apps to gain a working understanding of data analysis and its full potential.

Chapter **2**

Mining Data versus Minding the Answer

D ata driven decisioning is evolving beyond mere data discovery to results-based decision targeting. This newest step on the data science evolutionary chain is known as *decision intelligence (DI)*, a discipline that combines data science, social science, and managerial science into a singularly focused approach to making the best decision possible in any given circumstance.

In this chapter, you find out why targeting an outcome at the outset trumps the traditional model of mining the data first. The result becomes the prime directive in this 180-degree turn in the definition and execution of the oft-sought actionable outcome.

In other words, the focus shifting from discovering information within established data sets to deciding what you most need to know and then actively searching for that knowledge wherever it may reside.

In short, data takes a supporting role rather than a starring role in decision intelligence. The human mind also moves from a role as data/analytics organizer to that of a high-value player in search of the best decision possible. And, last but not least, artificial intelligence (AI) becomes a helpful assistant rather than a dreaded human overlord or job slayer.

In this chapter, you see why this rethinking on how to use data spawned a rising transformative and disruptive force in business as well as in people's daily lives. You also see why you should be quick to wield this force in any job role you may decide to take on over the course of your career.

Knowledge Is Power — Data Is Just Information

In the beginning, there was data. From the ticking of fingers and toes to stones stored in crude pouches and sticks bundled in vine, the early humans collected and recorded information. This recording of information continued throughout time unabated. The media that was used to record that data changed over the years, according to the technologies of the time. Eventually, however, the data outgrew the number of devices set aside to collect and store it, as well as the number of people using those devices. That's when we started calling it *big data*, in a nod toward its bigness overshadowing the capabilities of modern computing.

Folks tend to look in amazement at this growing trove of data, but the truth of the matter is that what seems like an immense resource is merely a mirror we humans are holding up to our world. And therein lies the problem: Possessing information that reflects the world back to us isn't the same thing as being able to use that information in a practical, real-world sort of way — let alone to do so with any sort of consistent accuracy.

Putting it another way, decision intelligence arrived as a movement when it became evident that mining data is like mining for any other valuable substance: The value lies not in the crude form, but in the polished gem. The goal now is to identify the gem you seek and then go find it. The trick here is do so with the understanding that the work isn't finished until you have achieved a high level of clarity in the decision-making process — a level of clarity seen only in the rarest of diamonds.

Experiencing the epiphany

To date, we humans have all been mining data to sort information into useful pointers — pointers to which products customers might want to buy now or next and which price they might be willing to pay, for example, or pointers on who on the team might have an edge to help win a baseball game or reach a sales quota, or even pointers on which activities might indicate the beginning of a data breach and which are the routine work behaviors of hundreds of staffers now working from home during a pandemic.

Pointers of all kinds — here, there and everywhere. And there's nothing wrong with any of this. Pointers can, and often do, direct people to a path forward in business, at home, and in various other endeavors.

However, pointers mark a path (often, one among many), but they don't decide which path you should take. In other words, pointers aren't the same thing as decisions. You're free to make the wrong choice as much as you're free to make the right one. But that approach falls woefully short of the tall promise in data driven decisions, doesn't it?

REMEMBER

"Following the data" was supposed to render some infallible truths and reliable actions. That's why so many analytics vendors tout actionable outcomes or actionable outputs. Short of automating that action, however, even recommended actions are pointers as well.

For example, predictive analytics might produce an actionable outcome, saying that a part in a machine will last ten more days and should be replaced on the ninth day. This action gets the most use out of that part with no interruption in the machine's performance. However, a decision still needs to be made. Company leaders may decide to order maintenance crews to follow all such directives and replace parts on the days indicated. Or, management may ignore the directive in favor of upgrading or replacing the machine instead.

That's okay for as far as it goes. But you need more from data analytics if the aim is to make correct or best decisions of a more complex and demanding nature — especially if they are grave decisions that can carry serious consequences.

For example, take a hard look at the COVID-19 pandemic and the many survival questions that sprang forth from it. Data and analytics can tell us how the virus spread, which virus variations exist, and who was most at risk. This was and is important information. However, data and advanced analytics — even the much-ballyhooed AI — cannot tell us whether it's safe to send children back to school. The information also shed no light on when, where, or how to safely return people to workspaces or to indoor dining and entertainment venues to help save the economy. In turn, leading public health authorities such as Dr. Fauci and others were unsure which actions to recommend.

In other words, all the data and all the analytics could not tell people what we most needed to know. And this is the recurring lesson that taught some data scientists to look for another way — perhaps by evolving current methods in analyzing data — so that outputs would consist of decisions and not mere information. In the wake of recognizing that today's data idol has feet of clay, we have come to this powerful epiphany:

Information is useful, but knowledge is power.

If you're thinking that we humans are rediscovering an epiphany first perceived many years ago, you are correct. Similarly, decision intelligence is not a new idea but rather a *renewed* one.

Embracing the new, not-so-new idea

The term *decision intelligence* has been in use for at least the past 20 to 25 years — one of its earliest mentions is in the scholarly paper "Knowledge Management + Business Intelligence = Decision Intelligence," by Uwe Hannig, a German academic specializing in information and performance management. The meaning of the term *decision intelligence* continues to change somewhat as vendors try to fit the term to their own products or purposes. Meta S. Brown, the author of *Data Mining For Dummies* (Wiley) and president of A4A Brown Inc., a consultancy specializing in guidance for launching and expanding analytics projects, says of decision intelligence that "solution vendors associate it with enterprise software, for example, though practitioners not tied to products see it as a broad set of disciplines brought together for decision making."

It's still very much a buyer-beware field, in other words. Products will be marketed as decision intelligence tools that aren't — or perhaps are but are also good for other purposes. Just as a clawhammer can be sold as a house-building tool and a nail-puller, so, too, can many techniques, tactics and tools be used for decision intelligence as well as for other analytical tasks.

Good analytics practice in general, regardless of labeling such as AI, data science, and data mining, are found in an existing open standard for data mining process called CRISP-DM. (Check out *Data Mining For Dummies* if you're curious about this standard.)

Many of the details in CRISP-DM are used by data analysts, business managers, IT leaders and others in a variety of business roles. Decision Intelligence extends on that idea.

But the distinction between the two concepts — data mining and decision intelligence — is perhaps best understood in their respective outputs:

>> **Data science** tells you what is knowable in any given universe of information. It can do so by answering your questions (data queries) or by automating pattern detection (advanced analytics or AI).

>> **Decision intelligence,** by comparison, integrates what's known into a decision process. It's the difference between knowing how COVID-19 spreads (data science) and using that and other information in a structured process to decide whether to allow people to return to work (decision intelligence).

REMEMBER

Impact is ultimately the answer everyone seeks. When every business and life question essentially boils down to the question of what you should do to achieve this impact, it makes sense to start the decision-making process with the impact you seek and the answer you most need.

Avoiding thought boxes and data query borders

Traditional data mining tends to box in your thinking and put borders around the questions you ask by simply focusing the work on the data in question.

For example, if you're mining marketing and sales data for insights, your thinking predictably shifts to a more or less standardized list of questions. That's natural because it's how humans organize information as well as their thinking about information.

In other words, people label data to organize it, but those same labels also influence how they think about the information so labeled. It's weird how that works, isn't it?

Nonetheless, labels are helpful to a large degree, and you can hardly function in using data without them. They're so helpful that Google's head of decision intelligence said that if data scientists and statisticians were left to their own devices, they would have named machine learning "the labeling of things" because these professionals prefer names that label what the thing actually does.

If you feel that this discussion is going in circles now, you're right. And that's the best illustration I can think to offer you on how traditional data mining limits everyone's thinking and querying.

Care to go around again? No? Well, people do continue to repeat many of their efforts in analyzing data anyway. Most often folks do that by refreshing the data and repeating the query — over and over again.

Models, algorithms, and queries are shaped accordingly. Machine learning, also known as AI in common use, is trained on this or similar data where it learns the most often asked questions and the common outputs. Querying is often automated, which results in a list of preselected questions. Even drill-downs in data represented by interactive visualizations are preset.

Those parameters form the box analytics software users find themselves in, the bordering that places restraints on querying, and the reasoning behind the repetitions in actions.

DATA ANALYSIS RUTS AND ROAMS

Traditional data mining processes usually look something like this:

1. Prep data from existing sources — such as systems used for routine business operations, streaming data, or data centers — for use in analytics.

2. Mine the data with a variety of tools, including analytics and machine learning (known commonly as AI).

3. Visualize the outputs — make graphic representations of the insights gleaned from analyzing the data, in other words.

4. Decide what action to take based on these insights.

5. Refresh the data and then rinse and repeat.

Unfortunately, data miners and data scientists often hand over the results of their hard work only to find that nothing came of it because there was no realistic business plan to use them in the first place. By comparison, decision intelligence ensures a plan is in place from the outset.

Still, there's no reason to throw out the traditional data mining process when you make your move to decision intelligence. Indeed, you'd be nuts to do that. This process works quite beautifully in many use cases — most notably, those that are unmuddied by nuance, gray areas, and language confusions. For example, is the color yellow meant to signify Caution or Coward in any given data set? That may depend on one of those gray areas, which, in this particular case, is bound up in context. Data scientists are quite familiar with these issues and deal with them every day.

More defined questions are arguably better suited to how analytics are positioned in this process. For example, it's true that predictive analytics will be correct more often than humans in determining the last day of usefulness of a machine part. It's also true that analytics will be accurate more often than people — even experts — in detecting patterns in massive amounts of data.

But it's also important to understand the limitations of this approach. Machines can do only so much. They don't think or learn as you and I do. For example, machine learning can sort data faster than humans in any this-is-a-cat-this-is-not choice of well-defined options. But even then, machines are likely to mislabel a few cat pictures that a human child would instantly recognize to be distinctly feline.

By comparison, decision intelligence melds your mind to the machine's "mind" so that the strengths of each one overcome the other's weakness. Obviously, it's not an actual melding of human and machine, but rather a blend of decision capabilities.

That's a vital advance because it renders outputs of greater significance to problem solving and additional analysis of real world impacts. An unintended side effect of using the traditional model was the devaluation of the worth of human input outside of programming and other software development activities. We humans got into the habit of putting total faith in algorithm outputs — even when the outputs are in conflict with our thoughts and experiences. We do this despite it being well known that data is rarely perfect or complete. But that's not the only problem challenging our blind faith in data analysis.

Unfortunately, as Cassie Kozyrkov, Google's head of decision intelligence, often reminds us: "Strategies based on pure mathematical rationality are relatively naïve and tend to underperform."

Anyone who has been chased by ads — for items they have already purchased and don't care to buy again — across social media and the Internet can attest to this most annoying "relatively naïve" underperformance of some analytics.

Even so, general wisdom still has it that data — and not people — should take the lead in business decisions. It's machine over gut instinct every time, goes the mantra, even when that isn't done in practice. But why must this be an either-or question? The correct answer, of course, is that it doesn't.

Enter decision intelligence, the practitioners of which "usually emphasize details of broad business decision systems; these include analytics, management of data and information resources, business rules, integration of decisions into operational systems and other functions," according to Meta Brown, the author of *Data Mining For Dummies*.

The aha moment here is that analytics and data mining are parts of the decision-making process rather than the whole of it.

Decision Intelligence is a huge umbrella under which all the activities necessary to produce decisions huddle and are put into practice to yield a preset, desired outcome.

Predictable and even preset questions are still good questions in many business pursuits. There's nothing wrong with continuing to interrogate the data in this way for many common use cases. After all, you always want to know your sales for the day and how that number compares to last year's sales. And, you likely always want to know which products are hot sellers this week, which employees were the most productive, and so forth. So go ahead and keep asking the data these questions.

But it's time to see what else you can do with data and analytics and AI. It's time to rethink how to go about the business of deriving decisions at scale as well. And that is exactly how some in the data sciences arrived at decision intelligence.

TIP

How do you break out of the boxed-in thinking behind traditional data mining processes? Think How before What. Figure out how to go about making the decision rather than focus in on what the data says in answer to your query.

Reinventing Actionable Outcomes

Perhaps no buzzword is more touted in the data analytics industry than *actionable outcome.* To be fair, some outputs are actionable and some of those actionable items can even be fully automated — no humans needed outside of those who built the machines that are now doing all that work.

However, more often than not, actionable outcomes are insights that *might* enable an action. That's quite a different concept than analytics that can deliver actual decisions, or a rated range of them, complete with expected impacts.

Decision intelligence aims to change outputs from insights to decisions, at any scale and by using varying blends of human and machine tactics. This is what Google's Cassie Kozyrkov means when she so often describes the difference between traditional data science with machine learning, and decision intelligence as "the difference between those who make microwave ovens and the cooks who use them." It's the recipe and the outcome that matter, she says, because the chef has no need to build a microwave or even understand how it works.

The focus is shifting, in other words, from data explorations and building more technology to delivering a specific payload.

Living with the fact that we have answers and still don't know what to do

Decision modeling is maturing to include more pointed pursuits, broader considerations in the decision-making processes, and more accountability for the results. It won't surprise you to hear that this new phase is also labeled *decision intelligence* and that it's measured by the value of its outputs, whether that's in terms of impact or return on investment or both.

There is no more time, patience, or money for fishing in data lakes or panning for gold in data streams in the hope of discovering valuable knowledge. Decision intelligence insists on moving with purpose to achieve a predetermined end whose significance has been well defined.

TIP

When considering where to apply decision intelligence to your own circumstances, boil down the problem to its truest essence.

Here's a handy example: You may ask the data what the weather will be like tomorrow. But that isn't the question. Nor will the answer "Partly cloudy with a high of 70 degrees" be of any significant use to you.

Think hard. What is it that you *really* want to know?

Perhaps it's whether to plan a picnic tomorrow. In that case, you likely need an assessment of the weather, plus pollen counts, projected traffic at the park, and maybe even water sports availabilities and/or wait times for picking up prepacked picnic lunches at your favorite deli.

Perhaps you wanted the analytics to tell you that your best pick for a picnic tomorrow is "Happy Park on the north beachside with shelter from the wind but not the warmth of the sun, and plenty of tables, because it's not a high traffic park. Also, your route has three delis, and two have less than a 10-minute wait for order pickups."

Decision intelligence can be applied for a relatively-speaking best decision for a problem or question of any size, ranging from the highly personalized (like the picnic questions) to the truly huge (like a global pandemic).

I talk earlier in this chapter about how the COVID-19 epidemic revealed the limits of a data driven approach to problem solving. Some of the lapses in the initial response to the epidemic were certainly caused by the urgency of the threat and the novelty of both the virus and the vaccines. Yet several factors worked in favor of making sound public health decisions under pressure. For one, Israel struck a deal with Pfizer to share patient data on the efficacy and side effects of the Pfizer vaccine in real world use. Israel also has one of the world's most efficient healthcare systems, complete with highly developed electronic healthcare records (EHRs) capable of collecting massive patient data in real time. The resulting database is well organized and filled with *clean data* — accurate and up-to-date data, in other words — which was vital to both understanding the disease and testing the vaccine.

Further, scientists, healthcare workers, and public health organizations around the world shared data and collaborated on finding insights and answers. The global response to the pandemic was a stellar display of how effective humankind can be in tamping down any threat when countries, health entities, and experts cooperate. The effort should be celebrated and commemorated for time eternal.

But all decision-makers can also learn from the shortcomings as well as the successes in this huge undertaking to end a dangerous pandemic. Chief among the shortcomings is that there is still uncertainty, after many months, about the specific actions that should be taken despite massive global data sets and ongoing analysis.

Businesses and other organizations find themselves in a similar predicament even in the absence of urgency, alarm, and dire consequences. In other words, even with the luxury of time and calmer heads, you can glean insights from data and still not know what to do about or with them. To put this in proper context, you should always remember this:

REMEMBER

Data will never be omnipotent, and you will always have to deal with some level of uncertainty.

Even so, you can and should improve how you make decisions and judge them by their real world impacts. That requires the combined applications of several disciplines and more human input — a more than fitting definition of decision intelligence.

Going where humans fear to tread on data

Though the processes used under the big umbrella known as decision intelligence vary from one entity to the next, they're likely to be more warmly embraced by people who were previously concerned that data analytics, and particularly those associated with AI, would eliminate their jobs.

AI, more often than traditional automation, is perceived by some as a direct competitor by managers and executives by virtue of science fiction depictions where AI is smarter than humans and capable of doing even high level jobs. That's also partly because of the frequent and often wrong assumption that automation is limited to replacing jobs on the lower rungs of the career ladder. By comparison, AI cuts directly from the top. That point was first driven home when Deep Knowledge Ventures, a Hong Kong-based venture capitalist fund, added an algorithm named VITAL as a member of the board of directors in 2017. After that, it appeared that no job was safe from a machine takeover.

OK, some did note that appointing an algorithm to the board was likely a publicity stunt, since most board of directors use data to inform their votes, but the scare that AI may replace business leaders nevertheless lingers.

Deep Knowledge Ventures credits its algorithm with saving the company from bankruptcy caused by "overinvesting in overhyped projects." Known as Vital (short for Validating Investment Tool for Advancing Life Science), the algorithm established itself as a seemingly crucial member of the board. It's interesting that the rest of the board — or perhaps it was the stockholders? — apparently had little regard for the directors' ability to keep the company financially strong.

Executives, whether at the head of business lines or at the top of the company pinnacle, typically fear data fueled algorithms. On the one hand, they're expected to toe the data-driven company line. On the other hand, data-driven decisions may make their own talents obsolete.

In doesn't help that executive pay, benefits, and perks are large line items in the biggest of company expenses: payroll costs. You can easily see where the same cost cutting logic that executives use every day could eliminate them as well.

Decision intelligence rebalances the scale by adding more weight to human roles in making key business decisions. That alone makes the concept welcome to leadership. However, decision intelligence is not a license nor the means to return to gut instinct, seat-of-the-pants, ego-driven, or agenda-loaded decision manipulations. The value in decision intelligence is that it is a far more effective way to make business decisions and savvy leaders will instantly grasp its importance to their organizations and careers.

In short, it is a rebalancing of how data is used and viewed. The evolution is in step with maturation patterns in other disciplines and a payback of sorts for data science's contributions to those developments. One example speaks for many: computing and data science spurred the emergence of Digital Humanities as a new field in the 1950s and has enabled its steady improvement ever since. Now a similar development process is flowing in the other direction.

Decision intelligence is a recipe wherein data, automation, AI and human decision-making capabilities are blended to bake better outcomes into the processes. Further, it is a renewed focus beyond mechanical and digital efficiencies to make the outcomes more meaningful in human applications and impacts.

For many experts and observers, including many executives who have always highly valued business acumen in themselves and other people, decision intelligence's acknowledgment and inclusion of the same is a natural progression in business applications.

It is a result of the formal recognition of another truth too: no matter how far AI/ML has advanced, combining it with in-house business knowledge always makes for better business outcomes.

Ushering in The Great Revival: Institutional knowledge and human expertise

Two of the biggest casualties in traditional data mining are institutional knowledge and human expertise. *Institutional knowledge* is defined as the knowledge within an organization about its own business and customers that's passed on from older workers and leaders to newer ones in informal and usually verbal person-to-person exchanges. Because much of it is stored in the minds of workers and executives, it's supremely difficult to identify, retrieve, and digitalize for inclusion in a data set. Therefore, it's often lost when a person with some of this knowledge retires, dies, changes jobs, or otherwise stops being an active part of the company. Without this key information, business decisions can be made in the wrong context for the situation and result in failure or undesirable consequences.

Human expertise works similarly: It's the knowledge gained by an individual by way of education, intuitive intelligence, talent, accumulated skill sets, experience, exposure, incidents of failure and success, encounters with anomalies and repetitious events, and a myriad of unique circumstances over the span of a career or lifetime. This information, too, is difficult to digitalize and add to a database. Therefore, human expertise also tends to be lost to illness, retirement, job change, or death.

The cost to any organization of the loss of either institutional knowledge or human expertise can be enormous in terms of money value, company culture, and the shape of the organization's competitive edge. These facts are not lost to many in business leadership and data science, which is spurring a revival in both valuing and capturing these deep wells of specialized and irreplaceable data.

Some think of it as a great revival as the pendulum swings from one extreme to the other. For example, disinterest in customers from a focus on profits alone has now swung to a near-fanatical interest in personalizing every customer encounter and ensuring a great customer experience for each individual. This swing comes from a renewed appreciation for the value of human expertise (in this case in sales and marketing) and in institutional knowledge of customers and operations with regard to improving profits. In other words, once data-driven process efficiencies had mostly or completely been realized, companies learned that profits cannot be separated from customers, as the latter begats the former. Hence the resumed interest in reselling to existing customers and retaining customer knowledge beyond basic financial transaction details.

WARNING

Though it's reassuring to many to see human expertise added back into decision-making alongside data, it's quite different to actually pull it off. Decision intelligence isn't an easy exercise in its formation or execution.

After all, data sets are still huge. Even if you use and find value in only 10 percent of data, that's still an awful lot of data to parse and analyze. AI is also faster than people at, well, everything. That's an advantage that organizations want to maintain. Then there's the need to automate tasks so that work gets done faster, more efficiently, and without the need to interrupt function, features, and the customer experience.

Where do all these factors come together in the decision intelligence effort? Well, that's what you and your organization have to figure out for yourselves. Certainly, there are guidelines on how to do it as well as tools at your disposal that I present in greater detail later in this book. However, remember that the first part of bringing humans more fully into the decisioning roles is in deciding the particular blend of human versus machine processes that are needed.

Or, to put it another way — and in keeping with Kozyrkov's earlier analogy — this is the part for the microwave chefs to work their magic in making the recipe. The job of the microwave builders is largely finished. You know you have the right recipe when you see the proof in the pudding, so to speak.

Chapter **3**

Cryptic Patterns and Wild Guesses

Yahoo! put the first Hadoop cluster — arguably, the first truly successful distributed computing environment designed specifically for storing and analyzing huge amounts of unstructured data — into production back in 2006. It's that date which, for most practical purposes, marks the onset of the big data gold rush and the hunt to discover unknown information buried in known data sets.

The results were largely perceived to be worth the effort and generally enlightening — even though most big data initiatives fail to this very day. Even so, the call for data driven businesses, to the chagrin of business leaders and managers everywhere, became the mantra in business and investment circles worldwide. Organizations were soon convinced that using data analytics meant the same thing as harvesting answers. The thinking was that the answers generated were perfect right out of the box and were produced by means far beyond mere human abilities. Gut instinct and human talent were summarily discounted and dismissed as little more than wild guesses. However, the reality was and is quite different, as analytics have limits, big data and AI projects have high fail rates, and business executives very often let their gut instincts override algorithm outcomes.

Fear of AI began to soar as people expected machine masters to leap from science fiction and rule the real world. But that's a far cry from what has happened so far.

The notion that data analytics was somehow churning out answers at a record pace gave way to the broadening realization that what analytics actually was producing were insights. Humans were still needed to glean understanding and perhaps inspiration from those insights and to turn them into decisions and actions.

It turns out that machines aren't the new masters of the human race, after all. And they don't provide the final answers humans seek. But that's more the fault of humans than the machines. People were so busy asking questions of the data that they forgot to look where the work was headed. Organizations often found themselves working in circles or solving problems that yielded no tangible benefits for the questioner.

REMEMBER

What organizations really seek is not so much an answer, but rather a path to a specific destination. In this chapter, you will find out why that distinction matters and how it changes the way you make decisions.

Machines Make Human Mistakes, Too

People commonly believe that machines are unbiased and more perfect than humans. Data analytics, automation, and machine learning (referred to as AI by marketers everywhere) are often presented as though the machines are capable of sorting out the data and reaching a perfect and fair conclusion on their own.

This simply isn't true. It's imperfect humans — not perfect machines — who make the technologies, set the rules, design the models, and select the training data. That means subconscious or intentional human influence can seep into every step: the rules, the programming and models, and the data selection. In short, the creation mirrors the creator. Machines are influenced by humans who build them and therefore frequently make many of the same mistakes humans make. Examples are numerous and varied. They include institutional biases, such as the (infamous) example of the continued use of *redlining,* a discriminatory practice in bank lending and other financial services that draws a figurative redline around minority neighborhoods so that those residents either can't get loans approved or can't get them at fair terms.

Such biases in computing are insidious and not entirely new. For example, a computer algorithm used in 1988 to select medical school applicants for admission interviews discriminated against women and students with non-European names. Similarly, Amazon ended a recruiting algorithm in 2018 that proved to be biased against women.

AI can ease such problems or make them worse. In any case, reverting to human-only decision making obviously isn't the answer.

REMEMBER

Whether you use traditional data analytics, decision intelligence, or a combination of the two, you need to take steps to guard against accidental or intentional biases, errors, and reasoning flaws. Here are a few important steps to take to ensure fairness in machine decision-making:

>> **Be proactive:** Use AI specifically to seek and measure discrimination and other known decision flaws throughout an entire decision-making process. Yes, this is using AI to make other AI and humans transparent and accountable.

>> **Recognize the problem:** Use algorithms to identify patterns, triggers, and pointers in actions, language, or rules that lead toward discrimination in order to set safeguards against discriminatory precursors in machine and human behaviors.

>> **Check the outcomes:** AI operates in sort of a black box, where humans can't quite see what it's doing. Yet AI cannot yet explain itself or its actions, either. But that's okay — you can still check and grade its homework. For example, when checking for fairness in data-based or automated recruitment and hiring, look to see whether the outputs meet current legal standards such as the 80 percent rule — the rule stating that companies should be hiring protected groups at a rate that's at least 80 percent of that of white men.

TIP

Software developers should also perform *disparate impact analyses* — testing to see if neutral appearing functions have an adverse effect on a legally protected class — before any algorithm is used by anyone. If your software is from a third party, ask to see the results of the analysis and a detailed explanation of how the product works.

>> **Do the math.** Statistical analysis has been around for a long time. You can perform an old-fashioned and routine statistical test to reveal disparities arising from unintentional biases based on gender, race, religion, and other factors. Be sure, however, to automate the math rather than do it manually, because an automated process scales better, speeds results, and is likely more accurate.

TIP

Be sure to compare your outcomes with the reality of the environment. Context is everything. For example, a low number of female members in the Boy Scouts of America is not indicative of a bias against females but is rather a sign of an emerging diversity and inclusiveness (D&I) program taking root. Sometimes, the results from calculating disparities in a given situation are more revealing of the environment than of a bias in play. If this is the case, be transparent about both the environment and how the disparate impact analysis was done. You might also want to set alerts for any change in that environment that would warrant a new disparate impact analysis.

Seeing the Trouble Math Makes

Math is at the center of data science — which isn't surprising, given that math is at the center of many areas, including music, computer programming, and the universe. However, though math may be the keystone of many things, it isn't the whole thing of anything.

In fairness to math, it's prudent to point out that math isn't a decision, either. The discipline known as decision analysis defines a *decision* as an irrevocable act — that means an investment of effort, time, or resources must be fully committed and deployed before it can be technically deemed a decision. Math doesn't commit, let alone act. It calculates. As such, it delivers a calculation, not a decision. The decision, my friend, rests with you, the diviner of the calculation.

It's worrisome news, I know. It is so much more convenient to praise or blame the math for data driven decisions and, in so doing, absolve ourselves of any responsibility or accountability. But no, at best math gives us limited cover for bad decisions. See? I told you math makes for trouble!

The limits of math-only approaches

When you come right down to it, math isn't much of a strategist. If your business strategy involves putting all your eggs in the mathematical basket, you're staking your business's future on a naïve strategy that more likely than not will underperform. That's what typically happens when strategies depend too much on quantitative values.

It's nonetheless true that quantitative values have fueled (and continue to fuel) the harvesting of big data low hanging fruit. That is to say that many of the algorithms that have been used until this point do have value and will continue to have value going forward — but only in certain circumstances. For example, an algorithm that predicts when a mechanical part will reach the end of its usefulness is a reliable indicator of when that part should be replaced. Such decision triggers — or decision recommendations, if you prefer a different term — will continue to be helpful. That being said, without the added qualitative inputs for balance and context in decision-making, pure math tends to go a bit sideways in real-world applications.

So, what could act as qualitative measures in decision-making? For the most part, they are things you associate with human qualities, such as behaviors, emotional responses, talents, instincts, intuitive intelligence, experience, cultural interpretations, and creativity. Folks often refer to them as *soft skills,* but Google's Cassie Kozyrkov hits the nail on the head when she says that it's better to think of these skills as "the 'hardest to automate.'"

I'm all for cultivating the soft skills, as my arguments throughout this book make clear. But I'm not about to throw the baby out with the bathwater. The points I make here in no way negate or contradict the usefulness of math in data science, data analytics, or decision processes. You can't just skip the math in decision intelligence — nor should you want to. The good news is that much of the math you need has already been built into many of the more useful analytical tools available to you, making them much less troublesome and far easier to use. (I tell you more about tools with automated math later, in Chapter 7.) For now, the point is that math alone does not a decision make.

REMEMBER

Decision intelligence adds to the data sciences; it doesn't lessen the value of the associated disciplines, experiences, tools, or lessons learned thus far in scalable decision-making. Rather, it involves a rethinking of how and when to use those disciplines, experiences, tools, and lessons learned thus far in the decision-making process. Make no mistake; math and algorithms remain important cornerstones in many of the tools. However, math and algorithms are decoupled from the decision-making process in the user interface and pushed to the background in emerging decision intelligence and related tools.

TIP

Think of decision intelligence as the next logical, evolutionary step in data democratization and interpretation.

The right math for the wrong question

Math is the cornerstone of data analytics in particular and of decision-making in general. However, the right math can deliver the right answer to a wrong question, which leads to nothing good in the way of making a sound decision.

How does that happen? It's the result (mostly, but not always) of communication errors and mismatched assumptions between people or groups. That's right — the problem has nothing to do with the math. The math is right and the answer is right, yet it's all wrong because the question was wrong for the result folks were looking for.

For example, it's quite common for a data scientist or a data analyst to query the data based on a question asked by a business manager or an executive. But managers and executives often pose questions from assumptions rising from their own (limited) perspective, often using imprecise language. Data scientists and data analysts, on the other hand, think and speak in the precise terms and statistical assumptions that are the norm in their crafts. The two seldom meet on the same train of thought.

TIP

If you ever want to develop a firsthand appreciation of what I think of as the great data divide, learn any programming language (provided you don't know one already). The first thing you notice is how profoundly it changes the way you think, the assumptions you make, the way you approach logic, and the expectations you have of machine performance.

The truth is, people fall into patterns of thinking and often can't imagine that any other pattern exists. Imagine a cake baker asking a bridge engineer to go outdoors and bring back some fruit flies. Never mind that what the cake baker really wants is a set of edible creations that look like flies made of fruit for that entomologist's birthday cake that's on order; the cake baker said "fruit flies," which the more technical-thinking bridge engineer took to mean those nasty little fruit flies that bedevil your fruit bowl. The bridge engineer may work diligently and for endless hours to collect fruit flies and deliver them to the cake baker who will then see this result as disastrous to their own efforts and squash the lot. That, in a nutshell, is why so many data queries end up delivering so little in terms of business value.

Real-world examples that aren't quite so fanciful are plentiful. As a science-and-technology journalist, I see news publications regularly derailed by their addiction to following the answers to the wrong questions. For example, it's typical for news media to "run the numbers" to see which articles attract the most audience eyeballs, clicks, likes, and shares. Whatever that outcome is becomes the next list of assignments for staff and freelance journalists. Sounds like a good plan, yes? Well, it is, but only for as far as it goes.

There's a problem with diminishing returns. Think for a moment: How many times can the same article be written in different variations before readers lose interest and the publications pay for articles that readers won't read? Those dead-on-arrival articles also impact other metrics, including the ones advertisers consider before buying ads or sponsored content with that publication.

In response, the publications run the numbers again to see which articles are trending now in order to repeat the cycle until it again ends in diminishing returns — all because of a wrong question, and even worse, a wrong question repeated endlessly.

The right question would be one that would put the publication in the lead position of trending articles rather than following the leader at the midsection or tail of moving trends. When a publication can figure out "what readers want to read about" instead of looking just for "what readers are reading now," they move to the top position in the competitive pyramid. Further, they stand a real chance of commanding more (and higher) ad dollars as well as greater industry respect and brand loyalty.

In this example, one could use the wrong question as a supplementary question or as input in the algorithm, in support of the correct question: "What do readers want to read?" But ultimately this formula falls short as well because the answer is based on the question instead of the destination. How so? Well, consider if I pose this same query and the answer is that readers don't want to read any of the tech- or science-related topics I write about — they want to read about the newest reality show instead. That's simply an output — an answer — I can't use, and neither can any science or tech publication. Magazines that focus on TV entertainment would give this answer a collective shrug, as in, "Tell us something we didn't already know." It's just not that useful of an insight for the work and cost involved for either genre.

Examples of the right questions for this scenario might include:

>> Which descriptive words appear most frequently across topics in the most read articles over the past year and how do they correlate with the number of likes and shares on this publication's articles across social media? (What I'm looking for here are reader triggers and themes of recurring interests.)

>> What are the top ten shared memes or social media post issues in my audience demographic and how do they correlate with current or breaking science or tech news? (What I'm looking for here are emerging or sustained interests that I can tap into as popular culture or high-interest angles for articles.)

>> How much did writer style and word choices vary between the top performing articles (in terms of eyeballs, clicks, or social media shares and likes) and where are the commonalties. (I'm looking for what kinds of story-telling readers prefer so I can change writer guidelines to improve readability of articles across the board.)

>> What is the impact of SEO keywords on article readership? (Here I'm looking to see if incorporating SEO keywords in the text and headline actually helped or hurt readership and to what extent, so I can adjust how stories are written accordingly.)

>> What is the overall pattern across all top performing articles over the past six months? (Here I'm looking to see what bells and whistles readers may be responding to, even if subconsciously.)

>> What are my competitors top performing articles according to readership numbers and social media shares and what are their commonalities? (Here I'm looking to see if my reader patterns match my competitors and where they diverge so I can consider topic options based on patterns my publication may not have previously considered.)

Now it's your turn. What do you think the right questions would be for a publication to increase its readership by taking the lead instead of following the crowd?

In decision intelligence, you decide first where you want to go or what you want to achieve and then figure out which tools, queries, data, and other resources you need to get there. Think of it as marking a destination and mapping the course to get there before you take the trip or take an action. In other words, decision intelligence asks you to regroup your decisioning processes so that they focus on specific goals — rather than formulate queries that may prove of little business consequence.

REMEMBER

The problem doesn't lie in the math or the data queries. Rather, organizations have a problem because they lack a clear definition of the desired business outcome, resulting in a lack of direction at the outset of the decision-making process.

TIP

Let the business outcome you seek define the queries you ask of data to ensure that your decisions lead you to where you meant to be.

Why data scientists and statisticians often make bad question-makers

Not so long ago, data scientist was the hottest job on the market. Everyone was in pursuit of these data gurus to unleash the value of data and help drive companies forward. And data scientists did deliver what was asked of them. Unfortunately, many of their projects still failed because what they delivered wasn't a match for expectations, although it usually was exactly as ordered. Organizations were and are notorious for not having a business plan in place for these initiatives from the start, and for not being precise in what they are asking data scientists to do.

In short, typically the data scientists didn't fail. Ill-defined expectations and the lack of business planning rendered their work moot. But that's not to say that data scientists' work is always perfect either.

At first, data scientists had free rein, for no one else in the business could quite wrap their minds around this big data tsunami. They experimented with new big data tools to explore possibilities and to educate their businesses on how useful data analytics can be. Then they included projects to answer their business analysts' and business users' most often asked questions. They built dashboards and visualizations, automated them, scheduled regular releases of updated insights, and eventually advocated self-service business intelligence solutions to provide some user autonomy (within carefully structured limits, of course).

But the further this work progressed, the larger the gap typically became between the data scientists/data analysts crowd and the business managers/business executives crowd. That happens when data scientists have too little an understanding of the business and when business leaders have too little an understanding of data science.

As the data analytics industry has matured, businesses are finding that they have little appetite or budget for data projects that fall short of producing business value. The definition of a *data-driven company* has also changed — now it means that data has moved out of the driver's seat and is riding shotgun. Data is an augmenter rather than a usurper.

By and large, data scientists are builders, and statisticians are largely data assemblers and interpreters. Data scientists and statisticians may still be building, assembling, and interpreting, but the problem is that almost everyone now has access to plenty of data tools — visualization tools and templates, model stores, sharable algorithms, specialized automation tools, AI in a box, and so on — to do those things in a more decentralized way. In addition, many of the queries data scientists and statisticians would come up with to ask of data now come prepackaged in modern, self-service business intelligence (BI) tools, complete with AI generated narratives in case the user has trouble interpreting the visualization correctly.

If you're in one of these professions, no worries. There's still plenty of work for data scientists and statisticians to do. But it does mean that the demand for new kinds of talent is rising. To borrow from Cassie Kozyrkov, Google's chief decision scientist, if you were to think of data scientists as microwave builders, you'd realize that the world no longer needs any more microwaves — what it needs now are better microwave chefs.

REMEMBER

In general, data scientists are tool and model builders, though statisticians are data wranglers and interpreters. Neither is a business decision maker. That's not a slam on either profession but rather a clear delineation of job roles. It's not entirely fair to blame either profession for failed projects if there was never a business plan to use their work anyway.

TIP

It's time to focus on the science as well as the art of making decisions. Decision intelligence is about leveraging both hard and soft skills.

Identifying Patterns and Missing the Big Picture

Data analytics, especially those powered by AI, are incredibly good at detecting patterns in data. They can not only find patterns in megasized data sets too large for human eyes to sort out but also find patterns in larger or smaller data sets that humans didn't know to seek. It's a little miraculous how well data analytics work, if you think about it.

Finding patterns is no small matter. According to global consultants, McKinsey & Company's report, machine learning models have outperformed most medical professions in diagnosing and predicting the onset of disease. For example, machine learning has outperformed board certified dermatologists in identifying melanoma and has beaten oncologists at accurately predicting cancers using radiomics and other machine learning techniques. Numerous other reports from other industry analysts detail a spectacular array of lifesaving successes from machine pattern discoveries.

Couple such successes with the proven success of recent mRNA COVID-19 vaccines and you're well on the way to significant breakthroughs for a variety of disease cures and vaccines. And a lot of the secret sauce is based on the patterns found in data. Nevertheless, I'm here to say that, though there's plenty to cheer about, it's also prudent to realize that it's eminently possible that one identifies the patterns correctly and yet can still completely miss the big picture.

It's time to take a look at how that happens in order to understand in later chapters how decision intelligence helps circumvent these and similar problems in the decision-making process.

All the helicopters are broken

The trouble with data sets is that no matter how large they are, something is always missing. That's because there's no singular, all-inclusive *data singularity* — no single data source containing all known information, in other words. There's only a hodgepodge collection of data scattered here and there and yonder. By its nature, any of those data sets is incomplete.

The thing is, people analyze incomplete data anyway because good enough is always better than perfect, simply because perfect doesn't exist. Even if there were a data singularity, data would most certainly still be missing from the pile. There appears to be no such thing as a true know-it-all in flesh or digital form.

That means data scientists and other data professionals must make assumptions, infer, augment, and otherwise tinker about to reach a reasonable output in the final analysis. There's nothing wrong with that. Your own human mind works that way. For example, if your eyes didn't catch all the details in a scene, your brain reaches back to your knowledge banks and memories to fill in the blanks so that you can better interpret what you saw. That method works well in helping you select an immediate escape action in an emergency, but it's pretty much a total fail when it comes to the recollections of eyewitnesses in legal testimonies.

People can often see many places where data is incomplete and augment it accordingly, but the other ways in which data is incomplete often escape notice, because again, your own brain is filling in a picture for you of what should be there but often isn't.

To hammer this point home, think of the problems associated with analyzing data in the hope of discovering what causes helicopter crashes. Data from helicopter crashes around the world and over time are carefully collected to be analyzed. So far, so good, right?! Yes — until the moment the machine informs you that all the helicopters are broken, which, of course, is untrue.

But the machine thinks it's true because the only data it saw was from crashed helicopters. To accurately analyze why helicopters crash, the analytics and AI need to see data from helicopters that didn't crash. In that data set will be helicopters that should have crashed but didn't, and those that nearly did but shouldn't have, as well as helicopters that functioned properly over numerous flights and in varied conditions. Now, there's a better view of helicopter crashes and the machine finally learns that, no, helicopters don't crash because all the helicopters are broken. It took a human to realize that fact first, however.

Decision intelligence adds more disciplines and methodologies to the decision-making process in order to move beyond (and guard against) faulty conclusions and misleading interpretations of outputs in order to move the organization forward to its desired outcome.

MIA: Chunks of crucial but hard-to-get real-world data

At a 2019 Microsoft workshop, the powers that be gave tech journalists and industry analysts hands-on experience in programming AI chat bots and a preview of upcoming Microsoft data-related technologies, including AI, quantum computing, and bioinformatics. One topic touched on was the need for synthetic data, although if I recall correctly, Microsoft called it something else at the time. (Virtual data? Augmented data?)

Regardless of what people call it, you might ask why anyone would need to use artificially created data, given the exponential growth of data from the real world. International Data Corporation, a premier global market intelligence firm, has reported that data from the real world expected to be created over the years 2020 to 2023 is growing at a rate that will surpass the amount of data created over the past 30 years. The analysts also say that the world will create more than three times the data over the next five years than it did in the previous five. Statista, another global leader when it comes to market and consumer data, pegs data growth to be more than 181 zettabytes by 2025.

I don't care how big your data center is, that's an overwhelming amount of data! So, why on earth would you need to create artificial data on top of what you already have? Well, it comes down to the fact that data sets are by nature incomplete. Furthermore, some real-world data is extremely difficult, impossible, or too dangerous to capture.

REMEMBER

Synthetic, augmented, and *virtual data* aren't the same things as false-made-up-out-of-whole-cloth data here, although false data or manipulated data can definitely be injected into real-world and synthetic data sets. (Those are problems for cybersecurity and data validators to address.) Here I'm talking about creating data that you cannot easily, safely or affordably obtain through other means. For example, you might think that getting wind speed data from the blades of a wind turbine, like the ones shown in Figure 3-1, would be a simple matter of taking reads from a sensor on the blades. But what do you do if those sensors fail?

You can't safely send a repairperson to replace the sensor in the middle of a commercial wind turbine farm where the wind coming off the blades of numerous high-powered windmills can be at hurricane force. You can, however, infer data reads based on previous sensor data relative to neighboring wind turbine data in current weather conditions — filling in the missing data with values inferred from previous metrics and/or neighboring devices' measurements, in other words. For example, one can infer without benefit of actually measuring it again that, since a specific structure measured 6 feet tall yesterday and it does not possess the ability to grow, that it is still 6 feet tall today. A better inference would also note that the structure has not toppled or sunk into the ground.

However, you can also create synthetic data sets based on known laws of physics, wind turbine specs, and other factors to create a simulation resulting in synthetic data that can be safely collected and used in decision-making. Most, but not all, synthetic data is created by simulations.

Another example would be facial recognition data. Many countries regulate how much (if any) facial data can be taken or used without a person's prior consent. This can significantly limit the amount of facial data available on which to train facial recognition machine learning models. To overcome a data shortage, companies turn to AI-generated faces of people who don't actually exist. Data from fake faces also helps machine learning know how to determine which faces are real and which are not. The distinction can be useful in many endeavors, including detecting deep fake videos.

REMEMBER

In decision intelligence, data considerations aren't the first priority. Focus on the outcome you want and then determine the tools and data you need to get there. Once you have a map in hand, it's easier to determine whether the data you need is available or needs to be obtained.

Evaluating man-versus-machine in decision-making

Business leaders often formulate a vision for their company or a particular project. This practice is not an attempt to predict the future but rather to aim for a specific future. This person is steering toward a future that they believe to be profitable or advantageous to the company. A *vision*, then, is a decision with a purpose.

How do you form a business vision? Developing an obtainable vision requires both creative and deductive skills. A business leader must be able to imagine possibilities, recognize opportunities, deduce their value and the probability of success, and shape a new or creative idea — a vision, in other words.

In short, a leader's vision is part imagination and part information with more than a dash of math. Business acumen is a talent based in large part on pattern recognition and the ability to see connections between heretofore unrelated items or pieces of information.

Given that data analytics and machine learning are particularly adept at discovering patterns and data relationships, why are they not good at identifying new business visions? Part of an answer might be found in W.I.B. Beveridge's *The Art of Scientific Investigation*, where the author explores the intuitive side of scientists and speaks of originality as "often consisting in linking up ideas whose connection was not previously suspected." Interestingly, that book was originally published way back in 1950 by W.W. Norton & Company Inc. Other great visionaries explain the role of imagination expressed in any form — whether it's art, science, or business — in similar terms. For example, the legendary graphical designer Paul Rand said that the role of the imagination "is to create new meanings and to discover connections that, even if obvious, seem to escape detection."

REMEMBER

Imagination is a critical element in making business visions and other decisions. It's a skill that machines do not possess.

What about logic and math and the other hard skills that machines do excel in? Do they not form the lion's share in importance and worth when it comes to making a decision — particularly in data driven companies? It's true that machines do surpass human skills in this regard. Machines can do math faster and usually error-free, but humans can do it without even consciously thinking about it.

The human brain runs a significant part of this work in the background, leading to the seemingly out-of-nowhere "Eureka!" moment in a flash of inspiration. It's called *intuitive intelligence* — the ability to use the subconscious mind to make faster and more integrated decisions.

Though both human and machine have pros and cons when it comes to decision-making, leveraging the strengths of each leads to decisions that consistently deliver a better value to the organization. This is why disregarding or discounting human instinct, gut feelings, experience, and talent is a grave error — just as overinflating the value of data and machines can easily lead you down the wrong path. Decision intelligence, acting as a multidisciplinary approach to creating balance between person and machine, is in a position to deliver targeted decisions for predetermined business outcomes that move an organization forward.

Chapter **4**

The Inverted V Approach

Traditionally, machine-made or machine-assisted decision making has always been *linear* — it moves consecutively from data preparation and selection to algorithm inputs and finally to an output. The output is typically an insight or a recommendation.

Sometimes, the output is integrated with an automated action. An example is a self-driving car that, at the direction of its onboard analytics' output, takes a left turn to detour around a car accident in the road.

Often, one straight line is not the only path to arrive at a decision. There can be several path options. Interestingly, if you do not retrace your steps, but instead plot a reverse path from your decision back to your starting point, you'll frequently choose a different route than you did initially to arrive at the decision. You may have noticed a similar effect in GPS directions on your vehicle when it directs you home by a different route than it directed you to take to arrive at your destination. Notice that the GPS chose the optimized path both times but even though both points remain fixed, the results are not the same route. When the two paths are joined at Point B (the original destination from your initial starting point), an inverted V is typically formed. This is what's known as an *inverted V pathway*.

In this chapter, you find out why adopting an inverted V approach in decision-making can ensure that you're using the best methods and following the best path to arrive where you meant to be. You may often be surprised to learn that the path you followed up the hill doesn't bring you back where you started at the base.

Furthermore, using more sophisticated tools to get you there or back again may end up leading you astray.

Finding your way to the best decision for the result you desire can be a tricky business. This chapter shows you how to determine the best path and hold the course.

Putting Data First Is the Wrong Move

When Hadoop and other big data tools appeared on the scene, back in the mid-2000s, the immediate mission was to know the unknown and learn the unlearned. Organizations sought to gain business value by first mining their existing data stores. That task quickly evolved into importing data from additional sources, and finally to adding real-time streaming data to the mix.

In short, it was all about the data, all the time. The appetite for data appeared insatiable and the supply of it unending.

Many of these data analytics projects proved successful, but many were also producing outcomes of little to no business value. Fishing expeditions, after all, add value only if fish are caught and tummies are full. Just throwing in a baited hook doesn't create success. Nor does pulling out a fish. A full stomach is the actual measure of success.

This is not to imply that all traditional analyses are essentially fishing expeditions, for they certainly are not. Yet even many of the outcomes that are deemed successful and do have business value fall short of the end goal. Decision intelligence is a framework designed to focus decision-making processes almost exclusively on accomplishing the end goal.

Back to my original (admittedly imperfect) fishing analogy. Think of all the data your company has access to or now possesses. Data analytics can pull a fish out of that data lake for you (yes, folks do call such data stores "data lakes"), but that fish may be poisonous or have a bad taste or be too small to make a satisfying meal — or result in a fine from the Fish & Game Warden, depending on current regulations. In this analogy, you were successful because you ended up with a fish. However, you clearly also failed because the fish, for whatever reason, was inedible. If you can't eat it, you're still hungry. That's a failed project.

By contrast, if you were to first decide that you want to satisfy your hunger with fresh fish and then select a rod, tackle, bait, and a location favorable to catching fish that you know are edible and legal to catch — you're much more likely to end up with a full tummy soon and no penalty for doing so.

By starting not with a question (how many fish are in the lake?) but rather with the desired outcome (hunger sated by edible fish), you can easily determine what steps and information you need in order to accomplish your goal. Decisions you make along the way are logical and purposeful and the final action predictable, measurable, and valuable.

If, instead, you had started randomly fishing in a lake to see what you find at the bottom, you may find items of interest — edible fish, inedible fish, bicycles, old tires — but my guess is that you'll likely remain hungry while you conduct this inefficient search. It's a lot of wasted effort and resources for little real gain.

Approaching data analysis by placing data first tends to have the same shortcomings. Finding lots of interesting tidbits in the data may be interesting, but you need to recognize that such results are not particularly useful and do not indicate a particularly wise investment in terms of either your time or your money.

REMEMBER

Decision Intelligence moves data from a starring role to a supporting role. The desired outcome determines which data, tools, and analytics capabilities are necessary.

What's a decision, anyway?

Time to get down to brass tacks, which in this context means coming up with a precise definition of the word *decision*. A *decision* is an act of choice from one or more options. A calculation or determination leads to the decision (the act).

Defining decision-making gets a little wonkier. Different disciplines define the process in different ways. Even so, no matter who or what makes the decision, the decision-maker for the purposes of this discussion is always a person. That's because a decision-maker is generally held responsible for the act. Machines bear no such responsibility.

For example, if a person drives a car into a crowd of protestors, the driver is held accountable for that act (decision). However, if an autonomous car drives into a crowd and kills people, it isn't responsible for the act even though the decision (the act) was executed by the car's onboard automation. The courts would have to sort out which persons are ultimately responsible for the car's actions, but in no case will the court blame the car.

REMEMBER

Decision-making is a process, whether that process is used by a person, a machine, or both. *Decision intelligence* is a multidisciplinary approach involving both quantitative and qualitative methods to begin at the end — in other words, begin with a desired action and then work backward in forming a decision-making process.

REMEMBER

When it comes to decision intelligence, the goal is not a decision (an act) but rather a specific result from that act. For example, neither the catching, cleaning, nor cooking of a fish can be considered the successful final result of a fishing trip. Success is found in a specific result — in this case, a full stomach. Start with the result — the impact — that you want and work backward to determine which team members you need, which roles they should play, and which data sets and data analytics capabilities you need in order to make it happen.

Any road will take you there

As an old adage says, "if you don't know where you're going, any road will take you there." The solution, of course, is to select a specific destination so you can then take the right road accordingly and ensure your arrival at where you meant to be. Decision intelligence helps you achieve this goal by keeping decision-making focused and on track, insisting that the decisions made provide business value and push the company forward to where it wants to be.

Obviously, it's not only the path that influences whether you arrive. Much like when you travel, you need to determine several other factors as well, such as which mode of transportation you're taking and the costs and logistics involved. You also need to decide which luggage to take, which clothing items to pack, and how to get around after you arrive.

Decision intelligence as a methodology works in much the same way: After you have determined the specific business state or impact you're aiming for, you assemble the elements you need to make it happen. To make such a list, the first step is to determine the essentials. First and foremost, you need facts. Good decisions are based on facts.

If all the facts you need are readily available, you don't need data to make a decision with a favorable impact. If only *some* of the facts you need are available, however, you need to find those missing facts (if you can). More likely than not, you find those facts in data, but sometimes a search engine like Google, a human subject matter expert (SME), or someone in the company's employ with institutional knowledge can deliver the missing information, and you still won't need data. In fact, just asking someone in the know first before you ask data often ends up being a useful way to shave time and costs off the exercise. Of course, the person you ask must be knowledgeable and trustworthy, but the point here is to get to the facts in the most efficient way.

However, if you find that you *do* need data to find the missing facts, you will have now narrowed down the list of data sets to analyze and likely have a good idea of where you can find them.

Not all facts are permanent, just like not all landmarks, roads, bridges or speed limits on a road trip are enduring. You may need to run the same analysis on refreshed data periodically to detect a change in facts. For example, last month's sales fact might be "blue coats are hot sellers," but this month sales data shows "no one is buying coats of any color."

If you're seeking to update facts with the help of sensors on the Internet of Things (IoT), look for change data (data points that differ from several identical data points before this change in value is detected) rather than waste resources on analyzing the entire set of data points, many of which simply repeat information.

Once you know what facts you need and where you're likely to find them, it's a relatively straightforward matter to determine which analytics capabilities and other tool options that you need, too.

In defining your desired business impact, be sure not to make it too broad or too general. Keep it narrow so that you have a clear picture of the direction toward which you must drive every action. Don't meander or wander in your efforts. Choose a business outcome and make every step in the process move toward that outcome!

The great rethink when it comes to making decisions at scale

When Hadoop came to be and the big data craze began in earnest, companies turned to data scientists to make sense of this technology and the truly mind-boggling stockpiles of data each company possessed. Most of the process was confusing and complex in the minds of top decision-makers. The result: Business leaders defaulted to putting data scientists in charge of framing the issues central to the survival of their businesses.

Data scientists decided what to do, how to do it, and how far to scale out or scale back. Data analysts served as human search engines, sorting through data to find whatever trends it contained for the period. Outputs were shuttled to business leaders, usually on an overnight schedule when bandwidth was more available. Business leaders made decisions based on the outputs they considered valuable enough and sufficiently timely.

In short, data analysis was centralized.

Since then, several important developments evolved when it came to how data analysis was done. Data digitalization became the new battle cry, automation tied to analytics was presented as the new norm, and built-in AI became a common expectation.

REMEMBER

AI in this context isn't the stuff of sci-fi movies or scientific aspirations. *AI* is a misnomer because in terms of modern software it refers to machine learning (ML). Everyone calls it AI in an effort to simplify a complex concept in the minds of business users and consumers. After all, everyone who watches TV and movies has some idea of what AI is (albeit usually the wrong idea) whereas your run-of-the-mill person on the street has never heard of machine learning. ("Wait, is that when you use a tablet in the classroom?" "Um, nope, it's not that at all. Let's just call it AI and go from there!")

Meanwhile, data science itself was becoming more automated and AI was increasingly playing stronger, bigger roles. Data scientists began to divide their attention between a) AI models and training and b) data science. Online marketplaces such as Amazon's AWS marketplace of AI models, Google's Public Data for public data sets and visualizations, and Figshare, where academic researchers share their research outputs, began to take up some of the slack. Each of the available marketplaces are filled with shared dashboards, data visualizations, templates, models, or algorithms that made using data easier for the uninitiated. As for the tools themselves, many began to merge as they matured, which is what happened with AI, data science tools, and business intelligence (BI) software.

In short, data science as a discipline was being pushed to the background and data scientists were steadily being decoupled from the lead as tools became more automated and user friendly. Businesses sought to leverage these tools to democratize data — decentralizing it so that nearly any job role had access to it to some degree. And yet, such tools ended up not being a silver bullet, because data continues to grow, becoming even more unwieldy, more of a nuisance to users, and a growing cost to businesses. Gains attributed to the data revolution that used to be substantial are slipping, either because the work isn't sufficiently aligned to business goals or because the problems ahead are increasing in complexity.

REMEMBER

Data analysis experimentation and data stockpiling are no longer in vogue. Tolerance for inefficiencies in outcomes is diminishing, and the holy grail of using data to drive a company — from reshaping the business model, reforming to be a business disruptor (or thwart said disruptors), and finding and providing the ultimate customer experiences to other complex but highly profitable endeavors — has not yet been fully realized. All these circumstances combined to create the need for a major rethink when it came to how one should make business decisions at scale — in other words, optimizing how one uses the decision-making process to handle the big decisions in the C-suite as well as the small decisions in the hands of business users.

That rethink resulted in a multidisciplinary approach designed to get you to the point where you can make decisions accurately, quickly, and efficiently using means suited to forming augmented analytics with unprecedented agility and flexibility. That approach, of course, is decision intelligence.

Applying the Upside-Down V: The Path to the Output and Back Again

Decision Intelligence is a rethink, not a redo of data-driven decision-making. You're not throwing everything out and starting from scratch — you're simply reimagining how you're going about the work and how you're using data and the associated tools. Part of the reimagining involves adopting the decision intelligence approach — the one that says you should begin at the end and work backward. In other words, you need to clearly define the business impact you seek, focus on the decision that will deliver it, and then work backward to the beginning. The idea here is for you to work out which steps will lead you to the exact decision you defined and the business result you seek.

REMEMBER

Don't feel bad if you sometimes get lost while you're trying to work backward on a path that doesn't yet exist. A lot of people get lost when they start using this method.

One way to wrap your mind around how this approach works is to use an inverted V to track the path up and then back again. Take a traditional decision process and follow its path to the outcome. That's the first leg of the inverted V — the leg that starts at the bottom and moves upward to the output or decision. (See Figure 4-1.)

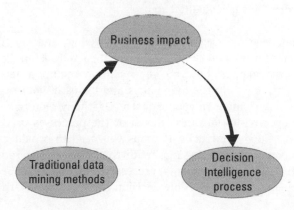

FIGURE 4-1:
The inverted V.

Now that you're at the top of the inverted V — at the decision — disregard how you got there and figure out how to get back down, which is to say back to the beginning query. This is the second leg of the inverted V model.

It's almost always an inverted V because, in the process of working your way back to the beginning, you make different choices in tools, processes, and data. You often find a better way than the one you took to the decision. In any case, compare the two paths. In all likelihood, other paths will also occur to you.

The point is that, whereas it's vital to fix the decision in your mind, it's not that important to set in stone either your queries or the path you're planning to take. It's this newfound flexibility in your choice of path that gives you room to discover and deploy efficiencies that may not exist in the traditional route. Settle on the business outcome you want first and then work backward to find the precise process, tools, data, queries, and other resources you need accordingly.

REMEMBER

Decision intelligence is a multidisciplinary approach. Among the varied resources you can use are inputs and direction from business leaders as well as what's generally referred to as the decision sciences: the social and managerial sciences, in other words. They're the ones that focus on the human-inputs side of the Decision Intelligence process.

Evaluating Your Inverted V Revelations

One of the first things you likely notice when doing the inverted V exercise is that you can consider more assets and employ more sciences. The traditional way of using machines to make or assist with decisions typically had you depend on established formulas, calculations, queries, data sets, methods, and so on to dictate how and what you do and when. This approach is similar to following GPS directions in prescribed, sequential steps.

By comparison, decision intelligence is a methodology and not an exact process, so the steps are flexible and customizable to fit each decision. You may find, for example, that the business outcome you seek may require a fleshed-out plan to prepare, support, and help the individuals and teams in your organization confront far-reaching changes in your industry. Or it may require a significant shift in either the overarching business model or the processes used to manage the company fleet of delivery trucks. Perhaps you need to consider possible public backlash or a potential incoming market threat from a known industry disruptor. The point is that almost all elements, processes, and assets can be considered and leveraged to make the best possible decision (act) and realize the business outcome you seek.

Your focus should be on *how* you make a decision. Which elements of the decision-making process require data analysis and which elements can be automated? That's a concise way of looking at the digital side of decision intelligence. But you should also ask, "How can I *make* this decision — whom do I need on the team, what soft skills should be added to the mix, which subject matter experts do I need to tap, how will the public or our customers likely respond, how should our existing talent be leveraged, what market forces should I consider, and what other elements pertinent to the decision should be under consideration as well?"

In decision intelligence, you can consider all influencing factors (whether digital or human), extract the elements that support the desired decision and outcome, and use them as inputs in the most efficient and meaningful manner possible.

REMEMBER

Decision intelligence allows room to insert creativity and other influencing factors into the decisioning process. Each step will thus be taken in context and within the parameters of the end decision.

Having Your Inverted V Lightbulb Moment

Traditional data-driven decisioning still continues to work well in many instances. For example, these days onboard analytics combined with AI enable autonomous vehicles to navigate roads and highways fairly well. One would think there is little need for any inputs beyond the facts currently fed into the analytics, which are mostly factors like real-time road, traffic, and weather conditions. Keep in mind, however, that (because change is the only constant) navigating in the future will happen under different conditions and this current method of decision-making may not hold up well.

The changes expected to impact the automotive industry and vehicle use are disruptive. For example, we already know that the move to electric-powered vehicles rather than ones running on fossil fuel is going to accelerate in the face of climate change. This, of course, will also change the refueling landscape and related vehicle services. We also know that smart cities are already in the plans and many cities have deployed at least a few of the features in traffic optimization already. Adoption rates of those features will in turn affect vehicle pathway designs — meaning roads and parking area designs and locations will change substantially.

Add to that the fact that in-city green spaces and multiuse developments are in demand, putting further pressure on current streets and parking areas. Roads may disappear from inside city spaces altogether, and parking areas may be located outside of populated areas or shrink, necessitating autonomous vehicles to park so close together or atop one another where human riders have no safe egress.

Maybe a public owned rideshare will eliminate private vehicle ownership altogether and the vehicles remain perpetually in motion, making parking arrangements moot.

Meanwhile, people will continue to make vehicle choices for entirely personal reasons, whether they own, rent, or use a rideshare to procure a vehicle. These harder-to-code preferences and experiences must be considered in the decision-making process as well. In short, car manufacturers will need to not only repeatedly and rapidly rethink their vehicle designs but also restructure their business model to better align with changing realities.

That is only one example among many across industries where current decision-making methods are working but may fail as time progresses. The ability to master the decision intelligence approach becomes even more of an imperative as the need to adapt to rapid change grows exponentially. Not that decision intelligence isn't an excellent fit for the here and now as a purely practical matter, because any use case that would benefit from tighter control over the final business outcome will benefit from a decision intelligence approach, which is to say pretty much all of them. So, too, is any use case designed to propel the company forward competitively, rather than tag along behind the status quo. A news outlet, for example, can choose to produce more content aligned to the most-read articles of the day, or its editors can choose to use decision intelligence to better predict which emerging news stories and topics today will be popular with readers tomorrow or next week or next month. Of course, news outlets can use decision intelligence methods to do both simultaneously, leaving no coin in their profit universe thus unturned.

REMEMBER

There will always be a host of mundane, practical decisions to be made, and decision intelligence can certainly help you make them. However, there are also the more creative endeavors — the ones that emerge as true innovations or as industry disruptors. Math alone cannot deliver to expectations in projects requiring the creativity, critical thinking, and genius demonstrated by those who can see connections between ideas and things where none now exist. Decision intelligence is a framework that includes in its considerations and calculations those inputs that are difficult or impossible to code.

Last, but not least, decision intelligence is a decision-making framework that fully deploys and leverages data democratization. It empowers start-ups, small businesses, and solopreneurs as well as most business users in organizations of any size. Done properly, decision intelligence is a powerful tool for agile small and midsize businesses in their efforts to become industry disruptors, compete against larger competitors, or make their companies more profitable. In larger organizations, decision intelligence tools enable employees to more fully apply their talents and make better on-the-job judgments to the company's benefit.

Recognizing Why Things Go Wrong

The defining line between hype and a true evolution in business tactics or technology developments like decision intelligence is in how it performs in real-life applications. In other words, the telling difference is found not in the promise of success but rather in the cashing in on it.

Decision intelligence aims specifically to deliver profitable business impacts. If it fails to do so, something is amiss in its execution, not in its design. We can know this because the decision science methods that are used are historically tried-and-true and merely combined and ordered in a different way. And, in any case, people can readily see and measure whether the targeted business impact came to fruition — or if it failed to manifest.

But given that any failures are a matter of botched execution rather than a flaw in the design, it's time to run a few reality checks on areas where fails are likely to occur and wins can be further secured.

Aiming for too broad an outcome

A common error is to make too broad a decision from which to develop the steps you need to get there. For example, a broad outcome such as "increase sales" or "broaden the product line" fail in terms of narrowing the path and defining the metric.

This is akin to saying you want to drive to California, without naming a specific place in California as your destination. You may find that you arrive somewhere over the California state line, but it's unlikely to be helpful or of benefit if it's a random destination.

If you were to instead state a narrower destination (Spago's, in Beverly Hills, for example) and used GPS to map a course, then it's pretty easy to calculate how much gas you need to make the trip, how many nights you'll stay in a hotel on the way, and how much you should set aside for your meal budget. And if you were to specify to the penny how much you were willing to spend on that trip to Spago's, these better-defined parameters would further define your path. The same is true if you were to specify making the drive in an electric vehicle, because your path would then be redefined according to the availability of charging stations.

REMEMBER

Be specific about the business impact you seek so that you can easily and clearly see how you might get there.

Mimicking data outcomes

It's a natural tendency to build on the knowledge you already have, and that includes using or mirroring insights from traditional data analytics and data mining methods. But you shouldn't be looking to validate or re-create earlier data insights, nor should you necessarily be using those outputs as your launching point.

REMEMBER

Insights gained from traditional data analytics and data mining methods aren't generally decisions, but rather pointers to a decision. Of those that *are* actual decisions, that are performing well, and that are fully automated, many can be useful as steps or inputs in a decision intelligence process, but they, too, should rarely be considered as the final decision you're chasing.

Sometimes you need data in order to realize the business impact you ultimately seek, but many times you won't in the decision intelligence process. Often, decision intelligence can be easily confused with *digital decisioning* — the process that focuses on machine decisions based on data.

You'll find many use cases in your business where digital decisioning is critical and ends up being all you need in order to resolve an issue. But that process, too, begins with determining the decision first and then figuring out what the machine needs in order to get to that decision in an automated and sure-footed way.

Failing to consider other decision sciences

Data science, when needed, is only part of the decision intelligence process. The other part is one or more of the decision sciences — the ones that are more human in nature and include disciplines such as psychology, human behavioral sciences, economics, philosophy, game theory, and management science.

REMEMBER

If you're using data alone, or data first, you're doing it wrong. Choose a business impact first and then use a blend of decision and data sciences as needed.

Mistaking gut instincts for decision science

Decision sciences, meaning mostly the behavioral sciences in decision-making, have specific methods and processes. You can't arbitrarily replace them with what is commonly referred to as gut instinct. This is no place for guesses. You want to make disciplined, highly reasoned decisions here.

However, there is some room for a few shortcuts, where repeated experience has formed rule-of-thumb shortcuts — heuristics, in other words. But be careful in using these, because they're common areas for mistakes and biases to happen.

Falling to change the culture

Though existing data teams can successfully execute decision intelligence processes, be aware that they may fall back into previous routines, which will diminish your returns. In other words, data teams may continue, or revert to, working as they had been working under data science models, either in part or wholly. If they do, this renders decision intelligence efforts pointless because the process isn't being implemented. In short, if the data team's mindset, culture, or routines remain or resume, it's time to reconfigure the team in order to disrupt what has become a stagnating environment.

However, it is equally possible that business leaders may commit the same sins in reverting to old decision patterns and mindsets, discount the results, fail to adequately explain the business decision target, or otherwise resist change or sabotage the DI project. Be sure to get leadership and rank-and-file buy-in as needed and early on. Also, deal with culture issues and resistance to change via change management throughout the Decision Intelligence process.

2

Reaching the Best Possible Decision

IN THIS PART . . .

See why the best decision may actually be the worst

Explore how to shape a query when you already have the outcome

Set up the decision

Take actions that lead to the targeted business impact

Chapter 5

Shaping a Decision into a Query

You can easily tell that it makes more sense to aim for a specific business outcome than to not do so, but it's a bit harder for most people to comprehend what to do next. After all, decision intelligence leans heavily on data — analytics that are typically set into motion with a query. But how do you frame a firm decision as a question that analytics can answer?

Put another way, how do you chase an answer when you already have the answer but are missing the question?

Part of the challenge in sorting this out comes from confusion over the terms and in looking at this puzzling quandary through a data-first lens. Keep in mind that a lack of consensus on the definition of key terms further muddies the issue.

Understanding the varying roles of data analytics in how smart things work — smart TVs, healthcare devices, and smart cities — versus the functions of intelligence as they apply to digital and human decisioning is the key to mastering decision intelligence and understanding where and how data queries fit into that process.

Defining Smart versus Intelligent

To get this chapter going, I start by defining the terms *smart* and *intelligent* as they are used in this book and most often used in broader discussions of decision intelligence. First, you must realize that the word *intelligence* in this context isn't synonymous with *smart*.

Intelligence means the ability to learn, understand and apply new information — a function in this context reserved for humans and the not yet fully realized Artificial General Intelligence (AGI), the AI portrayed in science fiction movies and books. (Apologies to dogs, crows, octopi, and other intelligent beings.) *Smart,* on the other hand, is most often used in the context of the Internet of Things (IoT) — in other words, referring to those devices or network of devices at the edge of computing that use data and analytics, often powered by machine learning (also referred to as AI), to automate a limited number of well-defined actions.

A smart TV, for example, recommends shows and movies based on what you've watched and/or rated in the past. The automated outputs from the recommendation engine are displayed onscreen for the users to review. When a selection is made, that item then plays automatically. A recommendation engine uses machine learning algorithms to filter data according to previous usage patterns in order to suggest similar selections the user might be interested in. Recommendation systems work the same whether they're on a smart TV or a smart couponing system at the cash register in a grocery store. They're data first (also known as *data-centric*) systems.

Other systems work a little differently but are still data-centric. For example, smart electric meters record and analyze customer usage data to enable adjustable pricing for peak periods, automated service problem reporting, and automated billing. Smart cities similarly record, exchange, and act on data from other smart products in their vicinity, such as:

>> Autonomous vehicles

>> Toll bridge passes

>> Automated road-violation ticketing sensors

>> Traffic flow systems

>> Emergency response systems

>> Carbon emission reads

>> Accident, traffic, and road hazard avoidance reporting systems

Any smart device out there follows the same pattern: data collection and analysis within a narrow focus for a well-defined and determined action. An autonomous vehicle, for example, fits the bill because it can take only one or two of five possible actions/decisions in any given moment or circumstance: brake, accelerate, turn left, turn right, steer straight. Though these systems are anything but simple, generally speaking, the decisions they make are simple or at least limited in available options: stop or go, turn or not.

Smart digital systems go beyond data comprehension to include learning from patterns in the data and continually improving the outcomes as a result. However, they don't understand the information as humans do, and they can only apply what they have learned to a pre-defined application, so they are smart but not intelligent.

The point here is that decision intelligence as a framework insists on focusing on the process as much or more than on data comprehension. Rather than shoehorn your desired outcome into a data query, you trust that the queries you need to put to data (if, indeed, such is even required) will come to light as you define the process necessary to arrive at your outcome.

Discovering That Business Intelligence Is Not Decision Intelligence

Not all products labeled *decision intelligence* truly deserve the title. That doesn't necessarily mean you should reject the imposters out of hand, however. Many of them can be helpful tools in the decision intelligence process. Business Intelligence (BI) applications are a prime example: These systems have evolved substantially over time and have proven themselves to be useful in understanding key aspects of your business' state and performance. However, all still require substantial changes before they can be deemed pure decision intelligence tools. Even so, several BI applications are well on their way to becoming decision intelligence tools, such as Qlik Sense (which leads the pack in my opinion), Domo, and Yellowfin.

BI apps are considered to provide intelligence in the sense that the fictional James Bond 007 would gather intelligence for the British Secret Service — but definitely not in the sense that the applications are themselves intelligent. However, these applications are smart as they go beyond data comprehension to provide further intelligence about the business through inferring and providing descriptive, prescriptive, and predictive outcomes. Given that context, think of business intelligence apps as functioning like your own secret agent out there, gathering data and inferring meaning on issues that are of most concern to you.

Despite the amazing advances these applications have made, including the incorporation of natural language querying and visualizations as interfaces, machine learning automation throughout most or all processes, machine generated narratives to explain the meaning of each visualization to the uninitiated, and increasingly sophisticated data pipelines and treatments, the outputs that BI apps come up with aren't actually decisions. They are pointers to decisions. In other words, they are insights that you can act upon but they do not tell you the best action(s) to take.

Further, BI apps are still data-centric, meaning they put data first and then mine it for insights — as is the traditional way. The use of machine learning models and algorithms do not change the course.

Put simply, BI apps still focus on data and AI models, whereas decision intelligence focuses on decision processes. That doesn't negate the fact that BI applications are wonderfully amazing tools. The point here is that BI apps are useful to the decision intelligence process but not yet capable of being true DI tools. I expect that to change soon, and a new category of pure DI apps (meaning something new and just not evolving BI apps) to emerge.

Discovering the Value of Context and Nuance

You want to know the difference between a best decision and *the* best possible decision? You may not be able to obtain the best decision for any given business problem — for a whole host of reasons, including cost concerns, insufficient deployment time, lack of company will, technology limitations, material shortages, skilled labor shortages, the laws of physics, regulatory restrictions, compliance failures, cultural relativism, moral absolutism, public backlash potential, licensing requirements, enforced industry standards, contractual agreements to wars, natural disasters, and economic upheaval. The best possible decision takes into account all circumstances influencing the probable impact of a business action before committing itself.

REMEMBER

Being able to come up with the best possible decision in the real world as it lives and breathes as opposed to chasing after the best decision in some abstract world that doesn't exist is the best argument I know of for the efficacy of a decision intelligence approach. With a DI approach, you can aim for the best possible outcome from the start rather than waste time and resources using traditional data analytics to arrive at a better-or-best decision that you'll never be able to implement.

TIP

Many factors that influence what constitutes a best possible decision are known or are calculable in advance. Considering them in the determination of the business outcome you seek is usually a straightforward exercise. However, it's possible to overlook an influencing factor, so it's important to be diligent at this stage as long as you don't let uncertainties push you into analysis paralysis. In all likelihood, your data will be incomplete to some degree, and your initial assessment of contributing factors may be imperfect as well.

Don't aim for perfect — aim for good and possible. As General George S. Patton is reported to have said, "[A] good plan today is better than a perfect plan tomorrow." That advice holds particularly true in this age of rapid industry and market changes wherein tomorrow's perfect plan might be obsolete.

Defining the Action You Seek

In the early days of big data applications (think Apache Hadoop), businesses were focused on learning the stuff they didn't know they knew. They were aware they had massive troves of data, but they didn't know what details the data contained. These new capabilities in affordable tools fueled a modern version of a gold rush. Organizations were giddy at the prospect, but the results were as mixed as the metaphors that ranged from mining data to fishing expeditions.

The point in data analytics, then and now, is to make decisions based on facts concerning the business, its customers, and market conditions. Yet many of these early forays produced little of consequence in real-world applications beyond the realms of marketing and sales basics. Not that this was a bad development, for any illumination is helpful when you're trying to navigate in the dark.

But to mix the metaphors again, not all illuminated insights amounted to pay dirt. Though numerous findings proved interesting for one reason or another, many failed to produce business value. And if there are ever two constants in business demands, they are business value and speed in realizing that value.

To say that continuing ineffective searches for mere nuggets of golden business truths is untenable is the understatement of the year. A rethink was clearly in order.

REMEMBER

The one true business goal everyone should strive for is to insist that every analytics output deliver business value in the quickest time possible. Once you grasp that fact, the value of replacing data-driven in decision-making with business impact driven becomes clear. Decision intelligence means committing yourself to business-impact-driven processes. It's a simple as that.

To arrive at any desired business impact, you first have to determine the necessary preceding action or actions and then you have to deploy them. You' work backward from an action (or actions) to determine the most productive and expedient path to bringing that action/those actions to bear.

The path you discover may or may not include data and analytics, but many business decisions, especially those with impacts that must be deployed and managed at scale, are sure to involve data, data analytics, automation, and AI. As such, these aspects will naturally play a significant role in digital decisioning. Just keep in mind that decision intelligence, as a process, involves tactics used in several disciplines and may or may not include data analysis or AI. Digital decisioning can be an element in decision intelligence, or it can be used alone to leverage AI in achieving specific business impacts. In either case, you must determine the decision (the action) first.

Setting Up the Decision

In any decision intelligence progress, the first thing you need to do is carefully determine your target — your desired business impact, in other words. A machine can't make this judgment call for you. Take your time and think it through carefully. Ask yourself the following questions:

>> **What is it that you want to make happen?** The answer is the business impact you seek.

>> **How can you make that happen?** Identify the broad action(s) you need to take.

>> **Which steps do you need to take to create that action?** Identify the specific steps you need to follow to carry out the broad actions you identified above.

Decision intelligence is the process or framework within which you will find the answers to these questions. It's a methodology that will enables you or your team to pull from tried-and-true tactics in a variety of disciplines so that your effort is neither guesswork nor solely reliant on gut instinct, creativity, or intuitive intelligence.

Decision science versus data science

Decision intelligence consists of two main parts: decision science and data science. Although it's not always necessary to use both parts as part of the decision intelligence process because not all decisions require data and analytics. It is nonetheless still important to think of these two general types of sciences as useful components inside the decision intelligence toolbox.

Decision science is the more general term of the two, encompassing several sciences and integrating analytical and behavioral approaches to making a decision. As a science, it's grounded in theories and methods drawn from a number of different fields, including psychology, economics, philosophy, statistics, and management science. However, it's not limited to these sciences. You can also incorporate other disciplines such as experimental game theory, neuroeconomics, psychobiology, anthropology, design theory, and cognitive science into your version of decision science.

Which blend of these sciences you use depends on the nature of the decision you're trying to make. Don't let this intimidate you. Odds are good that you're using many of these methods in your daily life, even if you're unaware of it, to help you decide where to eat lunch, which summer camp to enroll the kids in, and whether to accept the terms of a mortgage.

Even though decisions like these seem simple and mundane, the mental processes required aren't quite so simple. To speed things along, especially in emergency situations where you have to make a decision in a blink, your brain uses practical shortcuts. Collectively these shortcuts are called *cognitive heuristics*. While there's no guarantee that these shortcuts will render optimal, perfect, or rational decisions, they are so efficient and useful that they're copied in computing, such as in writing algorithms and other programming, such as software development and electronic games, where they are called simply heuristics.

REMEMBER

Even if much of decision science sounds mundane, it's important to recognize the crucial role your use of it plays in decision intelligence as a whole, and on both the human and machine sides of decision-making.

Think of decision science as the human side of the equation — the side of decision-making where machines aren't trending and where humans are completing tasks that machines can't reproduce. Generally speaking, the three aspects of decision science are:

> » **Normative analysis,** where you create formal models of choice to determine the most ideal decision for a given situation.

>> **Descriptive research,** where you study how cognitive, emotional, social, and institutional factors affect judgment and choice.

>> **Prescriptive interventions,** where actions are taken in an attempt to improve judgment and decision-making.

Historically, decision science has been applied in a variety of industries. Examples include (but are not limited to)

>> **Healthcare:** The focus here is on a variety of areas, ranging from forming a diagnosis to selecting from treatment choices to determining an acceptable balance in costs versus benefits in treatment options.

>> **Law:** Here, decision science insights can inform legal decision-making on subjects such as reducing the effects of bias in attributing responsibility to a party and aligning penalties and judgments with the crime and cost to society.

>> **Risk management:** Decisions in this area are linked to an organization's risk tolerance level, such as in prioritizing security measures, assessing climate change risks, and determining potential product liability, all of which can benefit from decision science methods.

>> **Marketing:** Insights gained from decision science can steer decisions linked to pricing strategies and customer reward incentives, for example.

>> **Logistics:** Warehousing decisions — from the order of product placement in the warehouse to facilitate efficiency in order fulfillment, to supply chain management and planning fulfillment processing locations — can benefit from decision science insights.

>> **General business:** Some decisions, ranging from identifying unrecognized conflicts of interest and biases to expansion and growth decisions, are common across all industries. Decision science can lead to better decision-making in these areas as well as others.

REMEMBER

Adding decision science to the decision intelligence methodology is a sensible and practical way to leverage advantages that can be gained from established and familiar disciplines and their respective tactics.

Data science, like decision science, is also one of those interdisciplinary fields encompassing several sciences, including data management, analytics, AI, computing in various forms from edge to batch processing, statistics, and others. If you were forced to describe data science in a nutshell, however, you wouldn't be far off if you simply said that it aims to prepare, process, and analyze data. As for the necessary skills involved in doing data science correctly, you'd have to include domain expertise, programming skills, computer science, and strong knowledge of mathematics and statistics.

Like decision science, data science is an established interdisciplinary field, as business and the sciences have used data in a computing sense for at least 30 years and counting. Despite its extensive use over many years, data science wasn't recognized as an independent discipline until roughly 2001. Now it's considered to be an essential business function, as businesses and other organizations become increasingly digitalized, making information largely unreadable without a computing device to view it, let alone analyze it.

Layering the data and decision sciences inside the decision intelligence process is the result of a rethink and reorganization of known methods for the purpose of deliberately and consistently harvesting value from business decisions.

Framing your decision

Decisions aren't executed in a void, and thus they shouldn't be conceived in a void. This is one reason the decision intelligence framework is so effective — it takes information and impacts not as isolated instances but rather as part of a larger context.

However, you must be diligent in extending impact evaluations to the degree necessary to ensure that the context holds and that impacts are acceptable in both intended and unintended consequences. For example, carefully consider from the outset whether a short-term decision will likely have long-term consequences — and vice versa if you're working on a long-term impact. It isn't the case that all negative consequences should be avoided, but you do need to know to expect and prepare for them. For example, you may find that a short-term negative outcome is acceptable when it also bears or contributes to a larger, long-term positive outcome.

Framing your decision — seeing your decision as the action leading to your desired business impact, in other words— calls for attention to detail as well as concision in specifying intent, action, and impact. You also have to take scale considerations into account and acknowledge that automated decisions on a large scale extends impacts over many instances, sometimes over significant periods of time, over vast spaces of geographies and governments, and across business lines. Reverberations in impacts, in the form of unintended consequences and unforeseen or unacknowledged risks, can be substantial.

You should be moving through the decision intelligence process with the clear intent of achieving a well-defined result with concise expectations on likely impact implications. While you're moving forward, however, make sure that you aren't (unintentionally) caught in the snares of a confirmation bias. This bias occurs whenever a decision maker seeks or considers only evidence that appears to support the decision maker's previously formed belief — and discounts or dismisses all evidence to the contrary. If you've already made a decision, or you don't want to make a decision, don't expect decision intelligence to give that decision — or lack thereof — its seal of approval. Odds are, it won't.

REMEMBER

Two ways to help guard against skewing the framing of your decision is to be on guard against falling prey to information bias (bias rising from measurement errors stemming from misclassification or observational bias) and data selection bias (where the data is not truly representative of the group, problem or situation and instead favors one element over others). Either or both can cause you to develop an incorrect or otherwise faulty decision frame that will then corrupt your DI processes and move your organization in the wrong direction relative to the optimal business outcome that could otherwise have been realized. In short, ensure the information you're working from to frame your decision is current, accurate, and fully representative of the situation, problem, or group.

TIP

Frame your decision in such a way that the intended business outcome is accurately targeted, the trajectory is predictable and manageable, biases are eliminated, and consequences are expected, acceptable, and manageable.

Heuristics and other leaps of faith

Cognitive heuristics is a fancy term for mental shortcuts — those tricks humans use in order to make instant decisions in times of danger. The fight-or-flight model is an obvious example.

But there are many more nuanced examples as well. Firefighters, for example, develop a sense for when a burning building will collapse, or a policeman reacts to the threat of a gun from seeing only a certain arm movement, or a schoolkid decides to catch or duck a ball that's fast approaching. All these actions rely on cognitive heuristics.

It's also how people make other types of decisions in a hurry, as in "Should I stop or accelerate for the yellow traffic light before it turns red?"

Cognitive heuristics is also how people avoid analysis overload — meaning making mundane, everyday decisions laborious time sinks by repeatedly considering the same information or beliefs. For example, your mind typically limits your breakfast options to two or three items or places that you commonly choose in order to shorten the decision-making process and speed you through the meal so you aren't late for work.

TIP

Be aware that as helpful as cognitive heuristics can be in framing decisions, they are far from infallible. Take the time to consider whether these mental feats are helping or hurting your efforts. In other words, check your assumptions and assess whether you have considered all pertinent options.

REMEMBER

Heuristics are helpful even though they aren't always accurate or don't provide the path to the outcome you would have preferred. When they fail, they're called *biases*. When they work, they're considered a rule of thumb to live and decide by.

When it comes to making decisions, think of heuristics as fast but uncertain, and algorithms as slower but definite. If you want to be quick, use the mental shortcut; if you want to be consistent, use the algorithm. Of course, in reality, that's a false choice because you can use both — yes, even in computing. And yes, definitely use both in decision intelligence.

Don't worry: Heuristics aren't blind leaps of faith. Heuristics in computing and analytics are tied to the same thing human mental shortcuts are — easily recalled and repeatable information. They are assumptions presumed to be true because they were preestablished as such and therefore don't require exhaustive examination to establish them as facts again.

There's no need to reinvent the wheel, in other words. In both human and machine decisioning, a wheel can be safely assumed to be a wheel, and any assumption based on that fact can be used to move the decision forward at a faster pace

You can use facts discovered and proven in various sciences as the basis for heuristics in decision intelligence, too. Just be sure that you're not using them as biases, but rather as acceptable assumptions that will speed your progress in discovering the path you need to follow in making any given decision.

Chapter **6**

Mapping a Path Forward

The 2020–2021 COVID-19 pandemic disrupted businesses significantly, breaking business and supply chain models worldwide. In so doing, it also made historical data practically useless, at least for the time being, because nothing that once was now exists in the same form. This has left every industry in a fragile and precarious position, with entire economies teetering from the aftershocks.

New data and new analytics methods are in urgent demand. By mid-2020 several global research and advisory firms were already praising emerging frameworks and technologies that aimed to define and grow a "new normal," drive innovation, and rebuild society over the next five years.

Additionally, industry analysts praised efforts to further democratize and scale data and analytics to help organizations regain their footing, reconfigure the economy, and reset society.

Decision intelligence fills that bill quite nicely. But understanding the value of a methodology and applying it in real life are two entirely different concepts.

In this chapter, you find out how to build a decision intelligence strategy that will carry your company and projects forward despite the uncertainties facing everyone. That strategy will also face squarely the human inability to rest on past laurels or rely on historical data that no longer tells you what you need to know.

Putting Data Last

Data sets have not converged into a single, all-encompassing data repository where all data in existence resides in a single physical or virtual space — commonly called a *data singularity*. That event is largely expected to be necessary for the emergence of Hollywood's famed depictions of a human-like AI. The concept is both feared and cheered by various data and AI luminaries.

But for now, at least, all that is available to humans and machine learning are pockets of data sets that reside here and yonder, from privately owned data centers on an organization's premises to a variety of private and public data storage in hosted and cloud environments and even inside those Internet of Things (IoT) devices found on the very edge of computing networks. This is to say that, rather than one large collection of data in a central place from which almost anyone can draw data, data is stored like nuts in trees by legions of squirrels fearing a hungry winter — almost anywhere and everywhere that data can be stored. In other words, data are sequestered in software silos. Therefore, you can safely assume that any data set, by the confines of its nature, is incomplete.

A variety of inputs from a collection of data sets will be more complete than a single data set, but even so, you cannot expect the results to necessarily present a complete picture. This inherent failure should tell you that you need to reformulate decision strategies in ways that enable you to obtain better business results through a more nuanced understanding of the problem and a more definitive approach to determining what data and/or additional resources are needed.

REMEMBER

Even if you could somehow rectify the inherent incompleteness of data sets along with the errors, repetitions, and lack of consistencies they contain, the fact of the matter is that the recent COVID-19 pandemic has rendered much of that data moot anyway. Historical data has essentially lost all meaning and relevance in the "new normal" context — not to mention that the new normal is still far from resembling any consistent state of normalcy.

Given this scenario of constant flux, why would any organization continue mining data in the usual way and call it done? It's not a given that recent data can even be used as historical data in future year-over-year (YoY) and other traditional financial metrics that companies use to analyze and judge their progress.

In short, many companies are adrift. Given that reality, organization leaders typically don't care as much about where they've been or even where they are. They want to know where to go from here. That's why you must reconsider doing data analysis as you have historically done it and decide first which direction you need to move the company in order to survive and thrive.

Solving that challenge often requires a new hybrid approach that harnesses the power of every asset at your disposal. Data is only one of those assets. You may need to plan its role in your calculations differently now.

Recognizing when you can (and should) skip the data entirely

It's amazing that it took just a few short years — since 2008, really — for big data analysis to move from an emerging trend to the backbone of every business. The mantra *data-driven company* soon emerged as a battle cry and evolved to a venture capitalist's and stockholder's base level requirement. Data are king; long live the king.

But, as it turns out, data isn't king at all — data are minions.

Evidence of this new reality is overwhelming. For example, machine learning (ML), also referred to as artificial intelligence (AI) in marketing hype, is no longer as helpful and certainly no longer scaling well on historical values made invalid by pandemic induced turmoil. Machines once thought to soon be masters of the universe look more akin to sad, deflated balloons now that data has tumbled from its throne.

Even customer recommendation engines — the software in the grocery store that offers in-store coupons and makes product suggestions, or a television streaming service that recommends other movies to watch based on a customer's purchasing or viewing data — are off their game because of data woes. Grocery stores dutifully offered coupons early in the pandemic for toilet paper that no longer populated store shelves. And TV streaming services were stymied when new content dried up, viewer tastes suddenly changed, trending towards older content choices which tilted more toward nostalgia and comfort. In my imagination I could almost hear them saying: "What is going on, dear movie streamer? Why do you no longer like movies about plagues in the apocalypse? We recommend these movies on contagious diseases and widespread death based on your previous viewing choices!"

Now organizations are left to sort through the data pieces and rethink their approaches. You'll likely have to start labeling data label pre-, during, and post-pandemic to prevent skewed results when seeking insights applicable to what's happening today. New machine learning techniques may be required, and ML certainly needs a training data reboot and maybe some reinforcement learning tactics to move it past the broken learning curves.

REMEMBER

Decision intelligence isn't radical or new or trendy. It's a broader approach to making informed decisions, which includes traditional data and analytics. That means you can still rely on current guidance such as the open standard for data mining process called CRISP-DM to help you evaluate data assets.

Leaning on CRISP-DM

Decision intelligence incorporates several existing methodologies and sciences. One example on the data science side is CRISP-DM, which stands for the Cross Industry Standard Process for Data Mining methodology. It's an open standard process model with six phases that together describe the data science lifecycle.

Note that this process also starts out from an understanding of the business need. That's the question it poses itself: "Which business need are we trying to meet?" In decision intelligence, the process begins with a statement, not a question: "This is the result (action) the business wants to take."

The six phases of CRISP-DM are described in this list:

>> **Business understanding:** The idea here is to get a firm grasp on the specific business need.

>> **Data understanding:** You come up with an exhaustive inventory of current data assets as well as a list specifying the kinds of data you still need to track down. It's vital to also ensure data veracity — that all data points are up-to-date and consistently accurate throughout the data sets, in other words.

>> **Data preparation:** Raw data can rarely be used as is. You need to clean and organize the data before using it in models or any other analytics tool.

>> **Modeling:** Here's where specific models and/or modeling techniques are considered.

>> **Evaluation:** Yes, at some point you have to select which model best meets your business objective.

>> **Deployment:** Here's where you deliver the results to interested parties.

REMEMBER

This step list doesn't necessarily denote a precise sequence of events, because it's common to revisit phases as the work progresses.

The six phases of CRISP-DM are repeated ad nauseum in every serious document or discussion on data mining. More often than not, such discussions go into more detail than anyone could ever need (you can easily get lost in the weeds when talking about CRISP-DM), so I've limited myself to offering just this quick glance at what that standard entails. For a more detailed — but weed-free — guide to CRISP-DM, read Meta Brown's most excellent *Data Mining For Dummies* (Wiley).

Using the result you seek to identify the data you need

In decision intelligence, you start by deciding the business outcome you seek and the decision that will cause that impact. From there, you determine which assets (including data) you need in order to arrive at that decision. Then you can determine which processes to use to derive the meaningful information you need and whether any of that can be automated. This is what is meant by working backward from a decision.

Traditional data mining efforts were supposed to provide actionable results — insights that a business could act on. Despite good intentions and best efforts, however, the results often weren't actionable. Sometimes the analysis landed far outside the mark, sometimes the data wranglers simply misunderstood the business goal, and sometimes the data requesters couldn't accurately convey what they were asking, because of their (unfortunate) word choices. Last but not least, sometimes company leadership lacked the will, the budget, or the risk tolerance necessary to pursue the recommended action.

In short, there was and is a lot of waste, delay, and other inefficiencies in the traditional manner of producing results.

Decision intelligence seeks to eliminate waste and inefficiencies by ensuring that the decision is defined first and properly vetted against company culture, goals, will, budget, risk tolerance, PR value, and other factors *before* effort and money are spent toward the work. The final action comes as a result (outcome) of the decision intelligence process and is aligned with the decision made initially.

Though some decisions can be made on the back of a napkin or in a simple spreadsheet by assembling the necessary facts and analyzing them manually, most organizations, even small ones, want to harness the power of digital decisioning. The next section points out why.

Digital decisioning and decision intelligence

Many people assume that digital decisioning means relying on doing whatever your successfully deployed AI tools tell you to do. It's much more than that, though. *Digital decisioning* is a methodology that also incorporates continuous improvement tactics, AI optimization, decision modeling, and decision testing and management as they apply to day-to-day operations.

Digital decisioning, like decision intelligence, begins with the decision — the final desired business outcome — in mind. Digital decisioning, however, is focused primarily on automation and on improving the decisions made by technologies that make extensive use of automation. That means digital decisioning is used primarily to continuously improve automated decisioning rather than to define a complete automation process. It's a manager of sorts of advanced automation based on an unfailing alignment to the desired business outcome and a determined effort to continuously improve how machine-made decisions contribute to the desired decision and impact — all within specified business rules.

Sometimes the terms *decision intelligence* and *digital decisioning* are used interchangeably. The notion of starting at the end first is a new approach for data science, data analytics, and AI professionals, so it should come as no surprise that, at this early stage, some folks are unsure about the terminology. Nonetheless, it would be more accurate to say that decision intelligence is the broader concept, one that incorporates digital decisioning to the degree applicable in realizing the desired business outcome.

Some decisions should be automated, and some should not — and it just so happens that the digital decisioning method can help you decide which ones are which. However, *soft information* — data such as opinions, ideas, commentary, and subjective observations — generally isn't part of digital decisioning considerations. James Taylor, the CEO of Decision Management Solutions and a foremost authority on the digital decisioning process, described to me recently in rather succinct terms which decisions are suitable for automation. In his eyes, such decisions have to be repeatable, nontrivial (when it comes to complexity and data intensiveness), and measurable.

Soft data, by comparison, are hard to code and often hard to measure as well, yet they can be equally crucial considerations in a business decision. This is the crux of why qualitative approaches like managerial science and other behavioral sciences are added into the decision intelligence mix.

REMEMBER

The two methods — digital decisioning and decision intelligence — aren't mutually exclusive. Both start out by determining the desired business impact — the decision — but then both make a mental trek backward, cementing the continuing escalation in the business world of the need to keep your eye on the ball — or on the decision, as it were.

Decision intelligence is the name of the game now. All business functions are now entering a new age of targeted accountability.

Don't store all your data — know when to throw it out

Before you start looking at how much data you have collected that the pandemic and other factors have rendered invalid and decide to do a major data purge, remember that data isn't your first consideration in decision intelligence.

Instead, start by reevaluating where your company stands now and what needs to be done going forward to continue to adapt to changes as they occur. Simultaneously, determine where you want the company to arrive on the other side.

These are the decisions that take priority as you deliberately move from a reactive to a planned and predictable response and approach. Use decision intelligence to help you make the best decisions to get you there, even (and especially) in these most trying circumstances.

Those decisions will lead you to other decisions you need to make, and every decision will determine what data and other assets you need.

If you nevertheless still want to clean up your data stores now and make some room for an influx of new and more diverse data, consider starting with these basic guidelines:

>> **Consider keeping "change" data instead of all data:** In other words, eliminate repetitious data, such as oft-repeated Internet of Things (IoT) or Industrial Internet of Things (IIoT) reads or file duplications.

>> **Consider deleting old and out-of-date customer data by determining sensible time cutoffs:** Examples are buying trends that are 5 years or older, IRS records that can be deleted after 7 years, and bankruptcy records that are 10 years or older.

REMEMBER

Data is not king; data are minions. It's not a crime to dump some of the minions! Much of the data that organizations store today are replaceable by updated data, but most of it's invalid for current decision-making purposes anyway, given the sea changes wrought during and after the pandemic. But don't be too hasty to purge data. Quite often it can have value in ways the organization has yet to consider.

TIP

Your wisest course may be to wait until you finish working through your new decision processes using the decision intelligence method and then, after you're done, note which of your stored data is never or rarely used. From there, you can pare down the data you ultimately decide to keep.

Adding More Humans to the Equation

Make no mistake, human decisions have always been an essential part of data and analytics, even AI. Data scientists, data analysts, and leaders in the organization all bring to bear significant influence when it comes to how data is cooked and served. Yet, none of these is a decision strategist, the most sought-after data skill set today and a role close to the center of decision intelligence.

REMEMBER

Professionals can take advantage of a number of different ways to add their inputs without having to write a line of computer code. How machine and human inputs are blended together in decision intelligence depends on the project and the data strategist's unique recipe.

The point here is that human decisions have led to the creation of all things data related and added significantly both to the pros and cons of various tools and projects. Decision intelligence isn't radical in suggesting that more human input can be advantageous, provided it adds to — rather than subtracts from — the substance behind a decision.

The challenge is that soft skills are *difficult* to code. Yes, it's true, but difficult doesn't mean impossible. Some sciences have worked diligently over many decades precisely to decode human sentiments, ideas, and behaviors. There's still work left to do in terms of developing definitive detection measures and analysis tactics, but some data is workable now, in terms of using it in decision intelligence projects. Further, some technologies are collecting data based on measurable observations of different aspects of the human condition and human behaviors.

For example, *computer vision (CV)* is an interdisciplinary field in computer science that gathers and interprets visual data inputs such as digital images, videos, and x-ray films. Essentially, CV works to enable computers to mimic the human eye-to-brain data analysis system. It's used with AI because the patterns within visual data are typically quite complex and unstructured.

One intriguing aspect of CV involves the ways it can be used to observe and interpret human behaviors. For example, CV is often used in advertising signage or videos displayed on gasoline pumps as a tool for tracking eye movement and thus accessing whether, how long, and which parts of the ad the customer looked at. CV also tracks and analyzes consumer behavior in stores, such as tracking which items and displays cause shoppers to pause and look, which items customers pick up and examine, how many clothing items they try on, where they're socializing, and whether they focus on procuring a certain item.

TEST THE RESULT YOU SEEK — IS IT THE ONE?

Any initial decision discovery you make may be exciting on the surface, leading to enthusiastic high-fives all around, but it may prove to fall short of expectations in the end. This is why deciding on the desired business outcome should be a disciplined process, not one where you pluck a decision from thin air or randomly choose one in response to an opportunity or a demand.

Some people rely on their brain to take its usual shortcuts and plumb its own subconscious to arrive at an inspired business decision pursuit. There's absolutely nothing wrong with that strategy. However, relying on decision science to move you from the warm-and-fuzzy to the cold-and-codable is a smarter approach in determining a business outcome as well as the decision that leads to it.

That's because you must make several real — and vitally important — considerations in that process. Those considerations include risk analyses, cost benefit analyses, and cost effectiveness analyses as well as simulation modeling, microeconomics, operations research, behavioral decision theory, management control, change impacts, statistical inference, cognitive and social psychology, and computer science, among others.

In short, decision science codifies your biases, quirks, talents, and genius inspirations (to a degree). (The technical term for this codification process is *heuristics,* but in layperson's terms, cognitive shortcuts and rules of thumb are used to simplify and improve the choices.)

Decision science guides how these initial decisions should be formed, from inspiration to a practical goal. This methodology is based on several quantitative techniques. The sciences integrated or combined under the decision science umbrella are psychology, economics, philosophy, statistics, and management science.

Decision science is the framework from which a decision is built to benefit an individual, a business, a nonprofit or government agency, or another entity. In this case, you use this framework to identify the initial decision, from which you work backward in decision intelligence.

And if you do make a gut-level or shower-inspired decision and have that Eureka! high going on, you can gauge its viability by using this same framework.

Either way, you can judge whether this result is the one to seek — the one you want to achieve.

Note that *decision science* is an interdisciplinary field which uses a collection of quantitative techniques to inform decision-making. *Decision intelligence* is a framework designed to tie the outcome (action) to a predetermined decision of well-defined business value. Decision intelligence is, at its essence, the combination of decision science and data science.

Similarly, diagnostic images such as those obtained by x-rays, MRIs, and mammograms can be "read" by CV applications, based on information and rules initially provided by human subject matter (SME) experts. The information and rules provided were then written as computer code and a collection of images illustrating that those were then presented to machines to "learn."

With all that preprogramming out of the way, AI and other advanced analytics can now catch other patterns in the visuals, enabling them to detect disease earlier than the methods doctors used. Those additional findings are a great benefit to medicine but also prove the value of adding human derived information and techniques to augment or accelerate machine efforts in analyses and decisioning.

The shift in thinking at the business line level

Decision intelligence isn't just a top-level exercise for data science teams and C-suite executives — all the executives in the organization whose titles start with "chief" such as chief executive officer (CEO), chief information officer (CIO), and chief finance officer (CFO), in other words. It's a method designed to leverage human talent across the board — from executives to business managers all the way down to the rank-and-file. This has always been the goal in data democratization — to get data into the hands of every worker in the company.

Data democratization seeks to eliminate bottlenecks and gatekeepers who hinder timely decisions and innovations at the source. An IT department that's doing its job well also seeks to eliminate barriers in accessing, analyzing, and acting on data.

Earlier efforts at data democratization relied on dashboards and visualizations to convey information to workers throughout the organization. (See Figure 6-1.) Despite data democratization being named by several industry analysts as a top trend prediction for 2020, adoption rates of the technologies used for this effort are commonly poor.

I'm a big fan of data democratization efforts, but I'm also here to tell you that there's a big difference between conveying information and extracting good decisions across the organization. For example, information and instructions typically flow down from executives and managers to employees as a matter of course. But when the goal is to ensure that all talent in the company is more fully exploited in order to advance the business cause, you need information to flow back up as well.

FIGURE 6-1:
Is a picture
always worth a
thousand words?

Put another way, simply conveying directions to employees is a one-way street. Harnessing all talent to make company decisions better and more profitable requires a two-way street so that information is exchanged. After all, employees' ground floor perspectives encompass different details than the executives' bird's eye view. Both perspectives are valuable and together provide better context. Leverage both perspectives.

REMEMBER

Most of the time, it won't be necessary to report decisions to upper management, because employee decisions are most often a common and routine aspect of their jobs. Decision Intelligence can be used to define the rules and scope for lower-level decisions to keep the company on the desired path. The degree of autonomy given to employees is a judgment call that must be made by every company.

In any case, expect companies to facilitate a shift in how people in the various business lines think in their decision making, which means that you empower more employees to make more decisions unilaterally. This will likely entail a new generation of virtual digital assistants (VDAs) for enterprises, in the vein of Alexa, to not only provide employees with relevant insights but also answer the question, "What will be the result(s) of this decision?" Enterprise VDAs already exist and are proliferating in business applications produced by a variety of vendors for just such business purposes. Examples include Oracle, Microsoft and SAP, all of which provide VDAs in their software to assist workers in customer organizations to do a broad range of tasks. VDAs can also be used to develop other assistant and skill chatbots (AI assistants specializing in specific skills). For example, Microsoft's Virtual Assistant is a Microsoft open-source template that enables you or others in your organization to create a chatbot to aid or augment workers with any task while also maintaining full control of user experience, organizational branding, and necessary data access.

Some old-school people managers may be troubled at the idea of empowering the rank-and-file to make decisions on their own. But this antiquated way of thinking will plummet as job automation advances. The naked truth is this:

The only people who will remain employed in the age of profuse automation are those who are the strongest in critical thinking skills, creativity, emotional intelligence, leadership, and other hard-to-code human-based skills.

A company will find such employees of little business value if they aren't allowed to work with some degree of autonomy. Admittedly, orchestration of their efforts will still be required, but that's just another argument for using decision intelligence — because it unites processes and guides them to a well-defined target.

TIP

Definitely prioritize collective intelligence, also known as *group thinking,* as a prime data source for some projects. Groups with high levels of diversity in background, culture, and profession who are collectively focused on solving a specific problem will prove especially useful in providing additional context and expanded perspectives.

Eventually, decentralized decision-making will become the business norm as companies seek increased agility, continuous business improvements, multiple paths to thwart or become disruptors, rapid business model changes, and other concepts not previously thought to be part of a business's competitive arsenal. But that's the subject of another book.

The point here is that the pandemic has permanently changed businesses and economies in fundamental ways, making the new normal anything but normal. The companies that thrive will be those that can thrive in a near-constant state of flux, through enhanced and targeted decision-making wherein every single ounce of talent and data is extracted and leveraged.

How decision intelligence puts executives and ordinary humans back in charge

There has been lots of handwringing over AI advances. People fear that automation and/or AI will soon take over all remaining jobs. The specter of mass unemployment hangs over worried workers everywhere. Even those working three or four minimum wage jobs simultaneously, just to eke by, are reluctant to ask for a raise because "the machines were coming."

The pandemic sped the adoption of automation far ahead of schedule, as most people went into lockdown to avoid the virus. Most of that automation is still in place, but the labor shortage that followed in the recovery period proved that automation isn't enough to keep businesses alive, much less set them up to thrive.

Further, despite the prediction from the World Economic Forum that automation will "displace 85 million global jobs by 2025," it also predicts that in the same period "97 million new jobs will be created that are better suited for a more heavily automated economy."

These better-suited jobs will be populated by people with strong domain knowledge, institutional knowledge, critical-thinking skills, problem solving capabilities, and a high level of creativity, among other specialized, distinctly human traits.

In other words, automation isn't eliminating jobs so much as it's changing the nature of work.

The C-suite of executive and board directors is seeing the beginning of a similar trend. This emphasis on what I call "specialized, distinctly human traits" is a welcome turn away from the earlier, data driven trajectory. To see what I mean, listen to the story of Deep Knowledge Ventures (DKV), an investment fund based in Hong Kong that made history in 2017 when it appointed to its board of directors an AI named VITAL (developed by the now dissolved Aging Analytics company). Further, DKV predicted at the time that AI would be running Asian companies within five years. It would seem that the venture capital firm was on to something, considering the fact that AI was steadily advancing inside many companies at the time.

Many a CEO was already chafing at having to substantiate every business decision with data rather than make a gut call or simply make a decision on their own. Many were quietly ignoring the data when it didn't agree with their own thoughts on the matter. Then, with the increasing incursions on boards and other high-profile placements, it appeared that AI would crack down on charismatic and crackerjack CEOs much harder than their part-time human counterparts. As far as much of the C-suite was concerned, this wasn't a welcome development.

Fortunately for them, the expected crackdown hasn't happened. A slew of legal and ethical issues soon had VITAL enmeshed in a PR nightmare, with many commenters on the investment scene labeling DKV's actions as a publicity stunt. By 2019, DKV had, without much fanfare, pulled the plug on VITAL.

More fortunate still, CEOs are slated to resume the helm more fully again, but that doesn't mean they'll make decisions *sans* data and AI. However, the tide is turning, and enabling greater autonomy for CEOs as well. As with the board of directors, there is now plenty of room to exercise creativity, domain expertise, experience, and talent — but to do so within the relative safety of this new decisioning methodology.

CEOs and other top executives will determine many of the big-picture decisions at the top of the decision intelligence process. Automated decision science tools can assist in refining and testing these decisions while decision intelligence will inform them of the likely real-world impact. In short, by moving data and AI to a supporting role rather than to a star position, humans in any job role can contribute more to their work and feel less robotic themselves. This should have a significant positive impact on morale, talent retention rates, and job satisfaction ratings.

Limiting Actions to What Your Company Will Actually Do

Not all good or even great decisions are executed. The phrase *action not taken* is often a startling and dismaying note to find on an algorithm's record. This phenomenon isn't new. Companies have chosen to pass on prosecuting counterfeits that copy their brand or intellectual property, pass on preparing defenses against ransomware attackers, and pass even on shoring up their defenses to prevent a second or third attack by the same party.

The list of seemingly incredibly bad moves after receiving sound information and machine assisted insights is long and notable and not limited to just a few industries.

If this statement flabbergasts you, join the club. Many a data scientist and data analyst has been frustrated by seeing their hard work ignored while untenable (but eminently avoidable) business conditions are willingly sustained.

Sometimes, the hesitancy or refusal to act proves harmful or even disastrous. Sometimes, however, taking a pass on acting on a good insight isn't such a bad decision when it comes to the broader scheme of things. The focus should be placed on a given business outcome — keeping your eye on the prize is everything. If the insight doesn't bring the prize closer, it should not be acted on. That means, before you get started on pursuing a specific business outcome, vet it first against company will, budget, resources, culture, and other known potential internal obstacles. This strategy saves you lots of time, money, effort, and frustration.

Looking at budgets versus the company will

Check the desired business outcome against more than one potential internal obstacle before doing the rest of the work in decision intelligence. For example, the company may have the will to see a decision through, but not enough budget to make the effort a success. Conversely, the company may have the budget, but not the will to deploy a decision.

Within these company bottlenecks threatening to block your way, you often find multiple layers of potential quagmires. For example, potential landmines in a company, for an otherwise well-crafted decision, can show up for the following reasons:

>> **Political orientation:** Sometimes a decision is made or discarded according to how it is perceived to fit with the political beliefs and affiliations of people in an organization. For example, a decision to provide a safe workplace by mandating masks and testing for unvaccinated workers is viewed by some to be a political stance rather than a safety issue. Some workers quit in defiance of such mandates because they valued their political opinion over any concerns about their health. Executives, too, sometimes make decisions that align with their political affiliation. The point here is that company or country politics can be serious obstacles for your otherwise non-political decision intelligence projects.

>> **Conflicts with the company culture:** If a decision is not a fit with the company culture, it is unlikely to be adopted and implemented. A company's culture is its commonly shared values. For example, if the company culture includes a commitment to animal welfare, then a decision for the company to test its products on live animals would be a direct conflict.

>> **Priority too low in the company's mission:** Every company has priorities on where to spend money, what jobs to fill, and other business issues. If the DI project addresses a decision that ranks low on that priority scale, it is doubtful that it will receive much support in seeing it come to fruition. Indeed, it may fast become a candidate for cost cutting. One example: a decision to buy more swans for the lake in front of the manufacturing plant. Yes, it would be nice to see the birds every day but it's clearly a low priority project. Another example: An insurance company may decide to exclude a more expensive drug from its formulary even when it is the superior treatment because cutting insurance claim costs is a higher company priority than improving patient health.

>> **Outside the company's mission:** It's easy to get caught up in an interesting new idea but if it doesn't fit or advance the company's mission, it likely won't be supported in the budget or by other resources. For an example, the data shows that the company could save thousands of dollars in energy costs by installing solar panels to power the cooling system in the company's data

center. While it's true that money would be saved, this efficiency does not move the company mission forward like the alternative decision would: to use cloud computing which has no energy costs for the company to pay and also provides features and capabilities above those obtainable for the same costs using the company's data center. In short, cloud computing saves money and advances the company mission. The decision to install solar panels would not be supported in this scenario.

» **Too controversial:** Most companies prefer to avoid controversy and any decisions on divisive topics that can spark customer, employee, or public backlash. For example, many employers rather avoid making decisions on whether its employee health insurance plans cover reproductive healthcare. Therefore, any attempt to decide whether or not to offer such would, in most cases, be shunned in favor of letting the insurance companies offer whatever they offer and thus escape making a decision that would be controversial either way.

» **Conflicts with the expectations of partners, vendors, or customers:** Identify groups that are likely to be impacted by your decision before you pursue it further only to find it rejected or abandoned somewhere down the line. For example, check vendor contracts to make sure you aren't breaking an earlier arrangement with one vendor as you decide how best to improve your supply chain or leverage a relationship with a new vendor. Another example: If customer expectations include a rewards program, don't decide to discontinue that program or replace it with another until you first address how customer expectations of the initial rewards program will still be met.

» **Public backlash potential:** If your decision gets the electric chair in the court of public opinion, the consequences can be costly. For example, if a big pharma company raises the price on a lifesaving drug like insulin, which is known to cost very little to produce, public outrage may eventually lead to a regulatory environment curtailing company and industry profits. Indeed, as of this writing, a prescription drug plan to regulate drug prices is before the U.S. Congress as part of the Build Back Better bill. No matter what type of decision you're making, it's wise to check expected impacts for potential public backlash before you get too far along in the process.

» **Outside the company's risk tolerance:** Like individuals, organizations have different levels of risk tolerances. In other words, some companies are more comfortable taking bigger risks than others. Make sure your decision is neither too timid nor too bold for your organization's risk comfort zone. For example, if the decision is to accept cryptocurrency in your organization's fundraising efforts, first make sure that your organization is comfortable with the risks, such as the fact that it has high value volatility, it's an intangible asset that can easily be lost to a forgotten password, and it is neither regulated nor insured by any authority.

>> **Interpersonal conflicts among decision-makers:** Turf wars between decision makers or business leaders can sabotage the success of your decision. For example, the chief technology officer (CTO) may want to add a new technology to the company's asset portfolio, but the chief information officer (CIO) had rather use the money in the technology budget to hire a managed service provider (MSP) to fill in during the labor shortage. The struggle for control of the budget can be loud and legendary but it can also wreck your DI project. Make sure you have a good read on the various turfs and turf protectors before seeking support for your DI project or pursuing its implementation.

>> **Pending regulation passage:** Fortunately, regulation rarely happens overnight. Even if a bill is put on the fast track and thus winds its way through regulatory bodies faster than usual, it still takes long enough that affected organizations can usually see it coming. It's wise to take these pending regulations into consideration in your decision making, along with the probability of their passing into law or becoming a new rule. Examples include potential Covid vaccine mandates under the auspices of the U.S. Occupational Safety and Health Administration (OSHA) and Austria's recent lockdown of unvaccinated persons — both of which affect workforces and the base of volunteers for companies and nonprofits respectively.

>> **Compliance issues:** Every organization has a set of policies, processes, and procedures that ensure everything the company does complies with all relevant laws, rules, and regulations. These are collectively referred to as "governance and compliance." Make sure that the decision you are preparing to implement is well within the boundaries of your organization's governance and compliance requirements. Examples of regulations you may need to comply with include (but are not limited to):

- EU GDPR (European Union General Data Protection Regulation)

- GLBA (Gramm-Leach-Bliley Act)

- HIPAA (Health Insurance Portability and Accountability Act)

- PIPEDA (Personal Information Protection and Electronic Documents Act)

  CCPA (California Consumer Privacy Act)

  SOX (Sarbanes–Oxley Act)

>> **Budgetary concerns:** The bottom line is till the bottom line. Here are some budget considerations that may derail the decision at the head of your hoped-for decision intelligence project:

- You might have a budget for both the decision process and the initial launch but an insufficient budget for follow-up actions or recurring costs to maintain the impact over time.

- One budget can't cover all the costs of the actions, but monies from several departmental budgets could. However, the business result doesn't satisfy the needs of all involved departments and therefore isn't justifiable on that end, so the funds are not made available.

- The action takes place beyond a single budget period, leaving a funding gap in one period or between accounting periods.

- The expected return on investment doesn't reach sufficient levels.

- It just isn't sexy enough to remove budget dollars from a pet project that's already on the schedule.

Budget constraints and a lack of will are the two top obstacles any project can face, but other roadblocks can prove just as fatal. Read on to see the bigger picture.

Setting company culture against company resources

Company culture is rarely a unified monolith of accepted behaviors, although it's usually presented as one. Companies often list the values they espouse in cut-and-dried terms as part of a mission statement or another official proclamation, but the actual workplace is frequently far more nuanced.

For example, a company may aim to honor and promote diversity but be biased, unintentionally or intentionally, in numerous ways. Checking the viability of a decision against company culture must be equally nuanced for it to succeed in deployment. The same issues in intentional and unintentional biases in the adoption rates of technologies apply to decisioning, albeit more in light of the outcomes than the technologies and methods involved.

The easiest course is to hew closely with culture statements documented by the company and be prepared to work through unstated points of resistance such as biases and fears of loss of job, autonomy, or authority. Vet the action against the company's stated culture before you proceed. However, that doesn't necessarily mean you should cave in to cultural pressures. If the business outcome is solid and ethical, you may need to revise the presentation to proactively address the deviation from the company's norms or rework your decision to proceed in accordance with company culture. Here are a few questions to consider:

>> Does the decision trigger known pockets of resistance within the company?

>> Does the decision meet the company's ethical standards and mirror its values?

>> Does the decision pass muster with regional societal values and mores?

>> Does the decision have a political or religious implication or connotation in the minds of leadership, employees, or customers?

>> Does the decision alienate market or industry allies?

Your decision must also be vetted against company resources. I talk about money and budgets earlier in this chapter, but here I'm talking about nonmonetary resources, such as available talent and person-hours, hardware and software assets, data assets, other assets, executive and employee buy-in, and other resources. Here are some common resources to check your intended action against:

>> Energy availability and costs

>> Supply chain considerations

>> Inventory availability

>> Key talent availability

>> Market timing

Once you have vetted your decision against these and other internal factors, you can calculate the probability of the act being realized. It may be that you need to scratch the decision entirely or couch it and pitch it differently to secure additional resources.

In any case, know where you stand before you proceed with the rest of your decision intelligence work.

Using long-term decisioning to craft short-term returns

One criticism U.S. companies often face is for thinking too much in the short term. The criticism is justified — company executives do tend to make decisions based on this quarter's likely stockholder returns. Admittedly, executives can do little to push back against this pressure, but that doesn't mean they have to cave to them, either.

Because decision intelligence begins with a business outcome, it can be used to plot out a long-term outcome and then work backward to identify and create a series of short-term outcomes that will deliver for stockholders but also keep the company working toward the longer-term strategy. However, decision-makers should also consider the advantages that come from making the company more agile in light of the pandemic flux that all industries find themselves in today.

Plotting a deliberate and accurate response rather than taking a reactive course may mean the difference between finding the company in bankruptcy court or finding it crowned as the industry king of the hill. This nugget of wisdom is well known, yet some companies still find themselves in reactive mode. That can be easily understood in the advent of a substantial economic shock, which was clearly the case with the recent pandemic. But the fact remains that the quicker a company can move out of reactive mode to responsive mode, the better its chances of thriving.

Decision intelligence can be of great help when it comes to righting the company ship and setting it on the correct course, but it can also be used to meet more immediate demands, from correcting supply chain breakage to delivering returns to shareholders.

Starting at the end is how you incorporate short-term decisions into the path of the long-term outcome. You can do that by

>> Using separate DI projects with short-term results at the end of each one

>> Dovetailing the DI short-term results with the DI long-term decision

>> Considering the short-term results as incremental results which you can imagine as rules to follow in backtracking from the long-term decision to discover the path to all those decisions

>> Evaluating your long-term decision against short-term impacts along its path to ensure all is in alignment and both individual results and the sum of the results are acceptable

Other ways may come to light as well. But the point here is that the decision intelligence methodology enables you to consider not only multiple factors but incremental impacts as well. That's the point of decision intelligence: Name the result(s) you want, and work backward from there to ensure the result(s) are delivered.

Chapter **7**

Your DI Toolbox

D ecision intelligence (DI) is a big, broad umbrella methodology that anyone in the organization can use to make sound decisions. It may sound similar to good analytics practice to you, and in many aspects, it is.

Decision intelligence differs in that it reaches beyond analytics, and even their ties to operations, to include a targeted outcome from the outset, domains outside of data analysts and data scientists, the automation of data science, and tools that greatly reduce complexity in data analysis.

Some tools may be familiar to you and likely are already in use in your company. Others are evolving and merging, and still other tools have yet to emerge.

In other words, decision intelligence is in a transitional state. Volatile market conditions brought about by the pandemic and subsequent recovery are spurring its adoption. The tools have yet to fully catch up.

Data science, which remains solid, is still used heavily in most DI projects. Those tools remain in play, but many of them are also undergoing a transformation.

In this chapter, I tell you about the current tools and describe the transformations you can expect to see in the near future.

Decision Intelligence Is a Rethink, Not a Data Science Redo

Decision intelligence is a rethink of the overall decisioning process and not a data science redo. In other words, DI is more of a decision process enhancement and reordering than it is a data science overhaul. Think of it as decision management in a broad sense, but not in the technical sense as the terms aren't truly interchangeable in terms of categories of software and systems.

Decision management systems treat decisions as reusable assets. In other words, they automate portions of the decision-making process. Actions based on the results can be automated (automated loan application approvals or rejections, for example) but are otherwise presented as selectable options that employees or customers can elect to take.

Typically, decision management systems don't begin with the result and work backward to determine the process, but instead focus on continuous improvements and the reuse of previous decisions in automated systems.

However, there is a movement to push for change in decision management systems. Pioneers and leaders in decision intelligence are leading the charge to use DI to improve decision management systems. Luminaries such as Google's chief decision scientist, Cassie Kozyrkov, Meta Brown (author of *Data Mining For Dummies* and the president of A4A Brown, Inc.), James Taylor (leading consultant and the CEO of Decision Management Solutions), and Lorien Pratt (pioneer in transfer learning for machines, a DI pioneer, and the chief scientist at, and cofounder of, Quantellia) immediately come to mind. Taylor, in particular, has laid out precisely how to adapt decision management systems and other technologies to the DI framework.

This rethink is driven in large part by the abrupt upheaval the world has recently experienced because of the COVID-19 pandemic. In a world where normal will never be normal again, decision-making has taken on a new urgency and importance. Because the pandemic and the various shades of recovery have rendered existing data and many previous outputs and decisions invalid, a great void of uncertainty exists where certainty was once assumed. Organizations of all types and sizes are now scrambling to figure out what to do now.

Current methodologies and technologies are confusing the issues somewhat. At this moment, analytics has many names, many purposes, and resides in many technologies, reflecting a variety of approaches such as (but not limited to):

- » AI

- » Data mining

- » Categorized analytics (descriptive, predictive, and so on)

- » Automation

- » Edge computing

- » Autonomous machine management

- » Decision management

- » Business intelligence

- » Streaming data

- » Gateway analytics

- » MLOps

Decision intelligence brings all these under one umbrella and treats them individually and collectively as assets in decision-making. They can be used or ignored at will, depending on the requirements in any given DI-identified process.

To some degree, the term *decision intelligence* resolves much of the confusion people feel over concepts that appear to already be fused, such as AI and analytics. Most business users don't discern the differences between the two, nor care to, because there is little value in sorting out the technicalities when your interest lies solely in the results. That's why the automation of data science and the addition of AI (plus removing math components from the general user interface of BI apps) is so effective in spurring data democratization and decisioning decentralization.

Stripping the science, math, and computer coding away from the user experience is how other technologies such as Apple operating systems and devices and all Microsoft Office products came to dominate their fields. Decision intelligence is highly likely to similarly dominate analytics and related technologies as products develop and new ones emerge that follow the same user-friendly path.

Taking Stock of What You Already Have

It's hard to imagine any company of any size having no decision assistance technologies. Even most microbusinesses have access to analytics and AI in a variety of third-party apps such as those found embedded in software, vehicles, GPS systems, and smartphones. For example, built-in banking and finance analytics are plentiful and range from those embedded in credit scoring apps like Experian to

Excel spreadsheets and a wide variety of accounting and tax software. Analytics are built into a lot of business assets too, ranging from company vehicle fleets and business web sites (often courtesy of the hosting service) to "smart" retail point of sale systems. Each of those tools is designed to assist with business decisions.

Larger organizations take a more hands-on approach and routinely build:

>> Decision services (found in the Service Oriented Architecture, where each service automates a separate and specific decision-making task)

>> AI learning models

>> Algorithms from scratch

>> Customizations of models inside of third-party apps

That's why I say that many of the technologies you'll need for DI projects are already in the hardware and software components that support the execution of an application. The technologies your organization is using to facilitate data transfers, storage, management, and analytics, as well as any decision management platforms, can typically be repurposed for DI use.

In any case, you'll likely find that much of what you need is already on hand and probably in use now, but you'll also likely find that you need to upgrade some of them to versions built to be more DI friendly — or that you need to add a few new technologies.

REMEMBER

Rethink and reorder how the decision-making work is done. Double-check the capabilities of all related technologies — rather than assume that those you have can do the job you need them to do now.

The tool overview

For microbusinesses and sole entrepreneurs, a gathering of facts from various analytics and other sources followed by a manual SWOT analysis — the tried-and-true examination of the strengths, weaknesses, opportunities and threats of the decision options — may suffice for some DI projects requiring fewer steps. Or you may choose to use a virtual whiteboard app like Lucidspark to map the logic in action to share or elicit input from other people. (Curious about Lucidspark? Check out the web site at https://lucidspark.com.)

But you can also use more sophisticated tools, such as self-service business intelligence (BI) apps like Power BI, which is now embedded in Enterprise versions of Microsoft Excel and Microsoft Teams apps. If you don't already have the Enterprise versions, you can access a free-but-limited version of the app online. Also take a look at other BI apps like Sisense, Domo, and Qlik Sense, all of which can be useful in DI work, albeit in different ways. Some of these apps are helpful because they have hidden the data science and computer coding almost entirely from the user interface, making it both powerful and easier to use. The data science and computer coding is still there, of course — it's just automated and running out of sight of the user. However, Qlik Sense stands apart because it goes further by serving the user insights related to their quest but that the user didn't ask for, which pushes the user's thinking outside of the box and into a realm of expanded possibilities. (For more on Qlik Sense, point your browser to https://www.qlik.com/us/products/qlik-sense.)

Larger enterprises will likely need far more technological muscle to enable them to develop or customize DI processes and to optimize existing related technologies such as AI. The technology ensemble should look something like this:

>> Decision modeling software

>> A business rule management system (BRMS)

>> A machine learning stack (an automated ML stack and/or a data science stack for your data science team to build ML algorithms from scratch)

REMEMBER

In the world of IT, a *stack* is that combination of technologies a company uses to build and run an application or project.

>> A data management platform with real time and streaming data capabilities

>> A BI system or application and/or data visualization tool

REMEMBER

Whether you're a small business, a medium-size business, or a large organization, if you find that you do not have every item, no worries. All of it is readily available in the cloud.

Working with BI apps

Self-service BI apps were developed with the goal of achieving data democratization through a degree of user autonomy separate from IT and data scientist involvement. Previously, decision-making was focused too heavily on data science and statistics — probably because most decision-making rules and programs were developed or implemented by data scientists and statisticians. It's natural to work within the familiar scope of one's own discipline.

Even so, data analysts largely found the tools to be a lot less clunky and far more useful with each iteration. Other business users, however, were typically stuck trying to figure out esoteric data science concepts, like data joins, dimensions, metrics, and visualization options.

But now, most BI apps are several iterations deep, and compatibility with the DI methodology is making a strong showing in certain brands. As of this writing, Domo hews most closely with its unique UI design: Their guiding principle is "If you can click and draw lines, you can analyze data." Power BI is also strong in terms of ease of use for general business users who have little to no experience with data analysis. My advice would be to test drive several BI apps using free or trial versions before deciding which is best for your purposes.

Several of these apps, as well as others not mentioned here, incorporate natural language querying and AI explanatory narratives, making them close to the ideal when it comes to promoting data democratization and decentralized decision-making.

Many of these apps are also now embedded in other apps. Examples include digital assistants like Alexa, Cortana, Hey Google, and Siri on the consumer side and chatbots built by virtual assistant applications in Oracle, Microsoft, SAP, and other enterprise software products. Further BI apps can be found inside of a variety of business apps like Excel spreadsheets, Microsoft Teams, Salesforce CRM, and many others. The increase in BI apps embedded in other apps also aids in DI efforts as users need not leave their work in one software application and sign on to other software to get the analyses they need to support the result they hope to accomplish.

Accessing cloud tools

The cloud adoption trend accelerated during the pandemic in support of the mass worker exodus from office to home environments. The trend will likely continue unabated even as the recovery gains speed, because the pandemic has permanently changed the future of work, business itself, and customer dynamics.

Many cloud services already offer analytics that are most applicable to realizing the most return on investment (ROI) for organizations. However, the analytics well is growing deeper as more cloud services are offering a wider array of analytics for business customer use.

One example is Power BI, tucked into the Enterprise Cloud version of the Microsoft Office productivity suite. The capabilities of Power BI are quite extensive, enabling users to draw on many diverse data sources for both historical and data streaming analytics on the fly. Now that it's a free embedded feature, business users can affordably use it in DI efforts as they go about their daily work or collaborative meetings.

Other examples include Domo (embedded in many business applications) and Google Analytics (embedded in many third-party web sites).

Other cloud tools pack powerful analytics, including Database as a Service (DBaaS) offerings such as Amazon Relational Database Service, Google Big Query, and Microsoft Azure. On the flip side, you also have several edge computing applications — those computing capabilities operating at the edge of networks, such as consumer IoT devices, manufacturing robots, and autonomous cars. Edge applications are often joined to the cloud as well and sport some serious analytics at both locales, such as Apple's recently acquired Xnor.ai, Rulex, Google Cloud's Edge TPU, and AWS for the Edge.

REMEMBER

What is most notable in cloud tools is the broadening of use cases for embedded analytics and the merging of work with analytics (as opposed to workers having to work with analytics in separate applications). It's both the broadening and the merging of tools via embedded APIs that brings cloud tool trends and capabilities in sync with the DI methodology.

The entire world seems to be moving away from the notion of *data-driven* to *decision-driven*. For example, Explainable AI (XAI), a set of processes and methods that allows human users to comprehend and trust the results created by machine learning algorithms, is also emerging to aid with making decisions that can drive the organization to its goals. Further, cloud tools are coming under closer examination for veracity in both the quality of the data and the soundness of the analysis to make the end decisions more trustworthy and accountable in driving the business forward.

Taking inventory and finding the gaps

The thing to keep in mind with decision intelligence is that the business result you choose dictates the data and tools you need in order to make that result a reality. In terms of tools, you need to look closely at features and capabilities to determine the fit, more so than the tool category.

For example, you'll need tools with very specific capabilities if the business result that you're after requires that every business user with direct customer contact be able to increase their customer experience scores via:

>> The use of customer-customized call center scripts

>> The capability for all sales reps and customer service agents to be automatically provided with real-time information on the customer and all their history of transactions and interactions with the company (typically pulled from customer relationship management (CRM) software)

>> The means to make real-time customer price quotes adjustable and customized by request on the fly

TIP

Maintain an accurate inventory of your current technology resources so that IT gains a good understanding of the precise capabilities within its portfolio of technologies. That information should then be part of the internal sharable knowledge base so that others can instantly search for the capabilities they need for a given DI project.

One way to fill in any technology gaps is to create internal app stores that would enable users to safely select what they need and pay for it as they go from budgets set up for just such a purpose.

REMEMBER

Given the fact that analytics are becoming a more natural fit with the nature of work and that quite a few workers struggle when it comes to data literacy, many of the most needed capabilities can be found in embedded applications, so be sure to note the availability of these in your inventory as well.

The good news is that whether you're a sole entrepreneur or a microbusiness, a small business or a global enterprise, analytics is becoming more ubiquitous, efficient, and affordable.

These developments also aid the adoption of DI throughout a workforce. For example, because BI and data industry leaders chose to work towards the decentralization of decision-making, each iteration of their products became easier to understand and use even if the end user has limited data science skills. However, current AI use brings forth various applications and projects, but oddly few to no tools exist to unify the efforts of related but independent AIs toward a single goal.

Adding Other Tools to the Mix

Your current technology stack or your BI stack may prove to be all you need for most decisions. However, after deciding the end result you seek, you may find yourself short on a tool or two. That's not entirely unexpected, given the rate of change in the technologies and the haphazard buying spree caused by the mass exodus of workers to their homes because of pandemic-induced lockdowns.

It's quite common for a business of any size to now find itself owning too much of one technology and too little of another. Companies had to rapidly equip most or all of its workforce to work from home and the speed led to some gaps in technology procurement and some redundant purchases. Those were strange times, after all, when toilet paper became a luxury item and employees took home items from the workplace with the blessings of the bean counters. In any case, now would be the time to inventory all those assets, too, before you make any additional technology investments.

In any case, the tools you tend to still need are nothing too radical or too singular in purpose for repeated use. These added investments, if they're necessary at all, should last you for a good amount of time. And, if you elect cloud versions, the constant updates will keep you supplied with added capabilities.

The sections that follow cover the tools most likely missing from the typical IT portfolio. Your mileage may vary, but these will at least help carry you to your decision destination.

Decision modeling software

To properly capture decision requirements, follow a standard like decision model and notation (DMN) to develop precise specifications of business decisions and business rules. The DMN standard is designed to work with business process model and notation (BPNMN), a graphical representation for specifying business processes, and/or case management model and notation (CMMN), which is a graphical representation expressing a case. (For more on DMN, check out the Object Management Group's take at www.omg.org/dmn. The Objective Management Group — OMG, for short — is an internationally recognized standards group, so everyone there knows their stuff.)

TIP

Don't let yourself be intimidated by these standards — they're designed to be easily read and used by all parties involved in specifying and monitoring business rules, including businesspeople with few technical skills.

DMN assists with capturing the decision requirements. You also need decision modeling software to support decision requirements gathering and modeling. Further, you need to add a business rule management system (BRMS) to manage the business rules where there is a high volume and low tolerance for delay (low latency) in the decision-making.

REMEMBER

Decision-making software (DM) helps you or a machine make decisions between choices, usually by ranking and prioritizing solutions to problems according to preset rules and processes. However, there's a distinct difference between legacy business rule approaches and modern decision modeling software. One major difference is that decisioning based on legacy business rules often occurs with one rule applied at a time, whereas decision modeling software uses a holistic approach to weigh the entirety of the decision rather than pieces of it.

Another major difference is that the technology-agnostic universal model of business logic in decision modeling software bridges the gap between business and technology management. It's helpful to be able to share the logic between both the business and technical sides.

At its purest essence, decision modeling software is how you manage logic from business decision to automation and in collaborations and understanding between business and technical audiences.

Managing models instead of rules lists is vital to ensure that the entirety of the logic is applied and not just individual rules. However, you also need a way to manage the rules, for various reasons, including where the need exists for speed or a high rate of repetition. For that, you need a BRMS.

Business rule management systems

A business rule management system (BRMS) is often the best choice to manage the business rules in high-volume and low-latency decision-making — in other words, for rapid, instantaneous, and repetitive decisions.

A BRMS uses business rules to define, deploy, manage, and maintain a variety of decision logic used by operational systems. In this context, *business rules* are logical statements that include policies, requirements, and conditional statements to determine which actions are taken within applications.

Legacy software typically includes embedded business rules, which become outdated, invalid, unwieldly, or in conflict with market or industry changes. As usual, legacy software is problematic and sometimes a serious obstacle to the current requirements in decision-making.

BRMS tools exist that can extract business rules embedded in legacy apps and implement them as loosely coupled decision services on the BRMS. Having all business rules outside of all applications and stored in a single repository gives you maximum control and flexibility, especially in terms of real-time adaptations and changes.

However, it's prudent to use decision modeling software to manage logic from business decision to automation, where speed and latency aren't primary concerns.

Machine learning and model stores

Machine learning (ML), also known as AI in marketing materials everywhere, is central to much of the work in decision-making, regardless of the method you use. Because a goodly amount of the effort in decision intelligence lies in determining and optimizing the process that leads to the predetermined outcome, you should consider how you'll tackle machine learning.

For organizations with the technical expertise and a set of onboard data science teams, sophisticated and enterprise-grade machine learning technologies should be added to the stack — if they're not already there.

For companies also interested in supporting citizen data scientists or companies that have no data science teams onboard, consider adding automated machine learning (AutoML) to the stack. Of course, organizations with data scientists may want AutoML in the stack as well, because it simplifies some of the AI work.

AutoML uses automation to apply machine learning models to solving real-world problems. Specifically, AutoML automates algorithm choice, feature generation, and hyperparameter tuning, among other topics relevant to machine learning modeling. Parameterization in machine learning involves using a set parameter to control the learning process. This parameter is configured outside of the model, and its value is established by a practitioner, not by the data. The practitioner commonly uses heuristics to speed and simplify its development.

Examples of AutoML systems are plentiful and include Azure AutoML, Google AutoML, and Tensorflow/adanet.

ML model repositories — meaning those ML models you've stored for reuse — should also be part of your ML strategy. In many cases, trained ML models can be shared or purchased from a variety of sources, saving you a goodly amount of effort.

But apart from that, you should store your own models for reuse. You can store ML models of less than 16MB in document storage in a database or in ML libraries that support model export and import. Generally, you train and store models before production.

You can find other types of ML-related stores as well. Enterprise feature stores are expected to take off in 2022 and gain steam thereafter. Such stores typically contain ML model features and consistently serve data for training and scoring, the entirety of which serves as an element of data pipelines feeding ML ecosystems.

Also, because ML is not the right tool for a lot of projects, keep non-AI automation tools (traditional automation) in mind as well as other emerging tools. One example is an interesting browser automation tool called Browserflow, a Chrome extension that lets you automate your work on any web site. Whether it is clicking, typing, moving data between apps, or anything else you would do in a browser, such as scrape user info from Twitter, you can automate the work with this tool. (Interested in learning more about Browserflow? See the demo at https://browserflow.app/.)

REMEMBER

It's a given that new ML models will need to be built to fit the process that decision intelligence maps out. But data science is mature enough now that ML tools and model reuse can reduce some of the work needed in a variety of cases.

Data platforms

In today's data-driven culture, most organizations are already using one or more data *platforms* — integrated systems that govern, access, unify, and deliver data stored in databases to applications and other technologies. Some examples are Microsoft Azure, Sisense, Collibra, Tableau, Domo, Oracle, Snowflake, Google's Cloud SQL, MongoDB, LumenData, RapidMiner, and Datameer.

But just because your organization is using a data platform already doesn't necessarily mean that you have available all the capabilities you need. Decision intelligence informs you of which data you need to use in the process to arrive at the business result you seek. That in turn dictates the data platform capabilities you need.

For example, is the data SQL or NoSQL, or a blend of both? Is the data historical and static or streaming in real time? The answers to these question and others pertaining to the nature of data can point you toward the capabilities, features, and tools you need in a data platform.

Data visualization tools

Look for data visualization tools that are automated and contain both graphics and text explanations. This curbs the likelihood of data misinterpretations considerably. In most cases, the automated visualization tools in business intelligence applications and platforms will suffice.

If, however, you need a visualization tool or three to do your own thing outside of BI, here are a few examples of the many options available:

>> **ChartBlocks:** An online chart building tool (www.chartblocks.com/en/)

>> **Chartist.js:** A charting library filled with templates (https://gionkunz.github.io/chartist-js/)

>> **D3.js:** A JavaScript library for making interactive data visualizations in web browsers (https://d3js.org/)

>> **Datawrapper:** A no-code-needed chart, table, and map visualization tool (www.datawrapper.de/)

- >> **FusionCharts:** A JavaScript charting library with over 100 charts and 2,000 maps for use on web and mobile applications (`www.fusioncharts.com/`)

- >> **Google Charts:** A free and easy-to-use visualization tool with a huge gallery of templates, many of which are interactive, pannable and zoomable (`https://developers.google.com/chart`)

- >> **Grafana:** An open-source analytics and interactive visualization app (`https://grafana.com/grafana/dashboards/`)

- >> **Infogram:** An intuitive visualization tool (`https://infogram.com/`)

- >> **Polymaps:** A free JavaScript library for making interactive maps (`http://polymaps.org/`)

- >> **Sigmajs:** A JavaScript library for rendering and interacting with network graphs (`www.sigmajs.org/`)

As a gentle reminder, choosing the wrong visualization can skew the information you're trying to represent. Unless you're skilled in statistics, data analysis, or related fields, you're almost always better served using an automated visualization, for accuracy's sake.

Option round-up

Though much of the discussion of tools centers on automation, you should note that just because you *can* automate something doesn't mean that you *should*. Use tools according to the job at hand. You can use a handsaw to pound a nail, for example, but it's likely to take more time and effort — and someone may get cut.

TIP

Use heuristics to shorten your tools and technologies options list to those that will deliver the capabilities you need, as dictated by decision intelligence, and to those that the human hands on deck can handle. Otherwise, choose tools and technologies that add additional (and measurable) advantages, such as efficiency, speed, or reduced complexity.

Taking a Look at What Your Computing Stack Should Look Like Now

Every organization's stack will look slightly different, because many DI projects will be unique to the organization's nature, intent, goals, condition, and market standing. Nevertheless, keep my general guidelines from the "Tool overview" section, earlier in this chapter, in mind when coming up with your initial checklist from which to refine points as you proceed with DI projects.

Most companies are operating almost entirely in the cloud now, making preinstalled on-premises data stacks unnecessary for a lot of DI projects. Be sure to look around and see what databases-as-a-service and other cloud services might contain the capabilities you need without having to shop for the elements separately. A complete cloud configuration can simplify your work and reduce costs too, although cloud versions aren't always cheaper than their on-premises counterparts.

If you're a one-person outfit or a small- to medium-size business, a spreadsheet or a BI app may suffice. But here, too, there may be other tools that will serve you better. Check for software containing other tools — Excel having Power BI embedded in the enterprise version, for example — to see if you don't already have better tools on hand or that you can access. For example, if you don't have the enterprise version of Microsoft Office, you can still use Power BI as a free standalone. You can find it here: `https://powerbi.microsoft.com/en-us/downloads/`.

Just as not every step in digital decisioning or decision intelligence needs to be (or should be) automated, not every business decision needs to be put through a long list of technology rigors. Many sole proprietors and small- to medium-size businesses can collect the intel they need to make a good decision using the analytics found in a variety of applications and other resources. Furthermore, simpler executions of data analysis, such as those made with the help of Excel or Google spreadsheets, with or without embedded BI, or a tool like Browserflow can also be enough to plot your course toward an outcome you seek.

REMEMBER

However you decide to use decision intelligence and the steps it indicates, be sure to use models from the decision sciences to guide your way.

3
Establishing Reality Checks

Chapter **8**

Taking a Bow: Goodbye, Data Scientists — Hello, Data Strategists

Though decision intelligence (DI) is an interdisciplinary approach where data science and data scientists can both play a role, neither is an absolute requirement in every instance. The title of this chapter is simply an acknowledgment that data scientists no longer take center stage in all decision-making (rather than a statement of the profession's demise). Plenty of work remains for data scientists to do; it's just not in much of the daily grind work they've been doing, nor is it still shrouded in mystery and glamour.

In a nutshell, data is only a single possible component in a DI process. When data is necessary, it's in a supporting rather than a starring role. By definition, that means data professionals may often (not always, mind you) find themselves in supporting roles.

Analyzing data is now a considerably easier task, given that most of the related software has matured so that it's AI-enabled and fully automated. You can thank data scientists for making those tools user-friendly. If not for their hard work and the hard work of software developers and other professionals, data democratization would still be little more than a pipe dream.

For the most part, data scientists (with some help from software developers) have completed their data democratization work and thus have enabled everyone to step up and do their own thing. Given the advances that have occurred in their field, data scientists are now freer to work on more complex AI models and projects, or even to work within DI projects themselves. After all, decision intelligence is a new discipline, uniquely suited to forging leadership in an era where AI is widely used but barely harnessed. It's a vital cornerstone in establishing responsible AI projects through accountable objectives and reliable monitoring through better design in metrics and safety nets for AI and other automation at scale.

Unfortunately, the world still faces a shortage of data scientists, so companies are well advised to look for and hire people with a different set of skills to help guide business decisions using decision intelligence. Enter the data strategist!

If you imagine the emerging new role of data strategist to be more than a little creative, you're spot-on. Specifically, ideal candidates would have talent for (and skills in) creative problem solving, creative opportunity building, predictive creativity, business acumen, critical thinking skills, logic, and experience in developing practical applications from creative inspirations. If they aren't already well versed in one or more of the decision sciences, they should be able and willing to learn the concepts and employ key methods.

Odds are that the role you're looking to expand first in terms of creative powers is now known as a business analyst. They're already creative data treasure hunters who write code often referred to as sloppy when it's really just different, faster and far more effective in data mining than the norm in software development. But there are other job roles where strong talent for this kind of work can be pilfered and built upon.

But here's the thing: these emerging and expanding professions aren't always necessary when it comes to making a decision via decision intelligence, either. But if data is important or critical to reach your targeted business impact, you need data strategists to work out a winning playbook.

Making Changes in Organizational Roles

Though the decision intelligence process can be completed by a single person, more complex and higher-impact decisions may warrant a skilled team of two or more professionals. The question is, which professionals should you place on a DI team? And which current roles need augmenting? Further, what old roles will new roles replace?

Data scientists are here to stay for the same reason software developers stick around: Business applications still need to be built, maintained, or expanded. That holds true in decision intelligence as well. But unless your DI project calls for significant digital decisioning or data analysis, these aren't the players you need on your team.

REMEMBER

The precise mix of skill sets and professionals you need on any given DI team depends wholly on the nature of the decision at hand. In other words, the tools and the humans must be selected as the project requires.

If the business impact you seek will come from actions engaged or deployed by AI, automation, or any application requiring extensive digital data analysis, you'll likely take a data engineering route to your outcome. These are the top roles to consider for this team:

>> A data engineer

>> A data scientist

>> A professional in the decision sciences

>> A data strategist

>> A business analyst

>> A statistician

>> An applied machine learning engineer

>> An analytics manager/data science leader

To round things off, I would also add to this list all necessary subject matter experts (SMEs). They should demonstrate a deep understanding of

>> The topic of the decision at hand

>> The business in general and/or the line of business the decision pertains to or affects

>> Any relevant decision sciences

>> Decision management systems or decision-making methods and models

TIP

Don't let this list intimidate you. It's merely an illustration of the types of professionals you may want to consider adding to your DI team if the decision is data-centric or requires a data engineering approach anywhere in the process. It doesn't mean you definitely have to have all these experts on your DI team.

REMEMBER

Always decide first what business impact you're seeking, and then work backward to figure out which tools, resources, and professionals you need in order to take an action that will cause that impact. If the business impact you seek is more behavior-oriented, your DI team may need to include one or more behavioral science experts, cultural specialists, decision maker experts, data analysts, public relations professionals, and others possessing skills and knowledge directly related to the decision you intend to make happen (the business impact).

If data has a central role, you'll need a data strategist or decision analyst to take lead. Typically, these professionals possess skills in mathematics, data analysis or related tools. They also excel in soft skills such as writing, interpersonal skills, creativity, emotional intelligence, intuitive intelligence, and the ability to integrate or connect seemingly unrelated ideas, concepts, or actions.

Leveraging your current data scientist roles

Just a few years ago, data scientist was widely proclaimed to be the hottest and sexiest job in the world. These folks seemed to be elusive geniuses who were uniquely capable of understanding data and technology on massive scales and in endless applications. Without the might and magic of this new class of technological wizards, it was believed that big businesses would succumb to competition overnight. The race was on to hire as many as a company could find.

Data scientists were in high demand, and they still are. Most of the people who filled this job role in the early days were skilled data managers and analysts by virtue of their jobs: NASA scientist, for example, any type of professional scientist, nuclear engineers, data managers, statisticians, medical researchers, and others. If you collected, managed, and analyzed large data sets in your current job, you could transfer or compete for a data scientist job.

A couple of years on, universities started graduating people with a degree specifically labeled data scientist. Many of those majors and schools are still churning out data professionals armed with the knowledge of using massive amount of data to drive companies, nonprofits, governments, stock exchanges, and other entities more rapidly and efficiently toward their goals.

Nowadays, however, the novelty is wearing off and too few data driven projects are producing value. Now board members, executives, and managers are looking at data scientists and saying, "Wait! Where did you say we're going with this?" To which the answer typically is "I didn't specify. I said that this information is contained in the dataset." That's when it occurred to business that maybe *data-driven* isn't so smart if you don't choose a destination in advance.

But that doesn't erase the fact that many data driven decisions did help companies compete and prosper. And they still will. DI isn't aimed at throwing out old processes in favor of new ones. It's about doing those things in a smarter way so that you also know the destination in advance and can be assured the company will arrive there.

That being the case, data scientists are in no danger of being laid off or sharing the fate of VCR repairpersons, because of wide acceptance of the DI framework. Instead, their efforts can be more strategically applied. Theoretically, at least, more of their time can also be freed to work on more demanding and complex business applications such as AI development and its expanding use cases. Elsewhere, modern software and other professionals can handle a considerable amount of the decision-making tasks, using the skills and tools now available to them.

TIP

Hold on to the data scientists in your employ, and reevaluate where their skills will be of most use in the business. Keep in mind that DI is useful in their work as well, especially in keeping budding AI projects on a profitable and ethical path. In any case, introducing them to DI concepts and processes will realign their efforts so that they're able to deliver value more precisely while pursuing company goals.

Given that most data and AI projects fail due mostly to miscommunications between business leaders and data scientists, most working in AI now will be happy to see meticulously defined decisions brought to bear. That is precisely the kind of clear communication they need to meet the expectations of commonly vague and ill described goals articulated by businesspeople in other working scenarios.

Realigning your existing data teams

Many organizations have data teams that are working diligently to render business value from both internal and external data sets. Odds are good that at least some team members have heard of decision intelligence already. (Admittedly, the topic tends to crop up more often in conversations among data professionals.) However, a considerable amount of confusion occurs, even in this group, over how to define the term and whether the tools that vendors have labeled as belonging to this category actually belong there.

Though a variety of vendors are working toward producing true DI tools, the majority that are so labeled and now on the market fall short of the mark. These tools tend to be heavily doused with AI, extensive automation, and features that appear or can be categorized as intelligent. But AI, automation, and next-generation software capabilities alone does not decision intelligence make.

However, decision intelligence is an important process in harnessing the power of AI for commercial use in that it focuses tightly on aligning the AI with the desired business impact. Arguably, it's the first process uniquely designed to both harness the power of AI and reign in many of its inherent threats and problems.

Gone are the days of turning machine learning (ML) loose just to see what it will learn, as Microsoft famously did with an AI chatbot that it set loose on Twitter to imitate a teenage girl. The chatbot became racist, with a penchant for profanities. The machine had learned, but it learned nothing of any business value and clearly could have become a business liability. It's not the only real-world case of AI gone wrong and straying far from business needs. Businesses have since discovered that they have no stomach or use for endless AI experimentation. This situation created one of the major drivers of the adoption of decision intelligence despite the popular mantra of "data-driven organization."

AI has also had a recurring problem from working in ways that AI teams didn't intend and couldn't predict. The *MIT Sloan Management Review* calls it the *expectation gap,* which it defines as "the difference between what people hope a particular AI solution will do and how it actually operates." It happens because most AI teams "are still figuring out how those solutions work even as they're being deployed."

For such irresponsible AI development to occur, companies must throw caution and prudence to the winds in the name of innovation at all costs. Obviously, this situation is untenable for most organizations.

REMEMBER

By using decision intelligence, data and AI teams can be realigned to regularly deliver measurable business value and thereby avoid much of this waste and risk inherent in their previous work methods.

TIP

Typically, it's unnecessary to replace data and AI team members — all you really need to do is change how teams make decisions and allow them to proceed with their work. You may, however, need to add team members to augment skills needed for DI methods to work — or, to simply reconfigure the team dynamics to ensure that old work patterns do not persist.

Looking at Emerging DI Jobs

Data science and statistics (and even AI) aren't magic. They cannot conjure a perfectly accurate picture of the future for you, nor can they provide you or your organization with even a single grain of certainty. You can only improve your odds while still recognizing that you're essentially gambling. Some gambles are riskier than others, but it's always a gamble when even a small amount of risk exists.

Rather than offer certainty, data science and statistics add assumptions to data so that you can make an informed guess about what's likely to happen. One chief assumption is that the future will mirror the past so that what was once true will remain true. Anyone even remotely familiar with Murphy's law, chaos theory, or the COVID-19 pandemic knows what a fragile link to reality that assumption has.

Even so, predictive analytics have proven business value. They will continue to inform organizations of probable future events and will also likely play strong and recurring roles in DI projects. As such, skills related to deploying or developing analytics will continue to be in demand.

However, many traditional analytics tools and platforms are now augmented by AI, making them far more accessible to users of any analytics skill levels. For job applicants, familiarity with and skill in using AI-augmented tools will soon be expected. Fortunately, consumer versions, like most technologies, tend to advance ahead of commercial versions, so most applicants will be initiated through these exposures. But in any case, few jobs will exist where analytics do not perform a necessary function.

REMEMBER

Decision intelligence addresses the future differently than predictive analytics do. Decision intelligence is a framework designed to keep your company on course in reaching and delivering the business impacts identified as possessing value to your organization. It's the means with which to map steps on a direct path to realizing a predetermined outcome. In short, DI isn't so much a prediction of the future as it is an effort to guide or control at least a piece of the company's future. That future may be just hours or days ahead — or decades or more. It's up to the organization to decide the desired business impact in context, with the context including a timeframe and other pertinent parameters.

REMEMBER

The future you're aiming for may not materialize. Imagine, if you will, the goals that various businesses and organizations were striving to reach back in the fall of 2019, just months ahead of COVID-19's savaging of countries around the globe. Every organization was disrupted shortly thereafter for a year and counting.

Despite the certainty of uncertainty, businesses must make smart decisions consistently and within the parameters of what can be known in that time. Further, businesses must be able to make new decisions in the heat of a crisis. Decision-making skills, though always historically important, will be in even higher demand across most professions and jobs.

Specific to new DI-related job roles, look for rising demand in the following professions:

- » Data strategist
- » Data engineer
- » Ethicist
- » Disruption risk assessor
- » Decision support analyst
- » Decisioning analyst
- » Decision-maker (the technical person responsible for AI decision architecture and context framing)
- » Subject matter expert (SME) analyst
- » Intelligence analyst
- » Chief AI decisioning officer
- » AI decisioning developer
- » AI research analyst
- » AI and human relations coordinator
- » Data analyst
- » Analytics manager
- » AI analyst
- » Applied machine learning engineer
- » Information intelligence officer
- » Idea integrator
- » Chief decision intelligence officer
- » Disruption appraiser
- » Situational intelligence analyst
- » Innovation intelligence analyst
- » Behavioral decisioning specialist
- » Qualitative expert/social scientist
- » AI feature store manager

- » AI model manager

- » AI project manager

- » AI product manager

- » Software engineer

- » Reliability engineer

- » Imagineer

- » Data collection specialist

- » Information locator

- » UX designer

- » Disruptor surveyor

- » Outlier surveyor

These are not the only job roles likely to materialize and rise in demand. Other jobs will be created as well, as DI takes hold and business models begin to shift as a result.

Hiring data strategists versus hiring decision strategists

The difference between a data strategist or decision strategist and a data scientist is that the first two are charged with taking command and delivering specific results, whereas the latter is responsible for fulfilling business requests and making it possible to find information in a sea of data. These generally aren't interchangeable professions, though one person may possess the skills of more than one of these occupations.

Data strategists are charged with developing a *formulary* — a mix of specific data sets from any number of internal or external sources — that can feed a DI process in support of a specific and predetermined result. For example, if you were attempting to cure a disease, you would first decide what point of the bacteria's or virus' vulnerability you would target for attack to destroy or disable it. From there, you can determine what data and tools you need to fashion a weapon (a medicine or vaccine in this analogy) to accomplish that end. A data strategist works in much the same way: Once a desired business impact is identified, the decision or data strategist sets out to determine the relevant data and the tools required to extract the needed information.

Data scientists traditionally do similar work, as do several other data professionals and data managers. Certainly, some of these professionals will add DI techniques to their repertoire. But, as a general rule, the difference is that data strategists are looking to fit the data to the output rather than extract an output from the data.

Decision strategists work within a broader scope. The formulary they're looking for may or may not include data. Further, determining and arranging the needed elements aren't all they're actively planning. They're also planning steps for implementation and beyond. They look at the decision and figure out which raw elements and special tools are needed to make that happen.

A decision strategist also determines which skill sets should be on the team as well as who has these particular skills and is available for this project. This person also looks to see what information is needed and where it's available — as digital data (either in storage or streaming or both), as information residing in a subject matter expert's head, or as best practices stored away in the memory cells of the longest-employed staff member who just happens to possess the most institutional knowledge.

A decision strategist will also likely make a preliminary list of needed collaborators (pending approval from the project head, of course). For example, perhaps key players in the supply chain should take part in this decision-making or at least provide valuable input from their unique perspectives. The decision strategist may also look to industry leaders, subject leaders, community influencers, and others from whom input or cooperation is needed to drive the impact the business is striving to achieve.

REMEMBER

A data strategist is looking solely at a data formulary. A decision strategist is looking at the plan for the entire operation.

However, the talents and skills that both roles need include soft skills such as intellectual curiosity, creative problem solving, emotional intelligence, and polymath inclinations as well as hard skills like data management and model building. Incidentally, these soft skills tend to be hard to find and harder still to teach. It's usually easier to form a team so that these skills can be obtained through several individuals working together, rather than try to find elusive individuals possessing most or all the needed skills.

Other types of data professionals can also play a role in the DI project, if needed, or other professionals outside of the data fields can use AI-assisted data tools to do so. The point here is that decision strategists and data strategists may or may not possess such hard (technical) skills, because the soft skills rank higher in their particular roles.

Onboarding mechanics and pot washers

The prevailing assumption in DI discussions is that the process pertains only to high-level decisions or to large-scale automated decisions. Though these are the primary focal points of many early projects, this process is applicable to all decisions at any level of the business and at any scale. In that regard, and in line with the democratization of data, anyone can decide what they want to make happen next and set their course to see it through.

This is clearly excellent news for solo entrepreneurs and small businesses, but it's good news for large organizations as well because it means that DI can be used to guide and manage decisions made throughout the organization. When every decision made anywhere and at any time in the organization is so precisely aligned as to collectively manifest the top objective, the business is operating at its absolute peak performance relative to that objective.

In the data driven approach I describe earlier, each line of business — and even each worker — was using data in the context of the job role and department goals, which often created conflict within the organization when interdepartmental goals weren't complementary or in agreement. It also created inefficiencies where priorities didn't match and became misaligned with a higher directive in the reconciliation process, where discrepancies and conflicts are intended to be resolved.

By contrast, decision intelligence, by always putting the decision first, aligns everything within the organization in the effort toward that end. If DI projects aren't so aligned, the cause is typically a failure to meticulously define the objective or put the decision in proper context from the outset.

This consistency in aligned efforts within a business is like a flock of migrating birds flying and turning in unison. Though DI isn't swarm computing or swarm intelligence — a concept often illustrated by this image of a perfectly tuned flock of flying birds — it can manifest distributed decisioning that's perfectly in sync.

Therefore, DI planning should include pushing it out into the business in much the same way that data democratization was, but with better guidance on the alignment of smaller decisions with the bigger ones.

The Chief Data Officer's Fate

When Hadoop arrived on the scene and the term *big data* became part of the everyday business lexicon, new job roles were needed to tend to all the moving parts that characterized massive distributed networks and then leveraged every advantage gleaned from such networks. That's when data scientist was declared the hottest new job. Only much later did the role of chief data officer come into being.

Virtually overnight, data became a hot commodity — a billable, salable, tradable, valuable business asset. With that rise in value came the responsibility to inventory data, manage it, secure it, and cash in on it in as many ways as possible. *Chief data officer* became the title of the person responsible for overseeing all of it.

REMEMBER

Back then, owning data was the quest. Think of it as a modern-day gold rush. The more data you found or acquired, the better off you were thought to be. After all, data had been declared to have bankable value. Everyone, it seemed, was on a mad search to figure out how to monetize data. Unfortunately, the data-has-value mantra was little more than lip service for many companies back in the day as data valuation is only now becoming a serious undertaking. Further, some companies are still dumping data because they don't understand its value and opt to cut data storage costs instead.

The point here is that earlier the focus was on data ownership while now its shifting to data access.

Though data has value today, ownership is less of an issue — the obvious exception being proprietary data, which will always be closely guarded and sold (or rented) at a premium. But data as a general resource is plentiful. For example, many governments from local to federal levels offer *open data,* which is data that's free for anyone to use and share. Data is frequently shared within industries, between business partners and in ecosystems like supply chains, or even between individuals.

Further, data value is affected by its usefulness. A good percentage of data has a short shelf life, meaning that it's useful only in the moment or for a short time. Once its usefulness expires, its value declines or disappears.

In short, data value ebbs and flows, but nowhere is it nonexistent.

Today, business value is found more in how the data is used than by who owns it. (The obvious exception here is company secrets and intellectual property data.) By and large, however, it's how the data is used that creates its worth.

Take for example, the various values for stolen data among criminals operating on the Dark Web. According to a Trustwave report, a healthcare data record may be valued at up to $250 per record while stolen payment cards are valued only at $5.40 per debit or credit card. That's because a healthcare record contains far more personal information, making it far easier to steal a person's identity or defraud health insurance companies for millions. However, those same healthcare records can be valued at $1000 per record or more in ransom when criminals use ransomware to lock down a hospital's data until the ransom is paid.

In more honest venues, data is also valued according to its use or usefulness. Rarity can also add value. For example, customer data may have a higher value to sales and marketing departments whereas patient drug trial data has a higher value to big pharma researchers and medical organizations than to commercial restaurants. In other words, everything is relative and so is the value of data.

Though this budding shift from a focus on data ownership to data access doesn't eliminate the role of chief data officer, it does change the list of duties and responsibilities somewhat. This executive role is still responsible for overseeing data collection, data management, and data storage at the enterprise level as well as for actively seeking ways to use and derive value from data. But these days, data acquisitions drop significantly on the executive's priority list, whereas dealing with threats (data security) and ensuring compliance rise in importance.

Where does this situation put the chief data officer in relation to the new role of data strategist? The data strategist is in charge of identifying and analyzing data necessary for a specific predetermined decision in a DI project. The chief data officer is charged with managing the company's overall data assets. A data strategist may or may not report to a chief data officer, depending on how the business is organized.

In other words, the data strategist and chief data officer are in somewhat of an awkward dance, much like the chief information officer (CIO) and the chief technology officer (CTO) are today. The CTO can report to the CIO, or vice versa. There's simply no clear chain of authority between any of these titles.

Freeing Executives to Lead Again

Many of the executives in the C-suite chafed at the idea of becoming a data driven company. More than a few top executives thought that data and the related technologies had robbed them of their agency and professional status. The common fear was that they were being demoted from leader to figurehead. More than a few resisted the call and continued to lead in their own ways. By extension, many react to the first mention of decision intelligence with similar distrust, foreboding, or outright rejection.

However, once top executives and line managers come to understand that their decisions and actions are no longer data driven but rather that they're free to direct the actions the organization takes, their comfort level improves dramatically.

This newfound understanding of a reversal of priority from data first to data last needs to be tempered, however. Decision intelligence isn't intended to replace data with gut instinct. It's a process where one directs activity to achieve a predetermined business outcome. Executives can certainly shape that outcome, but they should do so with the same meticulous care and consideration that any major business decision warrants. Still, many will be enthused to know that they have a stronger say than they perceived they had earlier.

REMEMBER

Many of the decisions in future organizations will be automated, which will further free executives to use their talents and skills on more demanding issues. For example, traditional banks are now locked in a dead heat with online lending disruptors in competitions for everything from car loans to mortgages.

Cloud native lenders tend to be more generous with lending amounts and terms based on access to more data and top-notch digital decisioning technologies. Traditional lenders could use decision intelligence to disrupt the disruptors or compete more aggressively for the business while still maintaining an acceptable amount of risk. If, however, a traditional bank sticks with its current data-driven loan approval processes, they'll likely lose more business deals than they close.

The shift from data-driven to decision intelligence is itself a decision. It's the first of many that will showcase the business acumen and competitive prowess of the decision-maker.

The feeling of returned autonomy and agency in business leadership can be quite breathtaking. The downside is that if the predetermined decision proves to be a bad call, the onus is also on the decision-maker, and that can be a breathtaking experience, too — in a bad way.

Chapter **9**

Trusting AI and Tackling Scary Things

When you think of the word *smart*, odds are good that the first thing to pop into your mind is artificial intelligence (AI) — either that or *smart things*, which are generally inanimate objects with built-in AI that are connected to the Internet.

Though it's important to acknowledge that AI is an essential tool for many decision intelligence (DI) processes and projects, it's equally important to recognize that AI isn't as smart as most people think it is. In doing so, it's easier to see why combining machine and human intelligence is a smarter way to solve business problems than relying on either one alone.

AI, the poor thing, is a bit dimwitted, you see.

For one thing, it can't extrapolate well. A feat that many small children can easily accomplish is beyond its ability. It also has an awful time trying to understand the spoken (or written) language used by folks like you and me. It can master the intricacies in syntax and semantics, but it can't parse the nuances of meaning. AI stumbles hard when it comes to the pragmatic function in language — namely, the influence on meaning of context, colloquialism, implication, inference, and relevance, among others.

AI also lacks experiences in the real world, primarily because it isn't connected in a physical sense to the many sensory and practical variations of life as humans know it. This means it lacks real-world experiences and reference points that humans lean on to help make sense of any given situation.

Moving down the list of AI's weaknesses, neither does it evolve particularly well. It mostly performs the same tasks over and over again. It can (and does) improve its performance, but it has no intellectual curiosity, so it doesn't wander far from its original purpose. It does commonly become lost, however, whenever the data its model depends on shifts, as the reality it was programmed to reflect changes.

But those aren't the only issues. AI is also an imposter. What everyone is working with today isn't really AI — at least not in the way AI is presented in Hollywood movies or on sci-fi television shows or in the expectations of most people and businesses.

Discovering the Truth about AI

Here's the deal: The technology actually used in decisioning and advanced analytics today is machine learning (ML), which functions as a subset of general AI. ML is quite impressive and is helpful in finding patterns in large data sets and making digital decisions at scale, but I'm not talking Arnold Schwarzenegger in the *Terminator* franchise here. That may not be so bad — Arnie is hard to beat — but ML has a few other pronounced shortcomings as well. More specifically, it consumes a massive amount of resources in time, effort, and data. It doesn't help, either, that it's often wrong!

To be fair, wrong interpretations of ML outputs are often caused by human error. A good percentage, however, come from ML's failure to either accurately distinguish between similar items or match the same items when the depictions have slight variations. (ML often can't correctly pick cats out of a photo lineup of furry creatures, for example, which truly enrages all the cat people out there on the Internet; see Figure 9-1.) Further, ML is highly susceptible to errors such as biased outcomes or outcomes based on wrong assumptions. A chain of errors can then occur, compounding the original problem.

Putting it rather bluntly, ML often scores worse in accuracy than a small child who is given the same task. But parents don't let small children make business decisions, because they have more than a few shortcomings as well. More specifically, they lack business acumen, work experience, and domain knowledge, among other characteristics.

FIGURE 9-1:
Machine learning
has trouble
accurately
recognizing
objects among
similar objects.

Adults who are seasoned professionals and subject matter experts (SMEs) also typically score much higher than ML, but they too fall short of making a perfect grade. Their shortcomings include heuristic errors, narrow perspectives, and an inability to swiftly assess or find patterns in large amounts of data. There are other problems as well. For example, who do you think gave ML its problem with biases?

However, when you combine machine and human approaches, you end up with a much stronger basis on which to make a decision, because you're leveraging the advantages of both. In so doing, you're also curbing or eliminating many of their weaknesses.

TIP

Think of decision intelligence as bundling human and machine intelligence.

Thinking in AI

Machines neither think nor learn like humans do. It helps to consider the difference in human and machine minds to understand how they work, together and apart, to make better decisions.

As I mention at the beginning of ths chapter, analytics and digitial decisioning do not now use AI in the truest sense. Instead, they rely on a subset of AI called machine learning. Some rely on a highly specialized form of ML called deep learning (DL).

Machine learning (ML) is a method of data analysis in which analytical model building is automated. It's this automation of increasingly refined models within the analysis process that people call *learning.* Machine learning algorithms "learn" according to preprogrammed defined criteria and adapt in each automated iteration, making the machine increasingly efficient at a specified task. It excels at performing tasks at scale, too — meaning it can perform the same tasks on a large and growing number of incidents simultaneously and without human intervention.

Deep learning (DL), a specialized form of ML, solves more complex problems using additional layers in its models and substantially more data in its training.

Both ML and DL are software based. However, both act differently from other types of software. For one thing, while bugs (programming errors) in ML and DL are fixed similarly to how they are corrected in traditional software, some ML techniques (most especially DL) are extraordinarily complicated making it hard to understand what they do and to find errors.

Small changes in the input data can lead to big changes in the ML model derived by the ML algorithm. Because of this, there can be instability in the results which is a problem inherent in the math and not the programming.

It may help you to visualize machine elements by comparing the human body and mind to ML or DL as the (software) mind and robots as the (hardware) body. But that's about as far as a likening comparison can go.

REMEMBER

No hard robots are actually used in data analysis, digitial decisioning, or decision intelligence. Robotics may be automated by the outputs from ML, but they don't serve a purpose in making decisions. Only ML or DL is used, and even then, neither is an element in all analytics or automated decisioning. Given the currently high adoption rates, however, ML is quickly taking over the field.

Typically, data scientists and other data savvy mathmeticians or engineers build ML models. Previously, a talent shortage in these fields created a bottleneck in ML development. The sheer complexity of ML put it beyond the grasp of most professionals in other fields.

But times have changed, and now you have more options in building and using ML. It is the arrival of these new options that puts more complex DI processes and projects within reach sooner, because they excel at reducing complexity and speeding up deployments on the production end. This in turn puts DI wihin reach for many more DI users throughout an organization — because ML powers other software and tools, thereby reducing complexity and increasing access there as well.

Automated machine learning (AutoML) is chief among the advances making the technology less complex and faster to deploy. All types of AI automation are hugely helpful, but feature engineering automation is especially so, particularly when it comes to rapidly building predictive analytics applications.

Feature engineering (FE) makes raw data ready for machine learning by applying domain knowledge to extract analytical representations. Relevant features are critical because no one can train a machine learning model without them, no matter which algorithms they use. And see, here's machine learning's little secret, which just so happens to be decision intelligence's little secret as well: Feature engineering is the most intense and critical part of the process because it involves the combination of domain knowledge, interdisciplinary expertise, and technology skills. Of these three, however, domain knowledge is the most important, with interdisciplinary expertise a close second and technology skills lagging behind both.

Interesting isn't it, that two human knowledge sets are needed *before* the data and technology skills? Kind of like the DI process, right? Moreover, if you thought AI was superior to humans or that humans have nothing to do with AI processes, you now know that they're two parts of the *same* process. Machines assist humans, and humans assist machines. They're meant to work together. And that has always been the case, even before software popped into the world's reality.

Back to automated feature engineering: With this technology, the processes for hypothesizing, transforming, and validating features can be machine generated so that data scientists can then plug them into machine learning models and rapidly move to production. This means that work that used to take months to complete can now be done in far less time.

Along those same lines of expediency, you now see the rise of *feature stores*, where features are built once and then shared across machine learning teams and machine learning models. (See Figure 9-2.) This eliminates the need for engineering support and further speeds assembling models in order to address new decisioning projects in record time.

Don't hesitate to use tools powered by machine learning in your DI process, if such is truly needed. However, sometimes machine learning is overkill and simpler tools such as more tradtional forms of analytics are a better fit for what you're trying to accomplish.

The precise blend of human versus machine processes is determined by the business impact you have committed to (decided on) and the steps you've determined as necessary to manifest that impact in the real world.

FIGURE 9-2:
Feast, an open source feature store.

Thinking in human

Human decision-making is much more fraught, complex, and powerful than many AI fans realize. Despite huge advances in machine learning in recent years, the human mind has yet to be successfully copied, much less surpassed by any form of AI. It just isn't that simple to replace the most efficient and brilliantly designed computer on this earth: the human brain. Though AI makers and builders continue to strive to mimic its near perfection, the human mind continues to consistently outperform machines in terms of accuracy. And it does so even though humans make the wrong decisions much of the time.

REMEMBER

We humans tend to make irrational choices even as we try to make rational decisions. In the case of a crisis, the urgency of trying to improve our chances of survival pushes us to make fast assessments and assumptions and then mentally leap to a quick decision. But just because our lives are at stake doesn't mean that we don't end up making irrational decisions anyway.

For many reasons, we humans make irrational or emotional decisions, and we end up giving them all fancy scientific names, proving that we're well aware of our shortcomings when it comes to making decisions. Yet we continue to make mental errors in our calculations leading to a decision. For a look at the infinite variety of ways we can fall on our faces, check out the following list:

>> **Follow the leader — off a cliff:** We humans have a tendency to see winners as good decision-makers, so we follow along. If a leader in industry shares anything from their stock picking methods to their morning routine, people

subconsicously assume that the ritual has a positive effect on the executive's abilities in some way. Hence, other people — even the CEOs of competing companies — tend to do the same or similar. No consideration is given to those "losers" who are completing exactly the same routine or following the winner now and achieving no positive results. This is a highly illogical way to decide how to spend your money or your mornings.

>> **Playing it safe — right to the poorhouse:** Another common mental error can be chalked up to loss aversion. Humans value what they already have more than what they might obtain. This is why a homeowner typically prices their home higher than its actual worth and a home buyer tends to price the same home much lower. It's also why people have a hard time downsizing — it's hard to "lose" something you own, even if you never wear it or use it. People often make decisions based on a fear of loss rather than on the anticipation of gain — which generally isn't a good plan in decision-making.

>> **Going for the tried-and-true behind door 1 instead of the hidden treasure trove behind door 2:** Repeat after me: Availability or familiarity doesn't mean value. The availability heuristic leads people to believe that things which come to mind first are more important or more truthful than things of which you're less aware. We humans overvalue the things we remember (even when we know that we may be misremembering), and we undervalue things we hear, see, or learn about for the first time. In other words, we value the familiar over the unfamiliar and the known over the unknown.

I could add many more items to this list, such as number anchoring (pricing an item according to whether the number you were immediately previously exposed to was high or low), confirmation bias and other biases, ignorance or neglect, overconfidence, moral lapses, and blind spots.

This is why making business decisions based on intuition — that curious concept otherwise known as instinct, which exists as the sum result of all of our past related experiences and/or common heuristics and biases — is considered a terrible idea and an error-prone way to lead an organization.

Letting go of your ego

In looking at ways in which business decisions can go wrong, one quite large target still needs to be addressed: ego. The other potentail pitfalls listed in the previous section tend to attach themselves to specific ideas or projects. Ego, however, is a free-floating menace that can attach itself anywhere.

According to a report in *Harvard Business Review*, business managers and leaders have historically thought of management in terms of "resource allocation" or "policy making." That is until Chester Barnard, a retired telephone executive, came along. He lifted the term decision-making from the public administration field back in the 1930s and put it in one of his books on executive functions and consequently forever changed the way businesspeople thought of their jobs.

Unlike more circumscribed terms like resource allocation, decision-making is more open-ended. Yes, you have a defined purpose, but it's more like a process, with a beginning, a middle, and an end — a thought or deliberation followed by an action, in other words. Rightly or wrongly, being a decision-maker (or the "decider," as U.S. President George W. Bush once decribed himself) is a status symbol and an ego boast, a moniker that instantly creates expectations in the business, in stockholders, in customers, and in others.

Ego being what it is, humans who invest much of their self-worth in their status as deciders are potentially weak links in the organizational chain of command. The human mind may well be the greatest computer on earth, but it — joined as it is at the hip to one's ego — also represents a considerable amount of risk to an organization relying on human leaders to make good decisions that produce good outcomes (not just once, but repeatedly).

REMEMBER

Several disciplines have studied human decision-making for decades, including mathematics, philosophy, sociology, psychology, economics, organizational behavior, and political science, among others. Advances made by these disciplines and in technology have improved business decisions and outcomes significantly. But we humans had to wait until decision intelligence came around for the focus to turn to determining the precise blends of human and machine decisioning necessary for achieving a predetermined goal as a recipe for optimal decision-making. That's why, in decision intelligence, you always let the predetermined decision dictate the tools and processes you use to turn that decision into a measurable business impact. This includes determining the precise blend of human and machine capabilities needed, or if any such mix is even necessary. Don't forget: An ego trip is a trip to nowhere.

Seeing Whether You Can Trust AI

The biggest non-secret secret in the AI field is that no one quite understands how AI works. When it comes to the most advanced algorithms, no one is quite sure how it makes its decisions. That situation can prove problematic, to put it mildly.

Professionals in the field do understand that AI — or rather machine learning, to be more precise — makes loads of mistakes, and at scale these can be a true horror show. The best minds in AI development understand, however, that mistakes aren't the problem. (Mistakes aren't the biggest problem in human decisioning either, by the way.) It's the belief that mistakes can't happen that creates the biggest disasters.

People who make decisions in the business world and who use AI-enhanced products to do so but who have little to no basic understanding of AI tend to believe that Data + AI = 100% Correct Insight. That assumption gets you into the most hot water.

What about AI's superhuman capabilities and the infallability of AI's underlying math, you might ask? And why are machine outputs proving to be correct so consistently, even at great scales, if AI can't be trusted to get things right?

Well, that's just it. AI *hasn't* proven to be always right. And, despite the raging marketing buzz, sometimes it's useless, and sometimes it's even dangerous. And, because there's no reliable way to figure out how the machine came to any given decision, checking its reasoning isn't possible.

One clear illustration of the fallability of AI is its recent and breathtakingly bad performance during the COVID-19 pandemic. Doctors and scientists around the world placed their hopes in AI to help diagnose, treat, and predict outcomes for patients striken by the disease. Some went further and hoped AI could quickly identify a cure or build a vaccine. None of that actually happened, despite herculean efforts and enormous amounts of data from China and Israel for training the machines.

Multiple studies — including a report by the Turing Institute, the UK's national center for data science and AI; a review in the *British Medical Journal*; and a review focused on deep learning models for diagnosing COVID, published in *Nature Machine Intelligence* by researchers at the University of Cambridge — found that of the hundreds of AI-predictive tools built and used to deal with the COVID-19 pandemic, none made any significant difference and some proved to be harmful.

Derek Driggs, a machine learning researcher at the University of Cambridge and a coauthor of the review in *Nature Machine Intelligence*, said in a related article in *MIT Technology Review* that much of the blame for multitudes of AI failures in COVID work is on *Frankenstein data* — poor-quality data, often spliced together from unknown and mutiple sources, containing errors and duplicates. As a result, some tools ended up being tested on the exact data they were trained on, which led to false accuracy scores.

Given the fact that AI a) makes mistakes, b) cannot currently tell us how it came to any single decision, and c) produces results that can even be dangerous, how can you ever know that you can trust AI to make automated decisions or to assist humans in making decisions?

The key lies in understanding that trust isn't always the primary or even secondary issue — or even an appropriate goal, to be honest. Trust isn't an appropriate goal in human decisions, either: You can build a DI process that doesn't rely on trust of machine or man but instead makes verification and validation a consistent part of the overall approach.

TIP

Consider *all* your options within the DI process — even if it requires some research first. For example, AI is neither the only nor (necessarily) the best intelligent computing option for analyzing big, complex data sets. Consider that bioinformatics, a computing technology designed to analyze the rapidly growing repository of molecular biology data, was far more useful in developing a COVID-19 vaccine and tracking the virus' origin than AI was in any COVID-related project.

You must carefully select a desired impact in decision intelligence because that choice points you toward the tools you need in order to achieve it. In the case of COVID-19, bioinformatics that aimed to prevent, maim, or kill the virus were more successful than the multitude of AI tools that aimed to help definitively diagnose, optimally treat, and ultimately predict outcomes for patients.

Finding out why AI is hard to test and harder to understand

Everyone agrees that it will be much easier to manage AI when it can explain what it's doing or what it did to reach a specific decision in human terms. For now, AI decision-making systems, especially those using deep neural networks (DNNs), are largely black box models — essentially, even the people who designed these systems don't fully understand how they work.

Further, they *can't* understand these complex and convoluted systems that are growing more complex, more ambiguous, and more autonomous with every passing day. This situation is untenable, requiring the development of new methods aimed at increasing transparency, understandability, and explainability of AI products, systems, processes, and outputs. It's a fundamental technological problem, in other words, and not a matter that can be solved by way of further education or by leveraging the experience of the human overlords.

In short, businesses are completely blind to what AI is doing (at least in its more complex forms) — but relying on it anyway.

As scary as that decision may sound, humans have a history of relying on products and concepts that have the potential of high negative impacts before completely understanding what they're dealing with — for example, antibiotics. Antibiotics have been used at least since the time of the ancient Egyptians to treat infections, even though no one understood how they worked or knew that infections were caused by bacteria until sometime around the 20th century. Why do humans use things before they understand how they work and what threats they may bring? The answer: Simply because they work. Users can measure the outcome even if they cannot see or understand the process that rendered that outcome.

REMEMBER

Ultimately, the test for anything — employee, process, or technology — is performance. Did it do what you needed it to do? If yes, keep it. If no, throw it out. And that's how AI is mostly judged today — AI works, so organizations keep using it and building even more of it. But it's only those in business who are completely unfamiliar with how the AI sausage is made who trust AI. Anyone who works with it knows better.

The answer to the question of why something performed — or didn't — is generally of less concern. Typically, the reason behind the results in a pass-or-fail test doesn't rise in importance and priority until something goes wrong. (Usually, something has to go horribly wrong, several times over.) That's why product liability laws exist — to force an investigation of the why and to hold someone or some organization accountable for any failure to subsequently contain the threat.

Interestingly enough, AI regulation appears to be entering the stage where older notions of product liability are taking hold. Several major government agency actions worldwide are converging on governing the ethics and regulating actions taken by AI or assisted by AI. For example, in the spring of 2020, the five largest financial regulatory bodies in the U.S. released a formal request, known as a request for information (RFI), to banks, seeking explanations on how they're using AI. This action is a strong signal that regulation over AI in banking and finance is forthcoming. Shortly afterward, the Federal Trade Commission (FTC) released unusually strong and preemptive guidelines for AI on "truth, fairness, and equity" issues. In so doing, the FTC made certain AI uses and abuses illegal.

The European Commission soon followed suit with its own proposal for regulating AI. It carries a hefty punch in fines of 6 percent of an offending company's annual revenues, making it a significantly higher penalty than the whopping 4 percent that can be levied under the General Data Protection Regulation (GDPR).

Though the regulatory environment worldwide is still evolving, some central themes surrounding concerns with AI are already apparent. Regulators clearly want companies using AI to

>> Assess and mitigate risks

>> Conduct impact assessments and resolve foreseeable unintended consequences

>> Ensure accountability and independence in testing and reviews

>> Insist on a continuous review of AI systems following all these steps and continuing forever afterward

REMEMBER

These same principles should be applied to the predetermined impacts of the DI process as well. After all, the entire point is intention. Anything that distracts from that intention is untenable.

To come anywhere near complying with the new regulatory demands I listed earlier, the infamous black box model that has been the AI standard for years must be replaced with full AI explainability and transparency. The old measure of trusting AI simply because it works is insufficient. Now, the problem of trust must be addressed head-on.

And, the results will likely go far in establishing trust in AI. Or it would, if regulators were ever to agree on what AI is in order to avoid unduly striking fear or overly limiting accountability. For example, the US regulatory bodies tend to define AI narrowly, such as ML models typically used in businesses and most software today. The European Union, on the other hand, tends to more broadly define AI as any software involved in decision-making.

REMEMBER

Decision intelligence is focused on discovering and taking the necessary steps to create a predetermined business impact. Part of that process involves mitigating risks and taking other actions to identify and, hopefully, prevent foreseeable unintended consequences. That means weighing the risks-versus-rewards in using specific tools as well.

TIP

Make sure every step in your DI process is fully compliant with current laws and be prepared to meet emerging or foreseeable regulation. That's the easiest and most efficient way to ensure that no new problems are created in your wake as you move forward.

Hearing AI's confession

DARPA wants AI to confess its secrets. DARPA, which is short for Defense Advanced Research Projects Agency, is a military R&D agency that has been persistent in its attempts to get AI to explain its actions — probably because automated military decisions are quite literally a matter of life-or-death. The effort to perfect and manage an emerging generation of AI machine partners for war service is in full swing.

When you think about it, though, DARPA isn't asking anything of AI that everyone else doesn't want to know. To ensure that the DI process and impact also comply with emerging AI regulations worldwide, organizations everywhere will need to be able to explain what the heck their AI has been up to. And they'll also likely have to explain which use cases they're sending AI to work on as well.

Furthermore, extracting the necessary confessions from AI becomes more essential, considering that some DI processes are executed entirely by AI. This technology is far too powerful to set-it-and-forget-it. It brings with it considerable risks, not the least of which is the guaranteed degradation of its own model over time.

REMEMBER

No one can fully manage AI unless the black box model is blown up and replaced with one that's a whole lot more transparent and easier to understand.

DARPA's goal here is XAI — shorthand for *explainable AI,* denoting what DARPA calls *third-wave* AI systems. (See Figure 9-3.) XAI developer teams in both the private and public sectors are hard at work to create next generation ML techniques to make AI understandable and trustworthy for users. One way to do that is to make the human-to-machine interface more user friendly, or at least to force AI to explain itself in clear human language(s).

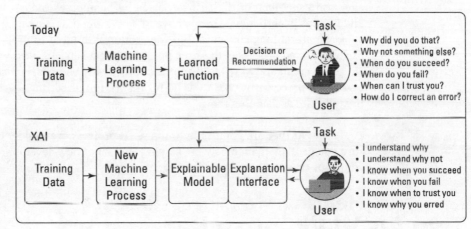

FIGURE 9-3:
Comparing what is with what could be.

REMEMBER

Creating explainable AI will make it easier to further democratize its use, thereby assisting more decision-making throughout the organization — and also making DI methods accessible to more users.

Progress is being made on the AI explainability front. In 2020, the National Institute of Standards and Technology (NIST) in the U.S. Department of Commerce produced a report defining the four principles of explainable AI for public review:

>> **Explanation:** Systems deliver accompanying evidence or reason(s) for all outputs.

>> **Meaningful:** Systems provide explanations that are understandable to individual users.

>> **Explanation accuracy:** The explanation correctly reflects the system's process for generating the output.

>> **Knowledge limits:** The system only operates under conditions for which it was designed or when the system reaches a sufficient confidence in its output.

Articles in AI and computing trade publications routinely cover related concepts, including premodeling explainability, explainable modeling, and postmodeling explainability.

In other words, serious work is underway to make AI easier to understand, manage, and use. Much of the software used by businesses today (decision-making and BI apps in particular) already have AI assistants that respond well to typed and spoken natural language cues. But that action is limited to preprogrammed and predetermined processes the user predictably expects. So, yes, when it's just as simple to command AI to build another AI — to any user's specifications and then reveal the processes it uses to do so for inspection or editing — then AI becomes the ultimate decisioning tool.

TIP

Tools like AI that are applicable to many DI projects are rapidly changing. Make sure you or DI team members are staying abreast of new developments to improve your tool selections and fully leverage their use.

Two AIs Walk into a Bar . . .

AI will no doubt play a meaningful role in many DI projects. In fact, you might have more than one kind of AI playing a role, meaning one of the two current subsets of AI called *machine learning (ML)* or *Deep Learning (DL)*. These types of AI are usually attached to a specific task and/or software. Which means you will likely have several AIs working on different tasks within your DI process. Add to that all the AI assistants hanging around in various devices like Alexa, Hey Google, and Siri all of which listen for voice commands so they'll know when to answer a request. Unfortunately, these AI assistants are likely to end up just eavesdropping in a business environment. That in itself is a potential security issue, but I digress.

Yeah, when it comes to AI, things can get a little crowded on your way to making great decisions.

Imagine, if you will, that AI in all its various forms, including chatbots, production projects, and AI-enabled devices of both the consumer and enterprise ilk, are individual beings who might a) work together or for the competition, b) be corporate spies or just plain mean, or c) be friendly busybodies. How might they act and interact in a DI process? And would it be a good thing or a bad thing if your decision pie had so many AI fingers in it? If you were to imagine only two AIs walking into a bar, would you trust them not to rob the place? Would you invite them to sit at your table? Are they the harmless targets of a funny work joke but otherwise hard-working, amicable chaps?

How can you tell how these AIs will behave and how they will get along with one another? Or should you expect them all to stare at the screens of their own version of smartphones and be oblivious to the presence of anyone else in the bar?

To be fair, conflicts, integration issues, and related problems within your DI process aren't limited to AI. They exist in software, tools, data sets, and other items you use. Once you have made your decision about the business impact you want to create and begin working backward to determine the processes, tools, and people you need in order to make it happen, remember always that every tool and process must work collectively toward the same goal — not individually, toward their own end.

So, when two AIs walk into the bar, take another hard look. Consider whether what they do is truly what you need in this scenario. Because the fact that AI works autonomously and largely in the dark is no laughing matter. And any of them will work "drunk" if they drink from the wrong data well.

Further, these machine coworkers may be central to your decision-making processes now, but you can expect them to eventually move on, like their human counterparts do.

AI experts, including leading pioneers and even the godfather of AI, Geoffrey Hinton, think we should throw out machine learning and deep learning and start over. Why? Because new obstacles are already cresting the horizon that these techniques can't overcome in decision-making. We'll likely need a different form of AI to deal with those.

The biggest shortcoming in ML and DL, according to Hinton, is that neither can become intelligent on its own, since neither is capable of unsupervised learning. He believes the fault lies in backpropagation which involves labeling and weighting data.

The consensus is that machine learning and deep learning will be abandoned in favor of nascent frameworks in the coming years to create a better path toward developing artificial general intelligence (AGI) for use in better decision-making. The point is that even if you think you know all the tools and techniques or consider yourself accomplished in the use of one or more, check your bias at the door and consider what else may be available to aid you on your DI project.

Don't let yourself become overwhelmed. If you think about it, machine learning and deep learning are just sophisticated statistical techniques. They're both just software, not alien life forms. So, those two AIs that walked into a bar aren't as intimidating as you might fear.

Furthermore, you won't have to learn everything about rising statistical techniques, because current AI subsets and increasing automation will likely do most of the heavy lifting for you anyway. Focus on staying on top of the options available to help you build out your DI process.

Doing the right math but asking the wrong question

Sometimes, when AI doesn't meet expectations, you should remember that it was born this way. Sure, it learns as it goes and can run off the rails in the process, but it got its start from the math-and-training data it was given, and it can do only so much with it.

AI experts work hard to get the math right in the models, and they almost always do. Unfortunately, getting the math right doesn't count for much if it's in response to the wrong question. Working steadfastly and using all the right math to solve the wrong problem is, well, quite a common problem. It often stems from a miscommunication between the businessperson who requested an answer but couldn't accurately articulate the question and a data scientist who thought the question articulated was the question to be answered. Hence the data scientist goes to work using all the right math in answering the question that the businessperson never meant to ask.

Put another way, this is the rabbit hole that has swallowed many a data scientist, and it's a common reason that many AI and data mining projects fail to produce a useful business result.

This same trap exists in decision intelligence as well. The problem you're trying to solve there is how to bring the decision you premade into a business reality. But if the decision you made is an answer to the wrong question or is an effort to solve the wrong problem, everything you do thereafter is just another rabbit hole.

At its best, decision intelligence is trying to build on a nugget of an idea, a flash of brilliance, a fresh, new innovative spark to fashion a business impact that will render a measurable gain in the real world. In all likelihood, a substantial amount of the work that follows will involve digital decisioning — either as part of a larger DI process or as the whole of a digital decisioning project. Either way, the question or the problem to be solved must make sense before anything else that happens afterward can make sense.

Business leaders must once again take the business helm, find the glimmer of a great idea, superimpose it over an imaginable and fact-based future of probability, carefully poke and prod it for weaknesses, and then, after meticulous vetting, set forth to design the DI process capable of bringing it to fruition.

Decisioning was never solely about the math, the algorithms, or the models. It was — and is always — about framing an idea first.

Dealing with conflicting outputs

In any process that involves more than one software program and/or related-but-separate actions, the potential for conflict exists. The rub might lie in integration efforts or in opposing results or outputs. Conflict can also arise in the decisioning team over which approach to take or which weights or values to assign to various elements under consideration. Turf wars or even disrespect or devaluation of diversity in professions, cultures, genders, or race can also be sources of conflict.

The fact is that conflict can bedevil your DI projects in so many different ways. Some of this friction is helpful and helps hone the business impact or the process to achieve it. A lot of it, however, is mildly distracting at best and destructive at worse. In data disciplines, it's known as *noise*. In people, it's known as noisy. In any case, squelch it quickly.

AIs can be in conflict too. Almost all of modern software has an AI component — virtually none of the AIs integrate or function in tandem with AI in other software. You can embed an AI-generated visualization of narrative in other software or websites and elsewhere, but you can't integrate software and make the AIs hang out at the virtual water cooler, share their datasets, and work out conflicts between them. Yes, ladies and gents, we have yet another silo — dozens more, actually.

AI is only as good as the data it is trained on, the data it retrained on, and the data it's working with now. Then there are all the other problems, like model decay, data drifts, and more data consumption for yet more model retraining. Add to that the fact that AI can also write algorithms for almost any purpose, from optimizing IT and cleaning data to refining automation. And those AIs, too, work largely without human supervision and with not so much as a by-your-leave to other AI it may come across along the way.

None of the AI in commercial software, consumer hardware (hello, Alexa!), or custom AI enterprise projects is trying to keep up with the Joneses. So, if one AI is performing better than the rest, the rest simply ignore it. So yes — conflicting results (outputs) can and do happen.

There is no single fix for this situation when it occurs. Just be aware of it, because it may foul the lines in your DI process at some point.

One thing that may help prevent such issues is ModelOps — those processes that operationalize and manage AI models in production (after deployment). ModelOps enables you to monitor your ML models through their entire lifecycle to ensure that they're performing properly, suffering no decay, and discarded as needed to prevent problems in decisioning and in security vulnerabilities. A good ModelOps platform also helps you keep your work with AI in compliance.

TIP

Add a feature store to decision intelligence AI toolsets and you can easily build and share AI models known to be already in compliance with your DI project — as well as with company rules and regulatory requirements. It's a shortcut that can save you time and lots of headaches. (For more on feature stores, check out the "Thinking in AI" section, earlier in this chapter.)

Battling AIs

AIs can engage in another kind of conflict as well. This one isn't quite as benign as the others and is about a thousand times more bedeviling. *Malicious AI* is machine learning that attacks other entities, such as businesses, infrastructure, and governments. It can be aimed at almost any target. In war, it drives drones to attack buildings and military personnel. Only the side it's attacking is likely to call it a malicious AI; the side deploying the attack will call it friendly. And that's pretty much how it works with outlaw cyberattacks too.

Malicious AI, which is also known as offensive AI, is the attacker. Defensive AI is the protector — except when malicious AI converts defensive AI to attack mode as well, or when defensive AI turns malicious AI against its owners, in which case it's now offensive/defensive AI. (Okay, I took a little creative liberty there in the naming of AIs that change sides during a conflict, but the fact remains that both offensive AI and defensive AI now exist, and both can be manipulated by another AI.)

At the business level, malicious AI is capable of a wide variety of attacks, ranging from deepfake videos for disinformation campaigns and infrastructure fails for real-world body counts to ransomware, whale phishing, and other forms of data attacks and data manipulations. Defensive AI, on the opposing side, mostly lives in cybersecurity products designed to protect the business from a variety of existing and emerging cyberattacks.

The bottom line here is that all businesses are now engaged in a battle of algorithms, some benign and some malignant.

What does this battle of algorithms have to do with decision intelligence? It boils down to the fact that the threat that AI brings to bear isn't that it will take over the human race, but rather that it increases the attack surface. Think of it this way: What one AI can do, another can do, because what one ML can learn on its own, another ML can also learn on its own. One malicious AI can attack your organization in numerous ways simultaneously — while also attacking hundreds, thousands, or even more businesses in the same ways, simultaneously. It's an onslaught that's impossible for humans alone to thwart.

REMEMBER

While that AI is attacking you, it's learning your defensive AI's tactics and instantly mitigating them while also learning everything about your business from its evaluation of your defensive AI, or just the AI it finds working elsewhere in your business. That means you must keep this real-world threat-scape in mind while deploying or engaging AI in your DI process. Use AI responsibly, in other words, and bake security measures into all your decisioning processes (digital and DI) to prevent a malicious AI from taking it over. And, of course, to prevent other security and compliance issues too.

TIP

Consider modeling AI development along the lines of DevSecOps (short for *development*, *security*, and *operations*) — it holds everyone involved accountable for ensuring security measures across all platforms of your organization. In short, it asks that you make it company policy to match security decisions and actions in perfect sync with AI development and operations decisions and actions. That way, your DI process is better protected from a wide range of security threats.

Chapter **10**

Meddling Data and Mindful Humans

F unny (and woeful) tales of data analysis and statistics-gone-wrong are plentiful. Statistical errors tend to fall into one of two broad categories: those involving bias and those involving inaccuracies. Traditionally, the five most common sources of statistical errors are in sampling, measurement, estimation, hypothesis testing, and reporting.

Unfortunately, these errors are still common, despite the many sophisticated advances in technology. You have to be diligent in weeding out these errors from all you do — from manual decision-making to AI decisioning calculations.

Keep in mind, however, that these errors all stem from humans rather than from machines, because software can do only what it has been programmed to do and AI can learn only from the training data it is given. The same holds true in decision intelligence (DI): Errors tend to spring from human sources but can lurk in human and machine interpretations alike.

In all forms of decision-making, you need to be precise, diligent, and forever mindful of details, pitfalls, and unintended consequences.

Engaging with Decision Theory

Decision-making is far more complex than it appears. Nonetheless, the science devoted to explaining its complexities has been able to produce formulas and processes you can follow as you work to make better business decisions. You should take full advantage of these methods, to ensure that your DI approach is based on solid priniciples and not just wishful thinking.

REMEMBER

Decision theory is an interdisciplinary approach to making sound decisions in uncertain environments. That's pretty much the case with every business decision because, if you were in an environment where all facts were known and certain, it would be easy-peasy to decide what to do next. But that's not the cushy, risk-free place you're in, is it? The devil may be in the details, but the unknown is where all future crises are born. So, back to decision theory and your journey to "out-science" the unknowns.

Decision theory taps into the knowledge and experience of several disciplines, including psychology, statistics, philosophy, economics, biology, sociology, political science, and mathmatics, according to their relevance to the decision problem under investigation. Decision theory is closely related to game theory, which can be thought of as the science of strategy because it's a framework for understanding decisions made by individuals affected by the actions of competing individuals.

REMEMBER

The main difference between decision theory and game theory is that game theory considers cases where decisions interact, and decision theory is the mathematical representation of a single agent's options with the goal of achieving the best possible outcome. In other words, in decision theory, you're looking for the best plan to lay on the table. In game theory, your best laid plan can be blown to bits by your competitors' moves. Both involve making decisions in uncertain situations. Both assume all parties are rational, which may be a stretch in some situations. Neither comes with a guarantee.

You win some, you lose some. That's just business. However, you use these sciences to win more often than you lose by consistently making good business decisions.

Decision theory contains three main model types: descriptive, prescriptive, and normative. Each applies to a different type of decision-making.

>> **Descriptive decision theory** refers to the observation of how people make decisions in practice. It does not imply that the facts are certain or that the decisions are obvious.

>> **Normative decision theory** models decisions made under presumed "ideal" conditions.

>> **Prescriptive decision theory** models how decisions should be made under realistic conditions. It considers both the situation and the decision maker's needs. Typically, it combines descriptive and normative theories in the calculation. You spend the bulk of your time charting decisions of this type, though risk levels vary.

If you're applying decision theory using AI in your DI process, a data scientist will likely need to build you a model that's relevant to your predetermined decision. Sometimes, however, you can find a shareable model in your company's AI feature store or ModelOps model storage, in an open source decision tree tool like Rapid-Miner (see Figure 10-1) or KNIME, and even embedded in a commercial product such as Microsoft Power BI.

TIP

In many cases, you end up using more than one model. Think of it this way: A single software application can use dozens or more models. Similarly, your DI process can easily contain several steps and that may entail several models as well.

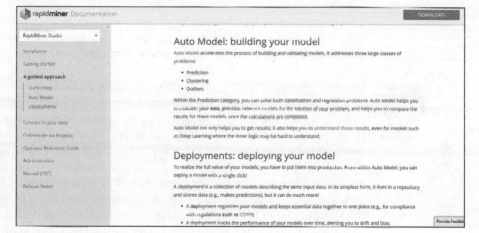

FIGURE 10-1: Looking at RapidMiner, a data science software platform.

Working with your gut instincts

Using decision theory to formalize decision-making processes may sound counterintuitive because anyone can make a decision at any time, anywhere, and on anything, with seemingly no structure to their mental work and with little effort.

The deceptive appearance of simple brain maneuvers coupled with the speed at which such maneuvers are made leads to common (yet dismissive) references to gut instinct and intuition. But it turns out that some science sheds light on these particular decisioning mechanisms as well.

Recent research has discovered a direct physical connection, via millions of nerves and one huge vagus nerve, between the human brain and gut. Because the neurons and neurotransmitters in the gut are identical to those in the brain, scientists are now calling the gut our second brain. Additionally, chemical secretions from the gut affect how the first brain works. The question remains of whether the two are actual parts of a whole or they form what can best be described as a symbiotic relationship.

On the other hand, intuition, specifically in regard to intuitive decision-making, is primarily based on strictly mental connections between previous experience and inherent talent. Put more succinctly, intuitive decision-making is based on near instanteous pattern recognition and prediction. The prediction part comes from rapid processing involving relevant rules of thumb or decisioning shortcuts in the mental caluclation. Those are called *heuristics,* and they're used in decision intelligence, digital decisioning, and other forms of human and machine decisioning as well.

The point here is that although someone can reach a decision quickly using only their own mental faculties, the process is never as simple as it seems. Further, these processes are discoverable, repeatable, and shareable.

REMEMBER

Organizations that deploy the decision sciences to make business decisions are largely seeking to mitigate risks and optimize outcomes. However, it's a mistake to categorically discard one decision process in favor of another, as has been done in recent years by always ranking data driven decisions over human made decisions. This machine bias rankled many in the C suite and often rightly so.

Some solutions require one over the other in the weighting of human-versus-machine decisioning, but many solutions benefit from the use of both. Decision intelligence allows for either digital decisioning or human decisioning to be used alone or in combination as the individual case warrants. You soon discover which processes you need along the way as you move backward from your predetermined decision to discover the path that leads to it.

However that process works out in each instance, business leaders will undoubtedly be thrilled to see that they have regained their status and value at the head of the decision-making table. But the truly smart leaders will hold on to digital decisioning to augment and guide their decision-making as well.

Looking at the role of the social sciences

The *social sciences* are a group of disciplines dedicated to the study and understanding of society and how individuals behave and develop a culture within it. In the purist definition, the social sciences are anthropology, economics, political science, sociology, and social psychology. These topics are also listed in the humanities, but that categorization comes from a philosophical approach rather than a scientific one.

REMEMBER

Other sciences and disciplines are often added to this core group of sciences as part of the decision-making processes. They include philosophy, neuroeconomics, experimental game theory, and human centered design (HCD), among others. Which sciences you use to draw your formulas from to add to your DI framework depends on the outcome you seek to cause and the circumstances needed to make such an action happen in reality.

TIP

The key to knowing which science(s) to incorporate in your DI process lies in understanding which aspect of human life each science addresses and how that directly applies to the decision you're making. For example, human centered design (HCD) defines and solves problems from the perspective of the people who must use and depend on a certain design. It's a good idea to include insights from HCD when making decisions that depend on high user-adoption rates, intuitive user interfaces, patient compliance, and/or overcoming cultural or language obstacles.

Using social sciences in decision-making models isn't necessarily a moral undertaking, although one would hope that the goals of the decision are for the good of all. However, their use in decision-making does tilt the scales in favor of humans over machines. The social sciences ensure that decisions are shaped according to their effect on people. In other words, they help decision makers understand how to interact with the social world and the impacts their decision(s) will likely have on others.

If the fears of AI overlords are to ever come to be, considerations of the human condition and the potential impacts on that condition would never be a part of the calculation. The social sciences make their impact felt by trying to ensure that all decisions are focused on improving the human lot rather than on replacing the human race. That's not to say that all decisions made under social science influences are benign for all humans. Social impact from decision-making in public policy, public health, political campaigns, corporate missions, and other efforts can benefit all, some, or none of the people impacted by a decision that ultimately was crafted to benefit a finite few.

REMEMBER

Incorporating the social sciences in the DI process, or in any decision process, for that matter, doesn't ensure that's there's no bias, inequality, or other negative social impact, even if it typically does make decisions more human friendly or humane.

Examining the role of the managerial sciences

Management science, like decision theory, is a broad and interdisciplinary field aimed at problem solving and decision making. That makes it a natural when deciding what should be included as part of most DI processes. It concerns itself primarily with management, change management, business process goal alignment, management consulting, economics, finance, business, and engineering, but it touches on just about any other managerial function as well.

REMEMBER

Managerial science differs from operations research in that the latter focuses on using tools like data analysis and statistics to increase the efficiencies of management systems, whereas the former applies those tools in a variety of fields such as data mining, logistics, engineering, and medical research.

Management science can include any and all activities involving a managerial function. But it usually entails these:

>> Discovering, developing, defining, and evaluating an organization's goals and then determining the steps necessary to achieve those goals

>> Persuading the organization to take the steps necessary to achieve those goals

>> Determining whether not the steps, when implemented, are in fact the most effective way to achieve the goals that have been set

>> When necessary, working to change processes that have shown themselves to be either ineffective or not effective enough

Most of these concepts were built from foundations laid by more established disciplines, such as business administration, economics, psychology, sociology, and mathematics.

All DI projects should include managerial science in the process because the success of the business decision, the processes supporting it, and the deployment of the action are all dependent on good management practices.

REMEMBER

Decision intelligence often relies on many intangible elements that are difficult or impossible to capture in traditional models, such as employee morale, opportunity costs, brand recognition, brand loyalty, intellectual capital, the value of institutional knowledge, and intuitive intelligence capital, among others. This is one of many qualities that sets it apart from the pursuit of data driven enterprises and AI operationalization.

The Role of Data Science in Decision Intelligence

Data science is the engine that powers modern organizations in every industry. That fact has not changed. Data science is a powerful element in decision intelligence, too, because numerous business decisions can benefit from a machine assist, and many others are — or should be — automated and fully scalable.

Data science plays one of two roles in decision intelligence. One is to augment or accelerate the decision-making process and the other is to fully automate and scale digital decisioning.

REMEMBER

In plenty of decision intelligence use cases, data science plays either no role whatsoever or just a limited role. That fact doesn't negate the value of data or its analyses to the organization in other applications or DI projects.

Fitting data science to decision intelligence

In numerous business decisions, the DI process is applied to how digital decisioning is done in a wide variety of use cases across industries. It's a rethink rather than a redo of how people use data mining and data analytics. The good news here is that it means this effort isn't the Herculean effort that some fear. The bad news is that you still have plenty of work to do to get it right.

First, let's get the terms and concepts straight. Decision management software, which has been around for quite some time, is typically known as enterprise content management (ECM) or business decision management (BDM). By any moniker, it uses tools such as business rules, predictive analytics, continuous improvement, business intelligence, and machine learning in its processes. Decision management software's primary goal is to operationalize business decisioning process systems, including AI/ML.

Digital decisioning also uses analytics and machine learning models in software and tools to automate actions and to improve automated decision-making. However, it focuses on delivering business impact from the decisions themselves rather than on increasing the efficiency in the automated decisioning process.

Thus, digital decisioning uses decision management software to deliver a precise and desired business impact from related decisions, but particularly from AI-based decisions. Given that the goal of digital decisioning is to deliver a specific business impact, it's a perfect fit and indeed difficult to separate from the DI concept at first glance. Both begin with the decision on a desired business impact and work backward to create the processes and assemble the tools necessary to make that impact a reality.

The difference is that, although digital decisioning (defined as focused on delivering business impact) mirrors or incorporates a DI framework, a DI process doesn't have to include a digital decisioning component.

REMEMBER

Digital decisioning is typically used to automate actions on a massive scale that affect people individually. Usually, the people affected by these decisions are customers or sales prospects. For example, you can use digital decisioning to determine which applicants to approve and which to decline for a home, car, or personal loan and to do so rapidly, despite a massive number of voice, mobile app and/or online applicants. The channel the applicants use (voice, text, app, or website, for example) is irrelevant to the decision-making process. Digital decisioning can handle it all in record time and not make a single mistake in observing the rules and pursuing the goals set by the decision-makers.

In other cases, digital decisioning is used to augment employee actions and responses. For example, it can inform a call center agent on the customer's product circumstances and path in the customer experience as well as prompt the best action for the agent or customer to take. Similarly digital decisioning can direct a field sales agent on the best offer to make to the prospect the agent is pitching at the moment. And it can do all that for many call center agents and/or field sales agents simultaneously and in a matter of seconds.

REMEMBER

Data science may very well be powering analytics and machine learning in digital decisioning, but it's the DI process that determines the rules and guides each individual decision toward a predetermined and overarching business impact.

Looking at a real-world example, imagine that a traditional bank is concerned that its current decision management software is governed by rules that are too conservative to be competitive and the bank is losing out on an otherwise lucrative market opportunity. Can this problem be solved by traditional means? Yes and no. It can certainly be solved at the applicant decisioning level. Data scientists or data analysts can reconfigure the rules so that more loan applications are automatically approved. However, just easing the rules in the existing decision management software adds risks as well as potentially rendering more closed deals. The resulting business impact can easily be negative for the bottom line or even catastrophic, which is why the original rules were so conservative in the first place.

The wiser course is to reconfigure the rules and processes to close more loans without substantially increasing the risks so that the business impact is more profit and a higher market share at an acceptable risk level. That decision can then be achieved in several ways, including adding inputs to the algorithm (perhaps by adding reputation and relationship scores to credit scores as part of loan application considerations), reweighting inputs, and/or by realigning the algorithm or retraining the AI to accept a broader range in output values.

REMEMBER

By making the business impact the target of the decision-making process rather than focusing solely on improving efficiencies in existing decision processes, the business ends up benefitting from every action taken throughout the enterprise. The entire point in decision intelligence and mirrored in digital decisioning is to massage every decision to the organization's ultimate benefit.

Reimagining the rules

Rules-based decisioning in automation is a logical approach to ensuring compliance with regulations, contracts, costs and profits plans, and customer expectations. Rules are also used in decision intelligence, but the idea here is to have business impact as the top priority. This change in emphasis forces you to take a different approach when writing up your list of rules, one quite different from the approach you would take if your focus was on improving efficiencies in the automation process or on updating processes.

Digital decisions are a series of small decisions made by algorithms and leading to an automated action. Business rules are used to ensure adherence to policies and compliance with regulations to ensure the business stays on track and incurs no penalties. Rules also enable digital decisioning to rapidly recognize and respond to threats and business opportunities alike. Rules enable the organization to drive down or contain costs when it comes to making changes to comply with a new law or reducing labor and human error costs incurred with manual decisions. As the volume of decisions goes up, the costs plummet. Further, rules enable the company to score higher in customer experience and customer satisfaction rankings by speeding customized, personalized responses to customers.

In short, rules are the very foundation on which a business prospers. That being the case, who in their right mind would want to mess with the rules in business decision-making? Well, actually, you do.

Throwing the rules out would of course be sheer insanity. But reimagining them can be a stroke of pure genius.

Take machine learning, for example. Models learn from the data sets they're being trained on. Rules are used to guide them in their task. Machine learning applications, for example, are often tasked with finding signs of fraud in banking transactions. For such applications to do their work, they are first trained on data sets consisting of bank transactions.

ML "learns" by successfully recognizing patterns and then responding accordingly with a predetermined action. In the case of fraud detection, the actions will likely be an alert to the bank and the affected bank customer as well as an instant decline of the transaction.

The machines then engage in continual improvement so that they are constantly improving at performing the task; the task itself, however, doesn't change. Business rules help keep the AI/ML on task, but as the data changes over time (commonly referred to as *data drift*), the AI/ML stumbles and even fails at its appointed task. That's because AI/ML doesn't adapt. It follows the rules and its training and stays on task. To remedy data drifts and other problems, the ML model must be retrained on a different data set.

By comparison, decision intelligence is highly adaptable. It assumes that change in business is constant. Decisioning processes are continually reassessed and adapted as needed. This means the rules change — and that means the ML models change.

Planning for the desired impact thus includes either overcoming ML's adaptability problem or using traditional analytics in its stead wherever it makes sense to do so. In traditional analytics, the programming is separate from the data, so changing data isn't typically a problem. In ML, the data and the model are heavily intertwined, which is why data drifting further away from the model as it changes and ages is a significant problem.

Due to these reasons (and others), a reimagining of the rules isn't a one-time exercise. This is why human involvement in decision intelligence is such an important element in many decision intelligence projects. Someone, not some *thing*, needs to be doing the imagining and reimagining of the rules and business impacts.

Luckily for you, there are ways to make changing rules and managing models easier and faster when it comes to digital decisioning — an area where, despite the problems, the advantages of speed and scale are king. For example, many organizations now have *feature* stores, which typically act as a dual database, where one side stores a huge collection of company approved features for machine learning and the other side provides low latency ML features to applications. Such features can be plucked from feature stores and plugged in a ML model, making a data scientist's work reusable, repeatable, changeable, and easy to expedite.

As for ML models already in production, ModelOps products can manage them by focusing on these tasks:

>> Preventing deterioration over time

>> Retiring or destroying them at the end of their lifecycle so that they don't become zombies with built-in security hazards

>> Retraining them on precise schedules to prevent model drift

>> Leveraging and even monetizing models

REMEMBER

ModelOps differs substantially from MLOps because the former manages ML models via rule based automation, and the latter unites ML development by data scientists with ML deployment by IT.

Decision intelligence can leverage all these tools to make and adapt rules throughout the process to make it more amenable to the needs of the desired business impact.

In digital decisioning, where the intelligence process is mirrored but in an all digital state, rules are typically changed in the operational and/or small decisions made by decision management software with a larger business impact in mind.

In any case, rules in machine decisioning matter a great deal, but they also must be continuously adapted to facilitate change.

REMEMBER

Avoid being reactive in making rule or model changes. You want to clearly be in a leadership role and ahead of the curve in your decision-making rather than reacting to a change that most likely puts your organization in a follower's role.

TIP

Keep the path to your decision easy to explain in business terms rather than technical terms, and make sure that the path is easy to change as needed.

Expanding the notion of a data source

In digital decisioning (which, when done correctly, mirrors decision intelligence — just in an all digital form), data sources are varied and often blended for the purposes of analysis. Sources include company owned data sets stored on premises or in the cloud, purchased or rented data from third parties, and streaming data, which typically comes in the form of machine data.

Subject expert knowledge, however, is a data source as well. That data can be captured in digital form — usually, from a long and arduous process of extracting the knowledge from surveys, long questionnaires, manual observations, and other techniques.

REMEMBER

In decision intelligence, you can certainly take advantage of subject matter knowledge in digital form, or you can ask one or more subject matter experts (SMEs) for the exact information you seek, or you can add such experts to your DI team.

More often than not, adding subject experts to your DI team is the best move. The DI process is designed to determine what impact the business should aim for, and that's rarely a question for a data scientist or a data team to make alone.

TIP

If your company's payroll record doesn't list a person or persons with the specific expertise you need for a specific DI project, consider turning to a consultant to fill the role. The point is that your team is both a data source to be mined and a group of collective intelligence to be leveraged.

REMEMBER

Not all data and data sources are equally useful, so be sure to judge them by their usefulness to your goal and not by their familiarity or by how they've worked for you in the past. Think of information as being everywhere in forms that exceed the boundaries of the digital world. But information can also be emerging within your existing data stores too. Look also for new, smarter ways to use data.

For example, using *change data* — data points that mark a change from proceeding data points in a repeated series of analysis — can substantially cut noise and overhead from your analyses in decision intelligence — just as it can in traditional data analysis. This approach means there's less data to move; therefore, it can be moved faster and cheaper. Change data also often represents the most useful data points in the data set, so you have reduced the data volume but increased the data quality, all other factors being equal.

Stay attuned to changes that collapse data to its essence that can further clarify the information you seek. Take, for example, edge computing, which is a term for data collection and analysis on an Internet of Things (IoT) machine (such as an autonomous car or smart home locks and lighting) or on a mobile device (such as a smartphone) or an Internet gateway near any of those things. Edge computing is already sorting what data should be analyzed at the edge (say, to enable an autonomous car to avoid an accident in real-time) and what data should be sent to the cloud for storage and further analysis there (such as how the car performs under varying weather and road conditions). AI will soon join edge computing and likely condense decision-making to its purest and most complete form at the edge. Reaping the AI's outputs from the edge is likely another advantageous data source — and a shortcut to boot.

You also need to take extra measures to ensure that data from emerging sources is trustworthy. While ransomware is stealing all the headlines today (along with locking down company data), manipulating data is an emerging threat that can't be ignored.

Everything from deepfake videos to data manipulated to cause harm to a country's citizens, organizations, and critical infrastructures constitutes a risk. Much of that data manipulation will be accomplished using malicious AI, which can in turn retrain private and public owned AI to turn on its masters.

Sometimes it's good to remember that some of the most profound knowledge gained by humankind was discovered by a man watching an apple fall from a tree — no data crunching, in other words. It's good to also remember that data isn't a god. Consider all sources of information and knowledge, but question all of it before you trust it to aid you in your decision-making.

Where There's a Will, There's a Way

Much of what I discuss in this book in the way of methods, tactics, tools, and processes assumes that the effort is rational. Sometimes, however, decision intelligence is used wrongly to "prove" a bias or another point that the decision maker holds or intends to create harm. Therefore, the will of the decision maker can pollute or corrupt the choice of business impact and the processes and tools used to cause that impact.

A single individual can make a decision — even a quite complex decision — using modern technologies, a spreadsheet, or the back of a napkin. But if you're unsure of your intent or another person's motivation and will, it's probably prudent to suspect the entire process. In such cases, another person's perspective may prove helpful.

In the case of enterprises, employing or building a DI team is usually better than depending on a single individual to make decisions that may be:

>> **Emotionally charged:** Examples are employee layoffs and environmental/climate change issues.

>> **Politically charged:** Examples are vaccine or mask requirements and business travel decisions during COVID-19 outbreaks.

>> **Subject to discipline biases:** A carpenter tends to think that a hammer will fix most problems, whereas a surgeon thinks surgery is often better than a

pill, and a software developer thinks more programming will finally squash the bug in the software. All such tendencies are examples of discipline bias.

Subject to turf protection: Here, the NIMBY attitude — *not in my backyard* — reigns supreme. Decisions should never have a negative impact on *my* department; they should always impact somebody else's.

>> **Subject to bias transference:** This effect often happens when old processes are repeated in a new process and the inherent biases are thus carried over.

Sometimes DI projects don't come to fruition because of a loss of will rather than evil intent. Often, the will simply isn't there to deal with

>> Budget constraints

>> Emerging regulations

>> Changes in political winds

>> A lack of interest or buy-in from leadership

On the flip side, DI projects can spring from

>> Intellectual curiosity

>> Creative problem-solving

>> Critical thinking on one project that sparks a new approach to another project

>> Discoveries made in exploratory or R&D decision intelligence projects

>> Other occurrences of intangible human talents and experiences, such as intuitive intelligence, gut instinct, Eureka! moments, and spontaneous inspirations

In the end, where there's a will, there's a way. It's the nature of the will that determines the value and intent behind the way. Be sure to build in safeguards and checkpoints in your decision intelligence process to ensure that that goodwill wins out over bad.

Chapter **11**

Decisions at Scale

A single decision can be large or small, depending on the size of its impact. However, small decisions when taken together can have as much or more impact as one very large strategic decision. Large decisions often require resources at large scales. Small decisions, meaning those made specifically for a single customer or transaction but repeated for millions of customers or billions of transactions, require elasticity in technology so that they can scale as needed to keep up. In each of these cases, scale is a significant consideration in decision-making.

For you to be able to accommodate high volumes of decisions at fast speeds, you have to rely on automation because humans cannot effectively, efficiently, and quickly perform such a feat. This kind of automation can be achieved with the help of an advanced analytics approach where AI is the top dog in the pack. AI can be accurately described (albeit a bit too simplistically) as automated decisioning at an extreme scale.

WARNING

Decision automation, whether AI based or not, is not a panacea. Automating decisions takes care of the scale issue in terms of volume, but also cranks up the scale in impact. And it may not be the business impact you had planned.

For example, consider iBuying, the algorithm-driven, home-flipping industry consisting of companies like Zillow, Open Door, Offerpad and Redfin, among others. In late 2020, real estate giant Zillow closed its iBuying home-flipping business, blaming a faulty algorithm for its overpaying for several thousand homes and predicting over $550 million in company losses as a result. In the third quarter of 2020, Zillow reportedly bought nearly 10, 000 homes but only sold about 3,000 at an average of $80,000 loss per home. It didn't take long — a single quarter at most — for the automated algorithm to run up huge losses.

Another example is in a 2021 Harvard Business School study that found automated hiring software has essentially broken the hiring system in the U.S. and is now blocking highly qualified people from gainful employment. These systems, deployed for their scaling and automated decisioning capability by 75 percent of U.S. employers and 99 percent of Fortune 500 companies, are worsening talent and labor shortages by rejecting millions of skilled job candidates.

The researchers identified the prevailing problem to stem from the selection of wrong keywords for screening purposes, such as *computer programmer* when the job actually only required *data entry*.

Other problems lay in the rules governing the automated decisioning in sorting good job candidates from bad job candidates. Generally speaking, the rules were too general, to coin a phrase. All kidding aside, the rules were too black-and-white, with no room for explanation or nuance. For example, applicants with a six-month gap in work experience are typically rejected rather than sorted to another system for further review. In some cases, applicants were sick or injured and unable to work for the period, or they were out for the birth of a child. Some had returned to university or focused on additional training and certification or simply couldn't find work in a recession. Further, some rules required candidates to essentially regurgitate the list of skills the employer itemized and rejected any who made other word choices for the same kill ("mopping" instead "floor buffing," for example) or listed higher skill levels than those requested.

Employers are reporting that they're now seeking alternative means to hire qualified candidates, but doing so is expensive because it requires "overhauling much of the existing hiring system," in the words of the Harvard Business School study

This example is but one of many where valuing scale over sound decision making tends to worsen rather than improve business impact. If scores of decisions are incorrectly made and executed on a massive scale via automation, even small decisions can have a massive impact on the business. This is why the focus must be on the decision first and on the data and tools later.

REMEMBER

Whether a decision is small or large, singular or many, it requires your full and focused attention from the beginning and then continued, careful management thereafter.

Plugging and Unplugging AI into Automation

When it comes to your decision intelligence process, you *must* know when to connect AI to automation — and when not to. Skipping AI altogether and sticking to a pairing of traditional analytics and automation might be your best option after all, for lots of reasons, chief among them that no one would seriously claim AI to be brilliant. The poor thing can barely pick out cats in various images. Yes, AI excels at performing the tasks it can do and in doing so on a previously unimaginable scale, but that doesn't mean that AI should automatically execute an action in *every* instance or use case.

REMEMBER

No one is claiming that AI is prone to missteps — you can't say that about something that performs its task in precisely the same way over and over again. The problem is that AI simply lacks good judgment. It can't adapt to change, and it can't explain to its human masters what it did and why.

These serious shortcomings can cause you big headaches in some business applications where machine learning is expected to both analyze and act outside of direct human supervision. Impact from this combined unsupervised decisioning activity can be substantial, embarrassing, or even devastating. That's why you need to understand the risks and rewards of AI before you plug it into your automation processes. It goes without saying that you need to test and retest the model before releasing it into production, but you also need to monitor your model's performance, its relevance, and its quality over time.

The reasons behind such a cautious approach are easy to see after you consider the sum of AI's evolution and performance. From the beginning, AI has always been seen as something that builds on a foundation provided by human subject matter experts (SMEs) — experts who have the time (or make it available) to share their knowledge in tedious and lengthy sessions to convert human knowledge to machine-speak.

Today, in a decision intelligence approach, the plan is to augment AI with human experts and then have AI augment human decision-making. If this seems like a never-ending cycle to you, that's because it is. But the line between human and machine knowledge is increasingly blurred because it's becoming harder to tell where the one ends and the other begins.

REMEMBER

After decades of work, software that learns does exist — yet even with its tremendous speed and ravenous consumption of data, AI still hasn't learned enough to perform like a human. Thus, human and machine remain enmeshed rather than separate elements in decision-making.

As I mention a little earlier, each AI application was planned to contain and codify the knowledge of human experts and automatically expand on it as the knowledge base grew — to learn from new, incoming data, in other words. These specialized systems conform to business rules and contain advanced capabilities in managing decision-making, using known logic forms such as tabular logic, decision tables, decision trees, heuristic logic, and fuzzy logic. AI continues to improve and evolve to this day and no doubt beyond.

In short, the plan was and is for AI to mimic human thinking. But it has never reached that lofty goal, nor does anyone in the field seriously think it will reach that goal anytime soon. Some thoughtful discussion even takes place in the AI field regarding how long it will be before what is now known as AI (but is actually a subset called machine learning or ML) is replaced by something entirely different. Current odds are that ML's days are already numbered.

For now, at least, two useful subsets of AI called machine learning (ML) and deep learning (DL) are the options. Of the two, machine learning is the more commonly used, with deep learning functioning as a much more specialized form of machine learning. More precisely, deep learning is a subfield of machine learning that is typically used for more narrowly defined and specialized tasks.

Machine learning, though not AI in the same way it's depicted in sci-fi movies and TV shows, is extremely capable when it comes to recognizing patterns and taking automated actions based on the outputs of its algorithms and in accordance with its internalized business rules. In essence, ML "thinks" and then does (via automation). For most business purposes, this is good enough on a grand scale — perfect, in other words, for many business tasks. But don't mistake that perfect claim for perfection in performance.

REMEMBER

Test and retest and always keep in mind that every AI model fails over time.

Dealing with Model Drifts and Bad Calls

A cardinal rule in decision intelligence is that you need to avoid bias in every step, whether that's confirmation bias, prejudice bias, or data/algorithmic bias. This rule applies to tool choices as well. For example, be careful not to be biased for or against AI but be cognizant of its strengths and weaknesses.

AI is more than "good enough" at many business tasks, but it's also far from perfect. AI models drift over time. This happens when the data they're working with changes but the AI model remains the same. This causes the data and model to drift apart in relevance and function. Something similar can occur when automated continual improvement in ML leads to the formation of errors in the algorithms.

The aim of automated machine learning (AutoML) is to aid and accelerate AI software development. Think of it as the automated production of AI models. Specifically, AutoML automates the selection, composition, and *parameterization* (the internal values ML can change as it learns) of machine learning models. Its intent is to democratize AI, meaning to automate the building of ML to such a degree that almost anyone can then summon and deploy an AI model to carry out their requests.

AutoML is definitely a good concept, but so far it doesn't look like it will consistently pan out in the real world. Several AI use cases have produced dismal results that appear to indicate that AI isn't ready to handle the work, let alone its own proliferation for general use. AI-powered Google Flu Trends, for example, promised to provide reliable influenza estimates for 25 countries, yet its estimates proved to be embarrassingly off the mark. It has since become the poster child for big data hubris, which held strong to the notion that machine reasoning, supported by huge amounts of data, would always be superior to human deductive analysis and hypotheses. (Oh, how the mighty have fallen.)

However, work continues to improve how AutoML performs too. The much-anticipated democratization of AI depends upon it.

Adding to the Google Flu Trends debacle is the epic AI fail in ending the COVID-19 epidemic, or at least in making it less fatal to people, businesses, and entire economies. Reportedly as of mid-2021, every single AI tool and project launched worldwide to address pandemic issues failed at its task — every single one. This comes as a shock to many people, who have tended to believe, ever since the infamous contest in 1997 wherein IBM's Deep Blue AI beat world chess champion Garry Kasparov, that AI will win any and every such contest, every single time. But, no, it doesn't. It was bioinformatics (also known as computational biology) and not AI that led to the development of COVID-19 vaccines and treatments and further insights into the virus structure, disease progression, susceptibility factors, and spread modes, among other important insights. Bioinformatics is distinctly different from ML and uniquely designed to compute biological data.

REMEMBER

Failure does bring some good with it: People started rethinking how and when to use computing in decision-making because of AI failures and the failures of other big data analytics projects. This is the impetus behind the rise of decision intelligence, which insists that you focus on the decision first, to ensure success via the proper alignment of tools and processes with the desired business impact.

The deliberate reweighting of the importance of tools and the value of existing processes isn't just a thought exercise but rather a carefully measured approach to tie business decisions directly to preferred outcomes. Ultimately, the effort is to eliminate or significantly reduce time sinks (large chunks of wasted time, in other words), effort waste, model drifts, and bad calls, among other negative effects in otherwise fruitless decisioning endeavors. You can scale decisions successfully and you absolutely should — where warranted. Just be sure to pick the tool for the job you need it to do first and its scaling capabilities second.

Reining in AutoML

Automated machine learning (AutoML) automates AI model-building to automatically create more AI models and improve AI by creating better models as well. But given that AI is decision-making at scale, it's not always a good idea to tie AI to automation in either its tasks or its proliferation.

But if you don't tie AI to automation, what's the point? You're likely back to making decisions on too small a scale to hit your business goals. It's a conundrum! Except it's not.

Follow these suggestions to reign in potentially runaway AutoML:

>> **Know the tools and when to use them.** The first important thing to remember is that AI/ML are tools and not panaceas or stars in the movie *Transformers*. Use them for the tasks they're suited for and skip them entirely in projects where they aren't needed.

TIP

If other advanced forms of analytics will serve the purpose, you're generally better off going with that. For one thing, traditional analytics are likely cheaper and faster to use than AI, and for another, they're probably a lot less complex to use.

>> **Start little, stay little, go big.** AI/ML works best in making serial small decisions that collectively lead to big or bigger decisions in automated digital decisioning or in a decision intelligence process. As long as you keep ML focused tightly on small decisions, you have less to worry about in terms of risk magnified at scale.

Don't be Google Flu Trends, in other words. Google Flu Trends appeared to depend too much on an algorithmic model as it went big in scope (estimating and predicting influenza occurrences in over 25 countries during flu season) but small on the number of data sources (primarily limited to social media data). Be more like Waymo, Google's autonomous car project. Waymo started small in focus (on optimizing multiple small decisions), stayed small in creating and testing data models (human drivers map each city, one at a time, to aid in the creation of the training data for the car's various ML models), and went big on the number of data inputs (collected through a multitude of sensors and redundant systems on the car, via satellite, and other data feeds) for a consistently safe and successful autonomous vehicle. In other words, go big on your planned business outcome, but keep the AI/ML focused on small serial or collective decisioning steps so that you can better control, adapt, and generally manage its performance.

REMEMBER

Small decisions in aggregate can have as much or more impact as one very large strategic decision.

>> **Realize that it isn't an all-or-nothing choice.** To automate or not to automate? That isn't the question, for the answer is to semi-automate! Well, not in every case. Sometimes you want to go full automation and sometimes not. In other cases, semi-automation will work just fine.

As a general rule, go for full model automation for well-defined, less complex tasks that are tightly guided by business key performance indicators (KPIs) governing the model. As complexity in the decision-making grows, scale back the automated model building to a level of semi-automation. For very complex decisions, consider whether automated decisioning is warranted and if it is whether the model you developed is sufficient to master the complexities in the decision.

>> **ML isn't a bridge for a talent gap — it's a service dog.** Don't treat AI as though it's the equivalent of, or superior to, human talent. It is not. But neither is ML necessarily inferior to human performance. It cannot replace human skill sets, but it can augment them extremely well. Hire the talent you need and bring the AI service dog to heel.

>> **Use representation engineering to add context.** I'm saying you should ensure that the data is contextualized in its presentation as training data to the student (the algorithm) so that it learns meaningful patterns specific to the problem or task the ML will be working on.

This task can be accomplished via *representation engineering,* a collection of techniques that *represent* (accurately portray larger data sets in smaller samples, in other words) to train the algorithm how it should detect or classify data or patterns. The idea here is to keep expectations aligned with the technology's capabilities to ensure that the training data is relevant, accurate and representative.

Though ML isn't programmed like computer software is programmed, it is and should be taught through guided learning — through exposure to appropriate training data and the use of business rules, in other words. Otherwise, you can end up with some bizarre results. When Microsoft released an AI chatbot called Tay on Twitter in 2016, for example, the only thing it learned on its own was how to be a racist — hardly the outcome any business would seek.

In short, the quality and contextualization of the training data set matter a great deal.

>> **Integrate complementary external data**. Leverage the *transfer learning capabilities* in AutoML — the process of applying stored knowledge obtained by successfully solving one problem to a different but related problem — by combining similar or related external data with your own, internal data to avoid *underfitting* (using a failed ML model that neither accurately mimics the training data or generalizes the new data it's supposed to solve the problem from) or *overfitting* (where the ML model mimics the training data too closely on a new dataset).

>> **Recognize that explainable AI probably will not be a reality anytime soon.** Much ado is made about how little is known about how AI/ML works. Many learned individuals, from the folks at the Defense Advanced Research Projects Agency (DARPA) to legions of data scientists to data privacy and equality experts, openly lament the fact that *explainable AI* — AI that can explain what it did and why or whose actions a human expert can explain — does not exist.

If AI could explain what it did or is doing, would we humans really understand it better? Maybe, but maybe not. And would you feel more in control? Also probably not. Is the ability to micromanage what AI is doing really what you were after? Or were you seeking a different result?

There are undoubtedly some important reasons for subject matter experts (SMEs) to have explainable AI — eradicating bias and other problems in its functions, for a start. But for most business decisions, the proof you need will come from testing its results rather than from reading the complex explanation behind the mathematical formula.

REMEMBER

Thoroughly test models in AutoML to ensure they're performing to your specifications and expectations. Retest often. AutoML is always evolving its model, so the model you tested earlier may not be the model it's using now.

Ultimately, the value in using AutoML depends on the talent of the user. Like any tool, it reflects the abilities of the craftsperson, and it has limitations the user needs to understand. A large part of your task, then, lies in deciding whether and when to add this tool, like any other tool, to your toolkit in your decision intelligence project and then to use it wisely.

Seeing the Value of ModelOps

Mathmatical models have always guided business decisions. People used them either intuitively (mentally) or formally (from prehistoric times in stick-and-pebble counting to more advanced abaci, spreadsheets, or computing). The models worked as long as they worked and were revised or discarded as soon as they didn't. Tweaking things or starting over from scratch wasn't difficult because the formula — the mathmatical model, in other words — exists separately from the data. You could ditch or revise the math and not change anything in the data.

Now that has changed because models have advanced to the point where they can "learn" in the sense that they can come to understand how to identify and react to patterns in data. However, AI models also suffer from *model drift* — deterioration, abandonment, security issues, and other aberrations typically associated with model aging but for other reasons as well.

Because the model and the training data are enmeshed, revising the model means that you must retrain it on new data. Retraining models is a constant and routine exercise, or at least it is when you're managing AI correctly. But constant retraining isn't the only drawback to AI models. The reality is that AI/ML doesn't display good judgment, can't adapt to change, and can't explain to its human masters what it did and why. If you decide to use ML in your decision intelligence processes, whether it's in a solely digital decisioning environment or in a hybrid human and machine decisioning process, you need to manage ML models to avoid these inherent problems and to leverage and even monetize them along the way.

REMEMBER

Model sharing and model management are critical elements in moving AI from project to production quickly and safely. They're also critical to democratizing AI. *Feature stores* — data warehouses that stockpile features for future machine learning use — enable projects to share features and data scientists to ensure that they're up to muster and properly maintained.

Feature stores are often a part of *AI model operationalization,* also known as ModelOps. Think of it as a platform to manage and govern the lifecycle of AI models. ModelOps enables faster deployment, added security, proper governance, compliance, planned model retraining, and the detection and destruction of degraded, abandoned, or aging models.

A good ModelOps system should be part of your maintenance program for your decision intelligence tools. The last thing you want to do is to use existing AI models simply because they are there or to delay a decision intelligence project from going to production because you're asking your team to re-create a model that already exists.

Bracing for Impact

Business decisions can impact your organization in numerous ways. Some are good, some are bad, and more than a few can ignite a chain of unintended consequences. But the reverse is also true, in that your business can impact your decisions in many ways — some are bad, some are good, and many are, well, totally mindboggling.

REMEMBER

To ensure success in decision intelligence, your organization must be committed to deployment and suitably braced for impact.

You must also prevent your business from getting in its own way. That's not to say that adjustments can't be made along the way, if extenuating factors arrive or change. And if at any time it appears that a desired impact is likely to turn undesirable, it's certainly okay, and probably prudent, to kill the effort posthaste.

But overall, your company must be committed to manifesting the decision you make from the start, or else all your efforts are for naught.

Decide and dedicate

Making the decision first is critical to staying on task, but nothing happens unless you also deploy the necessary actions via automation or another means. Therefore, let your mantra in decision intelligence be "decide and dedicate."

REMEMBER

Make a decision first — your desired business impact — and then dedicate the will, resources, and actions necessary to follow through.

If you think this general rule should also apply to decisions made outside of the decision intelligence process, you're absolutely right. Yet the vast majority of business decision failures — including AI failures — stem from a lack of follow-through in the space between taking aim and hitting the target.

The absence of follow-through can bedevil or derail decision intelligence efforts as well. Even though making a firm decision is the first step, nothing happens until that decision is acted on.

Working backward to decide the tools and processes you need in order to realize that decision is a huge part of manifesting the impact of that decision. But there's a marked difference between planning and mapping actions and deploying them.

Make decisions with a specific impact in mind

In decision intelligence, you *must* make a decision and then commit to seeing it through to the end. Even so, the resulting impact may differ from your carefully laid-out plans. The path of good intentions can lead to an unexpected result or even to several results. There can also be a difference between deploying the action and reaping the business impact. For better or worse, sometimes the impact isn't what you had anticipated.

You may find that the fruits of your labor result in a bigger harvest than expected. That can be a positive or negative business development. For example, your company may then need to scramble to hire more people, add warehousing space, pump up supply chains, or otherwise require last-minute and possibly substantial investments.

Conversely, you may find that the business impact falls short of expectations and that your return on investment (ROI) to date falls short of projections. This is generally seen as a business negative, of course, because money, time, and effort have been spent and usually can't be refunded or otherwise recouped.

Occasionally, you find a different impact or side impact that is a pleasant surprise — this is nothing new in the world of business. R&D often finds a pot of gold in an unintentional discovery on its way to finding something else. The Post-it Notes product, which grew from an attempt to create a superstrong adhesive (an attempt that failed miserably in the glue used on post-it notes) is a prime example of accidental profitable outcomes. That can (occasionally) happen in decision intelligence as well.

However, if you find unexpected business impacts to be a regular or frequent occurrence, your initial decisions for those projects aren't concise enough to keep the effort on target. Ambiguity or imprecision in naming the desired impact allows room for scope creep, interpretation variances, and loss of direction throughout the process. You must bring into clear focus the business impact you seek to materialize.

REMEMBER

In decision intelligence, you seek to accomplish a predetermined and specific business impact. And though steadying your aim in this way greatly improves your ability to hit the target, there's no guarantee that you will. There is *always* risk in business. Decision intelligence can help mitigate risk, but the process usually doesn't eliminate it.

Even so, intentions matter. The onus is on the talent and business acumen of the decision-makers as humans take a more upfront and pronounced role than in previous data-driven decisioning processes. Humans enjoy more open autonomy in decision intelligence but that also means that they bear more responsibility. The days of blaming the data for any bad calls are over.

It can be helpful to identify the scope and nature of the decision being made so that you can better grasp the intentions behind it and all the necessary moving parts that must follow. In its digital decisioning form, decision intelligence can be divided into these three categories of intent for repeatable decisions:

>> **Strategic decisions** are typically large decisions made only once. Any revisions are actually new decisions with different variables. Automation isn't typically involved, or at least not at the head of the process. Many options are considered, and some or all may be run in predictive scenarios to get a better read on probable outcomes and risks involved.

Typically, only a few executives (or even only one) are interested and involved in the exercise. The results may remain confidential. Strategic decisions typically lead to the formation of a spread of lesser decisions within the organization. Or the umbrella strategic decision may be shared with stockholders, key vendors, or other partners to help design or coordinate shared efforts towards a common goal.

These decisions need vast amounts of data and sophisticated analytics but are rarely scalable in terms of their deployment despite their vast reach and impact. Scaled deployments come from smaller related decisions carried out in affected divisions, departments, or external partners of the organization.

>> **Tactical decisions** are more about exerting control over business operations by human management. These repeatable decisions can be changed or adapted as management warrants the need. For example, a tactical decision may require the addition of seasonal, temporary, or independent workers to fill a skills gap or meet a seasonal surge in customer demand. They may involve the calculation of regional demand for certain goods or variants in pricing, the opening or closing of stores in response to changes in the economy, and other such factors.

Tactical decisions are often made by management in response to an immediate or predicted business need and are repeatable throughout the organization.

>> **Operational decisions** are decisions consistently executed at an individual level according to the rules of the group. A decision to extend credit, offer rewards, or complete a transaction for each individual customer based on the business' operational rules would be an operational decision. Similarly, decisions for staff, vendors, partners, distributors, and others are handled individually but consistently and according to the business' rules governing interactions with the group. These are high-volume, highly repeatable machine decisions.

In operational decisions, you'll likely find using AI to make microdecisions rather than sweeping decisions to be the better course of action. *Microdecisions* are a form of micromanaging because they allow for custom-ized or personalized responses rather than blanket responses. That happens through the use of more data, whether it's predictive, social media, or another type that lends nuance to the decision as it pertains to that specific customer.

This method not only tends to reap more profit and customer loyalty in those use cases but also helps prevent common errors such as is seen when a qualified job candidate is wrongly rejected by automated hiring systems where one-size-fits all criteria has failed miserably.

Ultimately, the big secret in machine learning is that it's basically a labeler. Now, as you can quite imagine, useful labeling requires meaningful naming. Even Dr. Seuss labeled things with no name as Thing 1 and Thing 2 so that enchanted children everywhere knew instantly to what or whom he referred in his storytelling.

You must be equally clear in the labeling of your decision and your intention behind it. If you cannot do that, you're most likely already adrift and your decision will likely fail. Name your intended business impact, and never take your eye off it throughout the entire decision intelligence process.

In short, you want to be successfully predicting a business impact and not merely producing a reactive response. However, you're not using a crystal ball here — you're making a decision and then working to make it happen.

Your job is to lead by making smart decisions, and you do that by the wise use of data, tools, and science to ensure that you have solid ground under your feet and aren't just flying by the seat of your pants.

Chapter **12**

Metrics and Measures

You can't manage what you can't measure, as the business adage goes. Measuring to manage the right elements within your decision intelligence processes is vital. But that doesn't mean that everything can be easily measured or even that it should be. Many things that are important to business are hard to measure — most notably, the monetary value of notoriously vague but indispensable soft skills such as leadership, judgment, talent, nuance, experience, critical thinking, creative problem-solving, and innovative disruption.

For example, what is the value of documentation for software or the value of the talented individual who composes such documentation? For another example, can a job applicant's critical thinking prowess, business acumen, or ability to innovate be predicted and/or measured? Whether these characteristics can be measured or not, it's undeniable that they do have value to the business and to decision-making processes.

REMEMBER

When it comes to building automation and AI decisioning models, incorporating soft skills is even more elusive, making taking their measure all but impossible.

Because of these innate difficulties, humans must bring soft skills to the table in the decision intelligence process. Among the many valid and valuable soft skill contributions are the anchoring of the decision intelligence effort to a human-centric reality and in identifying a business impact that's often imagined by a creative human mind rather than set forth by a data-informed app.

Keep in mind, however, that because of the inherent complexity of making decisions at high speeds and scales, machines bring unique and valuable capabilities to decision intelligence as well. AI is especially difficult to measure and thus monitor as it goes about its work at superhuman speeds and scales. But to be fair, it's difficult to measure and monitor a single human's thought processes as they go about their work, too. Even so, machine and human capabilities do have substantial worth individually and collectively.

None of these valid points and exceptions is an excuse to forego using metrics such as Key Performance Indicators KPIs — the performance measures over time towards key objectives and other measures (AI and bias testing, for example) to ensure you're on track at various critical points in your decision intelligence process.

In particular, monitoring AI automated decisions is critical to continual improvement long after the model is built and deployed. It's even more critical if the model is shared among use cases and applications. Model management is also crucial in spotting and replacing a decaying AI model before it causes chaos.

That said, let's move on to discussing what can and should be measured and how you might want to handle that.

Living with Uncertainty

It may seem counterintuitive that even final decisions are made and executed in the context of uncertainty. Nonetheless, you need to embrace the fact that despite your best efforts, it isn't possible to know everything. That means there will be gaps in the information and/or digitalized data you turn to, and where there are gaps, there will be uncertainty. When you keep this info in mind, you also keep in mind the associated inherent risk so that you can better mangage actions and expectations.

Simply being aware of what you're facing will serve you better than obsessing about the potential dangers facing you in an uncertain future. The fact is, there is value in uncertainty as well. After all, it is uncertainty that provides the room to question, create, innovate, invent, and disrupt. It is the space where change and strategy first form.

REMEMBER

Despite the potential upsides of uncertainty, your gut is right in that there is danger in unchecked uncertainity wherever it exists. So yes, you need to monitor what you can, test often, measure what you can, and manage everything throughout the decision intelligence process. There's just no way around that, unless you're comfortable with completely throwing caution to the wind.

Failing to make a decision in the face of uncertainity is a decision too, so even that isn't an option if all you want is to avoid risk. Going overboard in trying to mitigate that risk isn't particularly helpful, either. Micromanaging and fear of failure will be your undoing, just as it usually is in the business arena. At some point, you need to stop obsessing about the things you can't know and get on with it.

Often, you will be unable to assess the true value of a business decision until well after the fact, when you can view it through the lens of hindsight. That's because, ultimately, the value of a business decision is determined by its impact on the organization. Though you may do your best to predict the benefits of a decision, they aren't truly knowable until the action is taken and its reverberations have settled as measurable, historical fact.

The thing is, you will rarely have the luxury to wait and see what happens before you must make another decision and then another one after that. It's the nature of business to continuously respond to, change, adapt, and challenge the status quo. Anything less means that your business is stagnating and dying. From that perspective, almost any proactive decision is preferable to perishing. Therefore, almost every decision has some value in the larger scheme of things.

As true as that may be, the pivotal task in decision intelligence is to make the best possible business decisions so that you can reap a targeted value in the here and now. The decision may be made to increase efficiencies, create new value, build new revenue streams, or make steady progress in profitability, sustainabilty, market advantage, or other business goals. (Yes, the decision may point to a long-term impact, but even so, it consists of one or more actions to be taken now.)

REMEMBER

Even if your organization is a nonprofit, it must be able to sustain itself and produce outcomes of some sort, perhaps measured in lives saved, disasters thwarted or repaired, or medical cures found. A charitable organization must also gain market advantage — it must gain ground over its competition in order to attract more donations, build more political or lobbying clout, or attract more volunteers and support. In other words, decisions must lead to value for any organization, but that value can be measured in a variety of ways such as revenue, profits, donations, political power, efficiency, public perception or support, or industry influence — or by the sharpening of a new or existing competitive edge in the marketplace.

Whatever the value is, it's ultimately measured in terms of how it impacts the business or organization. Even charitable giving has a business impact and is measured as such. The value always lies in the impact on the organization. There may be additional or shared values for entities other than the organization as well, but it's a survive-and-thrive necessity that the organization gather value unto itself first. And though this is a certainty in business, it must occur despite some degree of uncertainty.

This approach may appear to you to be common sense, or at least common business sense, for why would anyone make any business decision without first weighing its worth? For others, it may seem daunting to choose an outcome you're not entirely sure how to make happen and pursue it anyway. Both reactions are common and correlate with varying risk tolerances among different decision-makers.

In any case, you're aiming to create value for the business by making a specific decision first. So, yes, you too must make the same infamous claim that former U.S. president George W. Bush once made and loudly proclaim (or maybe just under your breath): "I'm the decider!"

The good news is that you don't have to decide in a vaccuum. You can and should gather and analyze data, listen to key advisors, and make key strategic decisions with the aid of a trusted multidisciplinary team. Decision intelligence isn't about just listening to your gut instincts or making your best guess.

In other words, be on the ready to resume the timeless role of business decision-maker and take the helm and all the responsibility that comes with it. Data is now back in its vital-but-subservient role, and you, my friend, are back in the hot seat.

REMEMBER

The data-driven enterprise is evolving to a data-powered but decision-driven enterprise, and you are at the helm.

Making the Decision

If we humans live in a world of uncertainty (which, believe me, is demonstrably true), you may be thinking, "Well, gee, what's the point in making a decision first?" The answer is that if you can't produce business value from the exercise, there's no point in doing it. Ensuring every decision has business value is the key differentiator between decision intelligence and data-driven approaches.

Decision intelligence ties the work directly to a business impact at the outset, whereas data driven approaches are more often like running your hands along the walls in a dark room and hoping to find the light switch. A growing number of studies are finding that high failure rates for data mining and AI projects are caused by such projects lacking direction and a quantifiable business value. Certainly, lessons were learned along the way, but few such projects netted any real business gains in the end.

You must make the decision first and weigh its value in terms of the targeted business impact before you set out to organize the work to see it done. An excellent way to do that is to use a decision tree.

Decision tree analysis basically consists of a hierarchical drawing. A *decision tree* (see Figure 12-1) is a graphical representation of possible solutions to a problem, enabling you to weigh their probable outcomes. This organizes your thinking in a visualization that helps reveal the best course of action and thus guide your decision.

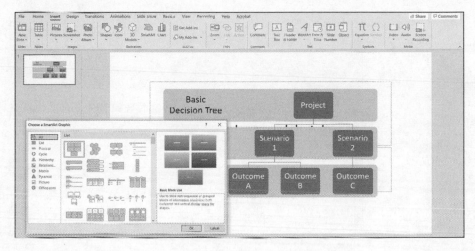

FIGURE 12-1:
A set of PowerPoint decision tree templates.

Four general steps in a decision tree analysis that apply, whether the decision tree is a crude drawing on the back of a napkin or a refined computer program within a digital decisioning process. And even though decision trees can range from being quite simple to quite complex, the basic steps remain the same:

1. Define the problem with structure and concision.

2. Model the decision process.

3. Apply probability values to potential outcomes.

4. Make a decision based on the weighting of the respective values of the outcome you choose.

Note that the outcome you choose isn't necessarily an outcome you want. Sometimes you must decide between two or more bad outcomes. Sometimes you get to choose between two or more good ones. The point is to choose wisely in order to realize the most gain or to minimize the potential loss.

A SWOT analysis can be equally useful in weighing a single decision choice in several contexts. SWOT stands for *Strengths*, *Weaknesses*, *Opportunities*, and *Threats*. A SWOT table is usually just a simple 2-by-2 grid with each of the four blocks labeled for one of the letters in *SWOT*. Deceptively simple corresponding bullet points are then added to each block.

However, a SWOT table can be expanded for use in comparison analysis as well. Figure 12-2 shows one template available in Microsoft Excel for just such a purpose.

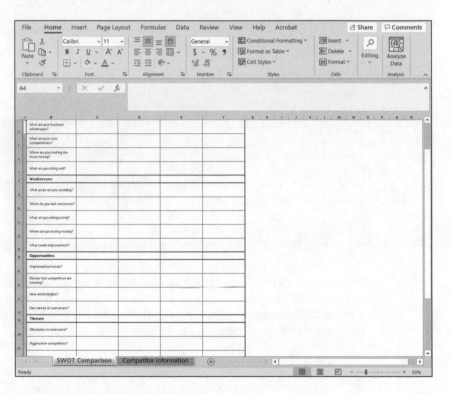

FIGURE 12-2:
A Microsoft Excel SWOT template.

You can also turn for help to the *decision sciences*, which is a collection of quantitative techniques combining decision theory, mathematical formulas, tech applications, behavioral sciences, design thinking, and managerial sciences. It combines the best of interdisciplinary tactics in both computer and human efforts in decision-making.

TIP

Be careful not to become confused over the terminology either while you strike out to use more complex decision science techniques on your own or in conversations with decision scientists. For example, in the business world, the term *decision maker* means the executive with the power and authority to make a business decision. In the computer and AI sciences world, however, a decision-maker is the data scientist or a similar professional who crafts a decision by concisely wording an objective that summarizes the context framing and decision architecture.

You can hire a decision scientist to make, guide, or assess business decisions for you to ensure that they're logical, free of biases and guesswork, and correctly aimed at delivering the best business value. That is certainly an option. Whatever you do, don't go for PFA decision-making. In this context, PFA stands for *plucked from air*, meaning it's factually baseless and devoid of substance. This is a decision based on little more than a whim or a guess.

Take the time to work through the process to make your initial decision from which you will purposefully bring forth a business impact. Leave little to speculation.

Seeing How Much a Decision Is Worth

If you were to suggest that that the decision made as the first step in decision intelligence is based on a perceived or expected business value as opposed to a definite or measured value, you would be right. But that doesn't mean that the decision is a guess or a wish upon a falling star.

Decision intelligence relies heavily on decision theory and the decision sciences throughout the process. The expected value of the initial decision on which every subsequent action is based is therefore calculable.

Before I delve into the math, I'm here to tell you that it's okay if you're not mathematically inclined. Don't let the formulas intimidate you. I will soon show you the tools that can complete the calculations for you. However, if you already have a track record of making good decisions, odds are good that you've been doing this math intuitively without consciously being aware of it. On the other hand, if you have a history of making bad decisions, now might be a good time to study the math so that you can improve.

If you're making business decisions regularly, become familiar with the math behind decision-making, if you aren't already. Many in the financial industry know it well. It may come as a pleasant surprise to those who routinely use these formulas in their work that the same math applies here.

Expected values in decision theory are how outcomes subject to probability or random variables are evaluated. In statistics and probability analysis, expected value (EV) is calculated by multiplying each possible outcome by the probability of its occurrence and then comparing their sums.

In short, expected values is a way to calculate the risks and judge whether it makes sense to take the leap. It also helps decision makers overcome psychological obstacles, such as fear of loss and biases, so that they can push forward to bigger rewards. Such obstacles might and often do skew a decision based on a simple cost/benefit analysis. EV enables you to quantify risks and use them as an element in the decision.

This is the formula:

$$EV = \sum P(Xi) * Xi$$

where EV = expected value and P(Xi) is the probability of the event and Xi is the event

Using the expected value of the outcome isn't a new way to make a decision. The formula has been around for a long time, and it's commonly used across industries. For example, investors often use scenario analysis to calculate the expected value of an investment. A start-up business can calculate its expected value to investors or lenders the same way, as can a more established business looking to compute expected business value in their exit strategy.

Typically, investors use estimated probabilities with *multivariate models* — forecasting tools using multiple variables. But there are plenty of options you can use as well, should circumstances present the need. For example, EV can be calculated using a random variable, a single discrete variable or multiple ones, and single and multiple continuous variables.

If you consider yourself more of a business leader than a mathematician, fear not: You do have options. Most of these formulas are embedded in spreadsheets like Excel and Google Sheets and are found in specialized or professional calculators (online, mobile apps, or palm devices). If those options still feel daunting, you can use investment or enterprise resource planning (ERP) software, hire someone to do the math for you, or turn to trusted advisors to guide you through it, such as professors at a local university or a mentor at SCORE, a nonprofit resource partner of the U.S. Small Business Administration (SBA). (Check out SCORE at www.score.org.)

TIP

If you're looking for an oversimplified shortcut, you can probably calculate expected value in many business decisions by determining the average expected financial outcome of the decision. Do remember that it's a shortcut, however, and its limitations diminish its value in decision-making.

REMEMBER

Be diligent about calculating probabilities correctly, because disaster looms ahead if you fall prey to your own hopes and enthusiasm. Common pitfalls include guessing the probabilities, basing values on little to nothing of substance, forgetting to reevaluate as needed, and forgetting that you're essentially gambling. Yep, business is a gamble. Never lose sight of that.

Even if you do the math right, the answer ultimately isn't a sure thing. It's a calculated risk. Your tolerance level for risk may vary from one probable outcome to another, or from one decision intelligence project to the next. That is as it should be.

Matching the Metrics to the Measure

Measure only that which truly matters and nothing more. You're looking for concision and clarity. Anything more than that will likely throw you into *analysis paralysis,* where you're locked into circular thoughts or overthinking, which is the opposite of making timely and sound decisions.

Some current metrics won't be useful to you, because your focus must now shift from adding efficiencies to improving performance. A recently published report by the Hackett Group found that most businesses have, or nearly have, exhausted all available opportunities to reap gains from increases in efficiency, given the wide adoption of automation and AI. The new frontier for bankable gains is now solidly in performance.

Accordingly, you'll want to focus on metrics that uncover problems and opportunities at critical junctures so that you can adapt and improve your processes as needed to hit your target. Ultimately, the measure of your performance will be in how well your decision delivered a positive impact for the business. You will be able to determine how well you're doing throughout the process by monitoring performance readings along the way.

Fortunately, a wide array of metrics, from change data to KPIs and numerous other measurements, can already be used to keep various steps in your decision intelligence process on track.

REMEMBER

Decision intelligence is often simply a rethink of how business decisions are made. Many of the tools, tactics, and formulas will already be familiar to you. You'll likely be using them in a different order and to a different end, but otherwise in much the same way. The learning curve should be minimal for most business leaders. If by some chance these terms and metrics are new to you, don't worry. Given that so many modern business software applications now contain automation, AI, natural language search and processing, and other helpful features, many of these metrics are now easy for novices to use, too.

Leaning into KPIs

Which metrics you need to use depends on the nature and specifics of your decision intelligence project. But, as a general rule, it makes sense to at least begin with the key performance indicators (KPIs) relevant to the decision you're undertaking.

Keep in mind that metrics measure daily operational factors and that KPIs measure processes at a high rather than granular level. So, though all KPIs are metrics, not all metrics are KPIs.

KPIs are quantifiable measurements of performance levels relative to business goals. They tend to be focused on *horizontal* functions and/or departments, such as financial reporting, customer management, and automated business processes that cut across all *verticals* — business sectors such as manufacturing, retailing, financial sector, and healthcare. KPIs can also be helpful in spotting trouble and opportunities early on. Because of this, investors sometimes refer to them as *key success indicators* (KSIs).

REMEMBER

Many of the KPIs your business now uses in making decisions in day-to-day operations and overall management will be helpful in some decision intelligence projects as well.

Like decision intelligence, KPIs focus on obtaining a specific objective. Top KPIs for chief financial officers (CFOs) of huge corporations and for small-business owners include cash flow, sales, and revenue. These are most applicable to financial decisions that keep a business viable and profitable. However, they can be too myopic to be used alone in a decision intelligence project. For example, during the 2020 COVID pandemic, supply chain disruptions, labor shortages, and business resilence rapidly became hugely influential elements in business financial calculations. Suddenly, costs spiked as businesses hurried to equip workers to work from home while continuing to pay regular business expenses such as monthly lease or mortgage payments and related expenses for empty office buildings.

Traditional cash flow and other KPI analyses were badly skewed by this particular *black swan event* — an unpredicted, sudden and surprise event far outside the norm and capable of far-reaching and severe consquences. Year-to-year figures now carry little to no meaning in terms of deciding what to do next. In other words, they're a marked transition between the past and the future with no real connection with either one.

The business landscape has permanently changed because of the pandemic. Organizations will struggle for years trying to decide issues once considered routine and steadily predictable. Now a fairly basic decision like what office space size and design is appropriate in terms of business performance, costs, and labor recruitment and retention requirements has become a tough nut to crack. As organizations adjust to fluctuations in these factors, the facility decisions will be made repeatedly over time.

Another example is that, based on current indicators in several countries, minimum wage amounts will increase to entice people to return to work. But wage hikes will transfer to a hike in the cost of goods and services, further impacting every organization's performance as measured in several KPIs.

In short, these are not the times in which to rely solely on traditional KPIs. But it's not the time to discard them either. Instead, you need to rethink how and where you're using them. Further, look at combining them with nonfinancial KPIs to get more comprehensive reads on where your business stands and to detect both good and bad changes in your company's performance sooner.

Examples of commonly used financial KPIs, beyond the previously mentioned cash flow, sales and revenue KPIs, include:

>> **Working capital requirement (WCR)**, which tells you how much financial resources are needed to cover any gap between incoming and outgoing payments. It's a real-time assessment of the organization's cash position between accounts received and accounts paid. Net working capital (NWC) also takes into account inventory management. The formula for that is

   Net working capital requirement = inventory + accounts receivable − accounts payable

>> **Debt ratio** measures the relationship between business debt and assets.

   The formula to calculate this is

   Debt ratio = total debts / total assets

>> **Profit margin KPIs** estimate the profit earned by the company. You can measure profit margins in several ways — the most common is gross profit, operating profit, and net profit. However you choose to forecast and monitor performance in terms of profit, remember that it will constantly change because of fluctuations in many influencing factors. That means you need to run this KPI frequently.

   The formulas to calculate these different profit margins are

   Gross profit margin =[total revenue − cost of goods sold (COGS]/revenue

   Operating profit margin = operating profit / revenue

   Net profit margin = net profit / net revenue

There are many options in KPIs, and, fortunately, most are embedded in software to make them easier to use. Look for accounting software, spreadsheets like Google Sheets and Microsoft Excel, and apps such as ERP and business intelligence (BI) apps to do this and other math for you automatically.

This list describes several examples of nonfinancial KPIs that you may find valuable combining with financial KPIs:

>> **Customer experience** measures how satisfied customers are and how loyal they're likely to be. The most popular metrics used are net promoter score (NPS), customer satisfaction (CSAT), and customer effort scores (CES). Most of these use customer self-reporting data such as online ratings, surveys, and social media sentiment analysis. The formulas are

> *For NPS, from the sum of responses, subtract the percentage of distractors (e.g. frowning face icons, for example) from the percentage of promotors (e.g. smiling face icons, for example). The score is not a percentage but a whole number between –100 and 100 that indicates customer happiness with your brand or organization.*

> *For CSAT, divide the positive responses (satisfied customers) by the total number of responses and multiply that by 100. Your customer satisfaction score will be measured as a percentage. The higher the percentage, the more satisfied your customers are.*

> *For CES, measure how much effort a customer must expend to complete a single process such as how much effort it takes for a customer to resolve an issue with your company, return or exchange an item, or complete a purchase, for example. To calculate these KPI scores, find the average in responses.*

>> **Employee experience** is customer experience for employees. You're looking for their satisfaction and loyalty so that you can improve your employee recruitment-and-retention strategies. These metrics are crucial during periods of labor shortages. Many of the formulae are the same as their equivalence in customer experience. You can use employee data such as attendance, payroll, internal promotions, and engagement from HR or enterprise resource planning software (ERP), or check employee responses to surveys and online or app ratings. Often, you can find the formulas for these calculations embedded in human resources (HR) software and spreadsheets.

>> **Competitive analysis** measures several data points to determine the strengths and weaknesses of your competitors in specific markets. The comparison should include competitors' features, market share, pricing, differentiators (distinctions unique to your competitor vs your company, and/or vice versa), vendor relationships, customer satisfaction scores, locations, and others.

You need to use a competitive analysis framework to make these types of calculations. Some commonly used examples are:

- *SWOT tables:* These list the *Strengths, Weaknesses, Opportunities,* and *Threats* of a particular endeavor.

- *Porter's five forces:* A model that identifies and analyzes five competitive forces that shape every industry: competitive rivalry, threat of new entrants, supplier power, buyer power, and threat of substitution.

- *Growth share matrix:* A chart that helps companies analyze their business units or product lines into four broad categories according to their growth rate and potential: cash cows, dogs, question marks, and stars. Each broad category has multiple subcategories.

- *Strategic group analysis:* Used in strategic management to identify and group organizations within an industry that have similar strategic characteristics, such as similar business models or similar strategies for their products.

- *Perceptual mapping:* Used by asset marketers to compare products and visualize customer perceptions of them.

>> **Distribution channel analysis** measures competitor channels and *exclusive* channels (those channels where distributors have exclusive rights to sell a brand's products within a set geographic area and win\thin the manufacturer's rules), the channel's cost and benefits to you, a ranking of your options, and an assessment of the channel as it relates to your growth plans. There are frameworks that enable you to easily make these analyses, too.

>> **Supply chain analysis** involves measuring performance at every stage of the supply chain. Begin by mapping out your supply chain so that you will know the stages and can see what should be measured to get a good read on performance relative to the the rest of the chain and to your competitors' supply chains.

Ultimately, the nonfinancial KPIs you choose to use in your decision intelligence processes depend on the dictates of the business impact you're trying to create. The point is to ensure that you're considering all extenuating factors.

Tapping into change data

A good way to quickly identify where business decisions are likely needed and whether your decision intelligence processes are taking hold is to monitor *change data* — data that is of particular importance because it flags a significant change of some kind. Noting the specific data points reflecting a change from previously similar data points is a good way to detect early movement resulting from the decision you've taken or to spot where a decision is likely needed. In short, it's where the rubber meets the road, so you'll know whether to hit the gas or slam on the brakes.

In a world that revolves around massive amounts of data, spotting a data point of interest — or several differing data points depicting a sustained change — may seem daunting. Fortunately, there are easier ways to do that. Change data capture (CDC), for example, is a set of technologies that work together to identify and capture data that has changed in your database. The change data is then available for use later as needed.

CDC presents a number of significant advantages. For one thing, streaming only *change data* — data pertaining to a marked shift in information — is faster, cheaper, and more efficient than moving all data somewhere to be analyzed en masse. This means that you can view and analyze the winds of change in data, so to speak, rather than try to make sense of the entire hurricane of information in the database.

CDC is also helpful in event driven architectures, where it helps deliver data between service boundaries. Basically, that means it moves any change in the data to wherever it needs to be without dropping anything, despite many moving parts. Regarding what event-driven architectures actually are, they use events to trigger and communicate between disparate services. The event can be anything, really. One example is a change in a real estate listing from For Sale to Sold. Another example is RSVP responses to an online invitation to an online event such as a music concert or a technology conference. Whatever the case may be, the event is a change in the data that is identified and then reacted to through a series of actions across disparate services as necessary to completing the required and automated reactions.

Change data is useful for both a heads-up and automated follow-throughs for many actions, including updates in search indexes, analytics, anomaly detections, production machine learning models, and others.

Your task for a decision intelligence project is to develop a strategy wherein you identify which changes in data you need to be alerted to, which changes you need to monitor, and which changes may require an automated response. Your strategy should allow you to either watch change occuring in real-time as a result of your efforts or clue you in to where you may need to add new decisions or processes to refine or improve your DI project.

To illustrate this point, think of a CFO or small-business owner who's finally able to identify change data that can be early signals of success or failure of an initiative or pointers to unexpected new opportunities or unintended consequences that now lie ahead. One way to make that possible is to identify change data in KPIs that can be combined or compared with change data from other metrics to reveal a reliable forecast or at least a strong indication of what you can expect to happen next. With that data in hand, you'd be able to customize reports, dashboards, and visualizations to show change data in new contexts and help you envision future opportunities and challenges.

Testing AI

AI is automated decision-making — no more, no less. You use it to scale decisions at superhuman speeds, so you had better be extra double-dog certain it's making the right calls. Unfortunately, AI has a heck of an unreadable poker face. No one is quite sure what it's doing most of the time.

Certainly, people are working on opening the AI brain boxes to read the machines' minds or free their tongues, but for most businesses, neither strategy is particularly helpful. Few business leaders can read such alien minds or know machine-speak well enough to understand the mathematical chatter. For most of us mere mortals, testing the outcomes is our best shot at evaluating how well AI is functioning. If, in the end, AI feeds the egg and scrambles the chicken, we'll know that something is amiss.

The true masters of AI *do* know of ways to effectively test AI performance at various stages before and after production, but that's a tricky business as well, simply because digital decisioning — automated decisioning, in other words — is far more complex and volatile than most business processes that are now typically automated. That's because change comes faster and in larger volumes in automated decision-making, and if IT has to step in and handle it, you instantly lose a big chunk of the benefits from using AI because of interruptions and lost time. The better course is to analyze decisions before deployment to ensure that the AI is making the correct decisions and then monitor decision performance thereafter.

You'll also be wise to proactively monitor for changes that drive reactions in the automated decision-making. To do this, you need to capture data on decision effectiveness using a decision monitoring system — systems which automatically document and checks results, processes, and experiences to see if they are aligned or diverge from your plan. These systems are also found contained in decision management platforms such as Red Hat Decision Manager, FlexRule Decision Automation Platform, and SAS Real-Time Decision Manager. Compare those results with correlating KPIs, regulations, and policies, for these are the business contexts within which AI decisions are made and judged.

You should note a few matters of prime importance when it comes to AI testing processes. First, the outcome you measure often isn't the AI output but rather the business impact from the automated action taken on the output. You also need to compare that to the corresponding KPIs, policies, and regulations for context, as mentioned earlier.

You may also want to measure against other automated decisions and the final outcome from these decisions combined serially or in parallel. Remember that context and business impact are everything. Taken altogether, this is known as *decision outcome data.* The bottom line here is that you have to evaluate more than the AI's analytical output alone. In short, taste the pudding, because the proof you need is in the pudding you made.

Here are a couple more items for your checklist: Be diligent about updating the KPIs, regulations, and policies affecting automated decisions. Slip up on any of those, and you're looking at a pot load of troubles, ranging from fines and penalties to lawsuits, missed targets, and wasted effort. You know — it's the standard business muck that everyone tries to avoid. And no, you can't blame the AI. The law says that the fault belongs with the operator, which in this case is the decision-maker in the technical sense as well as the business sense.

While I'm running down the list of matters to pay attention to, keep in mind that AI ages just like humans do, only a heck of a lot faster. You need to monitor AI models to catch decay and mayhem before it wreaks havoc on your automated systems or in any applications which share that model.

Use a good ModelOps platform to manage AI models. Be careful not to confuse ModelOps with MLOps because they aren't the same thing. *ModelOps* manages AI and ML models and helps keep your ML feature stores fresh and fully muscled. *MLOps* is what the IT folks use to transition (deploy) ML algorithms (ML models) to production systems. In short, ModelOps is usually a part of MLOps, but not always. Check on that and know what you're actually working with and what might still require some extra monitoring or tweaking.

One last note: You may also need to ensure that IT is orchestrating AI, because many organizations today have a lot of AI pieces, projects, and pilot programs inhouse already. These need to be gathered and managed so that they don't conflict with one another. You also need to see whether models there can be shared — the last thing you want to do is waste time reinventing the wheel at considerable expense every time you have a new project.

REMEMBER

The days when AI/ML was strictly experimental are long gone. Your business needs to treat these as assets and leverage the heck out of them accordingly.

Deciding When to Weigh the Decision and When to Weigh the Impact

A funny thing happened while you were busy measuring the various moving parts in your decision intelligence process: The decision directing this entire project turned out to be a stinker. Okay, that's not so funny, but even so, it's something that does happen sometimes. The processes, tools, and metrics you chose to execute your decision provided definitive proof that the decision wasn't feasible or that its impact was undesirable.

Usually, but not always, that happens because of a change in business goals, in politics, in will, or change in the business environment caused by the arrival of new economic or market challenges or opportunities. In other words, something beyond your control happened that requires you to reconsider what you're doing in a particular decision intelligence project.

Again, that's usually the case, but sometimes things go south because your initial decision was in itself wrong, inadequate, ill informed, or fraught with too much risk. This can occur despite due diligence in the beginning to assess the value of the decision through counsel and decision determinations such as risk assessments and expected value (EV) calculations.

If you find yourself in this situation, stop and reassess the value of the decision and its corresponding business impact. If the reassessment finds that the decision is still solid, your perception that things have gone wrong may be due to data drift somewhere along the decision intelligence process. In other words, somewhere along the way, you likely accidently introduced data or a consideration that was just enough off task to skew your insights away from the goal or just fresh enough to spark a better idea.

If the reassessment finds the decision is flawed or undesirable, scrap it and choose another decision. The sooner you make this discovery and change course, the better. This should be a relatively rare occurrence, but when it does occur, be thankful you discovered it sooner rather than later. It isn't a failure as much as it's a matter of finding ways to adapt to changing circumstances.

4

Proposing a New Directive

IN THIS PART . . .

Recognize that disruption is really creativity unleashed

See that disruption is the point

Know that disruption starts with intent

Affirm that decision intelligence is intention in action

Chapter **13**

The Role of DI in the Idea Economy

Because of the magnitude of current and predicted disruptions, ranging from industry disruptors to pandemics to climate change, companies will need to develop new ideas and make decisions at a faster pace and from a broader base of facts than ever before.

Decision intelligence is swiftly gaining ground as a means to overcome the short-sightedness of traditional data analysis methods in predicting, avoiding, and solving problems arising from disruptions of any type.

Note that the digitalization of organizations of all types proved critical to survival during the COVID-19 pandemic, for both humankind and companies. In countries with high digitalization rates, new business models were more easily and successfully launched and scaled. Examples include telemedicine, mobile banking, and grocery and food delivery apps.

But even in countries where most organizations were mostly or completely digitalized, production and supply still came to a screeching halt for many critical goods. Previous business concepts such as just-in-time manufacturing (also known as *lean manufacturing*) and supply chain models (most notably, the continuous-flow model) completely decimated the affected businesses' ability to function.

REMEMBER

No one experienced a shortage of toilet paper in the early days of the pandemic. Producers, because of their dedication to production efficiencies, could not rapidly adapt by shifting production from commercial toilet paper to consumer versions. Nor could the supply chains be redirected to deliver commercial toilet paper to retail consumer outlets, because retailers, such as grocery stores, were locked in to the continuous-flow supply chain model, or another equally rigid model. Though consumers perceived a shortage in toilet paper, warehouses were bursting with undeliverable pallets of commercial versions of the item.

This story repeated itself across many essential consumer grade items, such as hand sanitizer and surface cleaning solutions and wipes. In almost every case, the needed items existed but in a form that could be neither easily repurposed for consumer use nor shipped to retail distribution centers.

For the first time in a very long time, efficiency worked against businesses when it came to their survival and profitability. The lesson here is that increased efficiency may not be the best business impact to seek, after all — or at least not in all conditions.

Decision intelligence, because it considers a broader spread of facts and considerations, can play a vital role in finding alternative strategies and ideas to previously accepted business goals. However, it's up to the strategist and/or the DI team to avoid the trap of defining the desired action or impact as something that worked in pre-pandemic periods and may not work as well in the post-pandemic era.

REMEMBER

Choose your desired business impacts with care and revise them frequently. Conditions and circumstances change, data changes, and decision and AI models drift accordingly.

Turning Decisions into Ideas

In business, decisions are usually made using data science, often in the form of if-when decisions. For example, software may be programmed to make a decision like this one: If a loan applicant's credit score is within X-Z range, then approve the loan. This type of decisioning scales well because it produces consistent results every time, no matter how many such decisions it makes.

But these decisions are essentially up-and-down votes — meaning they aren't exactly visionary. They aren't ideas, in other words. They are choices between options.

In decision intelligence, you're looking for ways to capitalize on new ideas as much as you are in leveraging automation to keep more routine decisions on track. Make a point to routinely check for places in your business processes where you can infuse new ideas and creative problem-solving. Then use decision intelligence to figure out which steps to take to bring new ideas to fruition.

Repeating previous successes

The point of scaling decision-making is to rapidly repeat a model that has previously proven successful. The continuous repetition by automation ensures error-free and compounded success.

However, sometimes previous successes become irrelevant. For example, at some point manufacturers of stagecoaches had to recognize that the market for stagecoaches was dying and could not be saved. Whether those manufacturers could successfully pivot to producing a different product depended on how quickly they acknowledged this situation and decided to change their business model.

The same is true today: No previous success can be repeated indefinitely.

For many business functions, automating or using AI to tend to established and routine decisions at scale is appropriate and practical. But even these decisions can benefit from an update or a makeover from time to time.

For one thing, data isn't static; it changes over time, and so the models used to automate decisions dependent on that data change as well. (The technical term here is *model drift*.) AI and automation are not things you can set and forget. Indeed, the problem of model drift alone is so common that a new discipline to manage it called ModelOps is fast taking hold.

Beyond keeping automated decisioning relevant and current, even the most mundane of tasks can and should be reimagined to make the business more competitive and less susceptible to disruptors.

Consider using decision intelligence to help you assess the current and future business value in existing business processes and automated decisioning. Just like AI and decision models have a lifecycle, so too do the processes and operations these models address. Decision intelligence can expose the folly in pursuing "business as usual."

Predicting new successes

Predictive analysis often plays a big role in decision intelligence. That's because business decisions aren't limited to analysis of historical data or snapshots of performance in a particular timeframe. Forward-looking thinking is what keeps a company ahead of disruptors and maintains its edge in heated competitive environments. Forward-looking thinking — *predictive analysis,* in other words — is how companies make sense of what likely lies ahead so that they can make informed decisions and plans.

TIP

Predictive analysis doesn't necessarily require the use of predictive analytics, but in most cases that's exactly what will be and should be used. Predictive analytics and AI can sort patterns in data that help define an unfolding future well before humans notice any signs of it. But keep in mind that these predictions make certain assumptions — namely, that current conditions will continue unchanged. In other words, the predictions are based on patterns in historical data. When humans are doing the analysis, predictions are based, at least in part, on experience which also entails making assumptions. It is therefore prudent to periodically check those assumptions to ensure that they still hold true.

For example, predictive analytics may indicate when an automotive, commercial heating, ventilation and air conditioning (HVAC), or an airplane part will reach the end of its lifecycle and specify a replacement date just prior to its predicted expiration. However, if the part is used more heavily than expected in the next month or so, the part may need to be replaced earlier.

The same can be said of nearly any business decision. In decision intelligence, you check the assumptions in any predictive analysis used in the process just as you will need to check the integrity (drift) in your AI and decision models.

Weighing the value of repeating successes versus creating new successes

Decision intelligence is designed to ensure that you realize a positive business impact in every decision made at any level of the business. Current decisions in your business that are providing positive business impacts — including automated digital decisioning — may need to be revisited as you change decisions elsewhere. However, if those decisions will continue to perform well for the time being then it's likely a better use of your time and resources to first turn your attention to digital decisioning outcomes that are not performing well or to business problems that are not yet resolved.

In short, decision intelligence is about rethinking how business is done in your organization. It doesn't necessarily require wholesale replacement, rebuilds, or heavy lifts in making changes in your decision processes. The important thing is to start. Choose a simpler decision first to get quick practical hands-on experience in how the DI process works.

TIP

Evaluate which decisions are producing well and keep those that are in place for now. Remember to revisit these periodically to ensure which assumptions and resulting actions are still creating business value. Focus your decision intelligence initiatives on the current decisions in the company that are either failing to lead to business value or are no longer relevant in the face of changes within the industry or the market. The eventual goal is to convert all business decisions to the decision intelligence process to ensure that every aspect of the business is consistently rendering value.

Leveraging AI to find more idea patterns

AI performs best when all data is digitalized and properly labeled. Models abound, as do algorithms, and many are reusable, making AI use a bit easier and a tad less complex. Training AI is largely no longer an issue, but retraining is. The frequency of data deviations from the original training data set is accelerating the need for retraining

AI model retraining involves running the process again on new data (data that's different or updated from the original training data set). Everything else about the model remains unchanged. Sometimes, retraining must occur daily because the data changes that frequently. Sometimes, retraining can be scheduled monthly, quarterly, or even yearly, depending on how often the data significantly changes.

If you decide to change AI features, model algorithm, and/or parameters, you need to rebuild and test an entirely new model before putting it into production.

On another note, using AI in predictive analytics can prove quite useful in illuminating additional patterns in the data that may lurk there unseen otherwise. This new information in turn can spark new business ideas and innovation. Leverage this AI capability to test the validity of business impacts you seek in decision intelligence when applicable. You can also use AI-fueled predictive analytics to flush out new patterns you might need in the decision intelligence process.

THE NEW DIRECTIVE

The business world has been conditioned to expect disruption and to adapt or die accordingly. This lesson recently came in the form of industry disruptors like Uber and Lyft to the taxi industry, craigslist and Google Ads to the media industry, and Netflix and Hulu to the cable television industry. The idea economy had arrived in force, and disruption was the name of the game.

What businesses did *not* expect was the onset of a significantly larger and more powerful global disruptor: the 2020 COVID-19 pandemic. All aspects of every economy and business, every government, and every industry suffered a direct and massive hit.

Though warnings of a possible pandemic have been sounded over several years, few organizations considered this possibility in their business models, plans, or strategies — let alone in any predictions created by predictive analytics or otherwise. The result was a global scramble for economic survival on the part of many businesses and the rapid adoption of technologies and new models to make survival possible.

Though the pandemic and the subsequent recovery process coexist at the time of this writing, with each consuming attention and resources to varying degrees from one country to the next, ample reason now exists to rethink the narrow confines of the world's traditional business analyses and our definition of business data.

No traditional business practice in the use of data and analytics made allowance for such a massive disruption. The only saving grace was that this pandemic isn't likely to be permanent, at least not at the scale of disruption seen at its peak. However, more permanent disruptions are already cresting the horizon — monster disruptions such as even more deadly and sustained pandemics and the growing danger of climate change, which is negatively impacting vast swaths of our planet. Many effects of climate change will cause permanent changes to markets and geographies, like the predictable and permanent flooding of many of the world's big coastal cities.

In short, disruption is still the name of the game, but the stakes of the game are now much higher. The businesses that adapted and survived thus far will now need to turn their attention to making decisions that will ensure they survive and thrive in the wake of wave after wave of disruptors both large and small, manmade and natural.

The new directive is profit through resilience. That directive will, from this day forward, overlay every decision made in savvy companies.

In decision intelligence, when framing the business impact you want to achieve, make sure you consider and plan for added agility and resiliency. You can do that by either including such scenarios in your decision-making process or developing an alternative contingency plan in anticipation of the inevitable rise of forks in your path due to such factors — and including the means to instantly shift your decision accordingly.

Disruption Is the Point

Not so long ago, disruption was seen as a threat to established businesses and industries. It became apparent that *cloud-native disruptors* — those companies that exploited the advantages of applications built on the cloud delivery model to be always available and almost infinitely scalable to service millions of customers anywhere — were no passing fad but rather a sustainable and growing trend. This new market phenomenon spawned the *idea economy,* in which success is defined as the ability to turn ideas into value before the competition does. Disruption was the point, even if you became a disruptor only to your own organization. Change had quickened as the new heartbeat of capitalism.

In other words, disruption evolved from a business threat to a business goal. But here again, success is measured in terms of business value. It's fair to say, then, that disruption is the point precisely because it keeps companies and industries from stagnating until little or no further value can be realized.

This drive to continually create ever growing value in the business is why the traditional data-driven model doesn't perform to expectations. Just because a business decision is informed doesn't mean that it brings value.

Conversely, determining the desired business impact in advance informs the decision process so that each step is in proper context and framed to perform to expectations. And that's why decision intelligence is set to overtake data driven approaches. There's simply less waste and more bang for the buck.

REMEMBER

Often, following the decision intelligence process leads to disrupting other business processes and models. This is as it should be because, yes, disruption is still the point in the idea economy, where change is a necessity and a degree of uncertainty is a given.

Creative problem-solving is the new competitive edge

Efficiency is often trumped by creative problem-solving in modern businesses. A rather extreme but current example of why this distinction matters is the recent pandemic and its effect on banking and lending. As of this writing, a housing shortage, historically low interest rates, and extraordinarily high savings rates — savings amassed during pandemic lockdowns — are driving up demand, thus generating an unexpected but welcome opportunity for U.S. mortgage lenders.

However, automated loan processing soon became an obstacle. Traditional banks depend on IRS records to verify mortgage applicants' income, but because 2020 income tax filing dates were extended from April 15 to May 17, 2021, by the government in response to the pandemic, traditional lenders could not access 2020 IRS records for much of the first half of 2021. Further, the IRS experienced additional processing delays as it worked to process and distribute stimulus payments during the same period. This created greater risk as verifiable but prepandemic incomes are in many cases irrelevant to current earnings and the mortgage application process.

Traditional lenders were at a disadvantage. The very loan approval model they had depended on for years was now failing them. Meanwhile, other lenders, many of them cloud native and armed with innovative loan decisioning tactics, reconfigured their risk models to derive a current view of loan applicant risk without delaying their own capability in capturing pent-up savings now being spent on homes.

Lenders who came up with new ideas on how to manage risk and still rapidly capture a significant share of the home buying spree prospered nicely. Traditional banks that held on to their previous lending models for too long lost out. This is a prime example of how using an idea suited to the circumstances in order to shape your decision (desired business impact) changes everything about how and how much business you can do.

Traditional banks can continue to focus on adding efficiencies and improving profits incrementally by being solely data driven, or they can focus on remaining relevant and competitive in a market now teeming with disruptors using decision intelligence.

The single remaining competitive edge that traditional banks hold over their cloud native and nontraditional counterparts is cash disbursements — the simple ability to hand the customer cash on the spot either through an ATM or a teller facilitating an instant and in-person withdrawal. But it's questionable how long that edge will hold, given that the pandemic accelerated the movement toward a cashless society and given that new cash disbursement systems — including shared ATM schemes with no cost to withdraw cash from any participating banking app or company, and the far-off future possibility of 3D printed money — are already cresting the horizon.

These banking and lending scenarios are examples of why pursuing a data driven path in business will ultimately fail. First, you're moving forward by mostly looking backward. Second, when you do look forward (predictive analytics), you're still assuming that past patterns will continue to be relevant in the future. Third, you're largely trying to improve on existing business patterns and processes rather than trying to disrupt them so that the business value can continue to rise.

Bending the company culture

It has been a long haul to persuade company staff and partners to accept and adopt the data driven mantra. Many were concerned that they would lose their job or senior status or even general agency and respect if they were reduced to executing only the actions that data and AI dictated should be done. Changing company culture to now accept decision intelligence as a guiding light to how work is done may be challenging as well, particularly where suspicions of a threat from machines still linger.

Some people will readily embrace decision intelligence as they immediately recognize that this is a demotion of sort for data and a promotion in kind for human talent. Members of the C-suite in particular are likely to feel greatly relieved to know that they are officially empowered again and that data is now their assistant rather than their overlord.

Others, like data scientists and business intelligence analysts, may feel threatened as they perceive their importance move from the forefront to the background. Still others in an organization will appreciate being asked to bring their expertise to the decision-making table, or they'll delight in machines serving as assistants on the job and delivering both valuable points to consider and, ultimately, political cover for any controversial decision taken.

In short, different people throughout an organization will react in different ways to the switch. This will produce ripples in the company culture and eventually cause it to evolve as well. It's prudent, then, to implement change management from the outset. This structured process, with its specific steps and tools, is used to prepare and support employees and executives in accepting and adapting to organizational change. A well designed and consistently implemented change management initiative will facilitate decision intelligence adoption overall and guard against resistance to the actions taken in any given decision intelligence exercise.

Competing in the Moment

If you want to avoid driving off the proverbial cliff, you should assess the long-term impact of short-term decisions. However, it's equally crucial to focus on making decisions in the moment as the pace of change in business and market conditions is now at a record high and both appear to be continuing that trajectory.

This brings up the question, of course, of how long the decision intelligence process takes to complete. The short answer: as long as it takes. A more definitive answer: It depends.

Some computations — namely, those wherein the facts are readily accessible, data confirmation isn't required, appropriate heuristics are used, and the user has the necessary smarts — can be done on the back of a napkin or in a simple spreadsheet in a matter of minutes or hours.

The same speeds or faster can be obtained in some AI-driven applications, such as GPS mapping and digital assistants in computing, where the user can add inputs to push the data analysis to create the impact they desire. In the case of GPS routing, that may be customizing the trip to prioritize using highways in the name of shorter travel times or scenic routes with multiple stops for a more refined experience.

Likewise, once digital decisioning processes and rules are in place — meaning the DI process is completed and the subsequent decision management is in place to ensure the required business impact is derived from AI decision-making — automation will scale and accelerate affected decisions thereafter. Many will take mere minutes even at extreme scales.

The time it takes from start to deployment of a fully realized DI decision in its truest sense depends, however, on several variables. In the case of more complicated decisioning, the time needed is directly related to the level of complexity of the process and the corresponding skill sets within the DI team or the individual conducting the effort.

Assessing whether current digital decisions are now rendering business value should be a straightforward matter. Challenging the business assumptions in these decisions may be less so because it requires, at minimum, a heightened degree of intuitive intelligence and at best a command of the decision sciences to discern which assumptions will hold for any given period.

Tackling decisions with pronounced disruptive or significant impacts should take longer because extraordinary care must be taken to ensure that no biases or errors seep into any crevice in the process. Though this precaution may take longer, it also tends to have the highest returns because it seeks to create new value where previous value is stagnating or eroding.

In any case, be sure to stay in the moment while working out these decision processes to prevent missteps, misapplied heuristics, false or outdated assumptions, and ill matched metrics and resources. In other words, if you're working as the decision chef, focus on refining the recipe and not on reinventing the tools or taking sketchy shortcuts that may backfire.

Developing the decision recipe, preparing, cooking, and serving it to perfection takes as long as it takes. In the real world, however, it takes whatever length of time you have. For example, you have less time to make this work if a pandemic is threatening your business's survivability and more time if you're searching for new ideas to use as profitable disruptors.

You may be unsettled by the idea that DI has no set time frame for creating value. Experience has taught IT and company leadership that projects can roll on forever before a useful product gets rolled out. If that happens with DI, the business impact has been poorly framed and the effort is virtually aimless.

When business impact is properly framed — that is, in full context, including a time component — the process unfolds under those constraints. As long as the scope or parameters don't change, the process should remain on course and on target. How long it takes is then of importance only to the time component to which it's bound. Ultimately, achieving the stated business impact is all that matters.

Changing Winds and Changing Business Models

Predictive analytics are only as good as the data they analyze. The data is always historical, even if it's streamed in real-time because some amount of time, no matter how miniscule, has elapsed from the time the data was collected to the time it was digested in analytics and an output was spit out. Clearly, they're still largely useful predictions, but they're still predictions based on historical data, even if only barely so.

That's neither a fanciful criticism of the time expirations on data, nor a wringing of the hands over the nature of time. It's simply an acknowledgment that even predictive analytics are basing predictions on what happened in the past — not on what is happening now.

That means that current events can run even the best of business decisions right off the rails. That is to be expected because change is the only constant in this world, leaving every judgment call vulnerable to uncertainty.

REMEMBER

Predictive analytics and predictive analysis of any sort aren't true predictions of the future. These analytics and decision processes aren't crystal balls, in other words. No one knows for certain what will happen in any aspect of life. Do not think that decision intelligence will entirely remove uncertainty, for it certainly will not.

Any business decision is based on probabilities. In decision intelligence, you're aiming for a definite target (business impact) using a multidisciplinary process to perfect your aim — you'll probably hit the target if you did everything right. But even if you did everything right, you may still miss the target because something in the here-and-now changed the probability of your success.

A big, crystal-clear example is the pandemic, which effectively blew up everyone's business decisions, plans, and models. All that work just disappeared — poof! — and it was gone in the minutes it took for the powers-that-be to finish reading the lockdown order in a public announcement. Other examples with a truly hefty punch, but not so easily recognized early on, is the U.S. labor shortage, despite high unemployment in the early days of the recovery, as well as the strong surge in demand for housing despite the ongoing threat of mass evictions.

The point of that in this discussion is that decision intelligence will always be an ongoing effort because your business will always be operating in changing winds and because your business model will always be subject to threats you likely won't see coming. However, if your focus remains on business impact for every business decision, you can respond in a timely and effective manner. Making good business decisions has always been the crux of a successful business. Getting better at it bodes well for your organization's future — no matter what obstacles lie ahead.

Counting Wins in Terms of Impacts

Decision intelligence is all about staying focused on creating an impact of value to the business. By definition, these impacts have value, and value is measurable. That means a win or a loss, a hit or a miss, is readily discernable.

When you count business wins by the impacts of decisions rather than by more nebulous markers, the focus remains on profitability in both the short and long terms. Perhaps counterintuitively, this emphasis on profitability doesn't mean that there's no room or place for the soft skills. The truth is, because these skills cannot be automated, they must be tapped directly from the source: talented people. These skills must be added to the decision process so that they can help refine and bring about the desired business impact.

Skills referred to as *soft* skills are numerous and include such characteristics as intuitive intelligence, human integrators (intuitively connecting seemingly unconnected ideas and facts), creative problem-solving, critical thinking, nuanced valuations, object recognition (why yes, AI, that *is* a picture of a cat!), emotional intelligence, and human relationship management, among others.

Historically, soft skills have been dismissed, devalued, and even scorned. That is a serious business error. But it's an error that makes it difficult for some to readily recognize the consequences.

REMEMBER

Decision intelligence frames a desired impact in context. This means that considerations such as potential for public or customer backlash (human relationships), integration of disciplines and ideas (human integrators), avoidance of unintended consequences (critical thinking), elegantly refined heuristics (nuanced valuations), disruption by design (intuitive intelligence, creativity), and new approaches to old and new business issues (creative problem-solving) are all necessary soft skills in establishing the context.

Rather than fall down a rabbit hole trying to assign values to human and machine contributions in the decision intelligence process, just focus on measuring wins in terms of the value of business impact alone. This keeps the processes on course and tensions lower because value — perceived or real — isn't assigned to individual components (human or machine).

IN THIS CHAPTER

» Using what-if analyses to make decisions

» Recognizing that data-driven means driving ahead while looking in the rearview mirror

» Learning that decision intelligence is forward looking

» Leveraging industry convergence

» Harnessing continuous disruption

Chapter **14**

Seeing How Decision Intelligence Changes Industries and Markets

D ecision intelligence can lead to changes in markets, industries, and societies. It's not that the decision-making method itself is an earth-shattering force, nor is a conspiracy afoot or any industry-wide effort to push the future in any given direction using DI tactics. Rather, change is more likely to come to markets and industries after enough organizations successfully pursue purposeful impacts that together create a tide of change that washes over all of us. The effect is comparable to business trends that cross the threshold into sustained and accepted practice over time. It's not so much an industry goal or effort as it is part of its evolution.

Now, whenever a single entity's decision reverberates throughout a market or industry, it's called a disruptor if it creates a disruption to the norm via innovation. People who are creative, critical thinkers, and skilled at decision intelligence may purposefully set out to either become a disruptor or to counter one. Or they may just be focused on improving their own companies and later find their role in changing the industry a complete surprise.

In any case, harnessing the power of good decisions comes with consequences. Keep in mind, however, that not making a decision can be just as much a decision of consequence. Better that you aim for the consequences coming your way than to be subject to them. Decision intelligence, because of its focus on creating a desired business impact, can help you predict outcomes — consequences, in other words. In the business world, "predicting consequences" is better known as *forecasting*, and it can pertain to internal decisions or be applied to competitor, market, or industry movements.

Facing the What-If Challenge

Decision intelligence is a discipline that aims to make good business decisions using data. The decision is the star of the show, and data plays a supporting role, which is the opposite of previous data-driven or data-mining models. Typically, decision intelligence is used to make AI more productive from the organization's viewpoint. (AI is essentially automated decisions at huge scales, so getting those processes right is absolutely essential. Imagine making a mess of things and then watching it as it rapidly spreads to infinity — or your entire customer base which is just as bad.) But decision intelligence can be used, and is used, to make decisions without AI and without large data sets and analytics as well. It's a versatile methodology.

Your mission, should you decide to accept it, is to ferret out the best business impact to pursue and then choose the decision that will deliver that precise impact. Yes, that's often hard to do, but presumably that's what you get paid the big bucks for. (I'll leave for another day the discussion of what constitutes "big" in bucks in data.)

The good news is that you don't have to read a crystal ball or, as the Facebook meme goes, "mess" around and find out. You can choose from more scientific ways to go about this process, and even choose from a bunch of tools available to help you do the math. For example, you can predict outcomes to a variety of what-if scenarios to help you choose a decision on which to build out a more involved or complex decision intelligence process. Or you can just run with a decision you choose from your what-if analysis and call it a decision intelligence project well done! You're in charge. You get to call the shots.

Playing out several possible scenarios is a well-established method in decision-making. The point is to weigh options based on costs, risks, potential benefits, and resource availability. For some what-if scenarios, using comparative or SWOT tables or even just a pros-and-cons list on the back of a napkin will suffice. But if you want more sophistication, plenty of more advanced what-if analyses tools are available to you as well, such as the analysis tools in the Microsoft 365 Excel spreadsheet program. Check out these tools yourself so that you know all your options. While you're at it, check out the embedded Microsoft Power BI tool because it's helpful for lots of different kinds of decision-making.

Taking a closer look at Excel, three what-if analysis tools are built into the program: Scenario, Goal Seek, and Data Tables. Of the three, Goal Seek is more representative of a decision intelligence process in that you enter a result and it calculates backward to determine possible input values to produce that result.

Three other options are built into Excel as well. For example, the Forecast Sheet feature lets you look at data trends using different forecast options. Another option would be the Solver add-in, which is like Goal Seek but can contain more variables. If you need more advanced tools and models than these, you have to load Excel's Analysis ToolPak add-in. (I talk more about these Excel tools in the later section "What-if analysis in scenarios in Excel.")

Don't think that Microsoft is the only game in town, however. Google Sheets has the same or similar tools as Excel, but you need to first install them as add-ins from Google Workspace Marketplace. Causal – Scenarios, shown in Figure 14-1, is the Google Sheets version of a scenario manager.

FIGURE 14-1:
Causal – Scenarios, as shown in the Google Workspace Marketplace.

TIP

Test your choice of outputs before you designate it as your final decision. When you know that the decision is solid, you can start working backward to determine which buttons to push and which levers to pull to make this train leave the station and head for that precise destination.

What-if analysis in scenarios in Excel

A scenario feature is one of the three What-If Analysis tools built into Excel and available for Google Sheets as well. In this tool, you provide scenario inputs, and it calculates the results. In Excel, you can find it on the Ribbon's Data tab, on a pull-down menu under What-If Analysis, as shown in Figure 14-2. (In Google Sheets, you have to install the add-in from Google Workspace Marketplace.)

FIGURE 14-2:
The home of what-if on the Excel Ribbon.

The What-If Analysis menu

Scenarios can calculate results from sets of input values. It can handle multiple variables, but only up to 32 values for each variable. Excel's Data Tables feature works similarly to the scenario features in Excel and Google Sheets in that it calculates results from the inputs you put in the tool. The difference between the two is that Data Tables works with only a couple of variables, each of which can handle many values. In short, the scenario features use more variables but fewer values, whereas Data Tables uses fewer variables but more values.

TIP

When using Excel, enter and save sets of values in scenarios so that you can easily switch back and forth between them on your Excel worksheet to view their different results. You can also collect information from several sources in separate workbooks and later merge all scenarios into one workbook via the Merge Scenarios command in Scenario Manager.

REMEMBER

If you plan to merge scenarios from two or more workbooks, make sure the cells of each one are labeled and hold the same type of information. Without this conformity in workbooks, merging is a hot mess. Consider setting the example for other sources who have scenario info (accounts payable, for example) by providing your scenario first and asking them to follow suit with the structuring of their inputs.

You can also create a scenario summary report to compare all scenarios in one place. Go to the Data tab in Excel and then to the What-If Analysis group to manage scenarios with the Scenario Manager Wizard. (See Figure 14-3.)

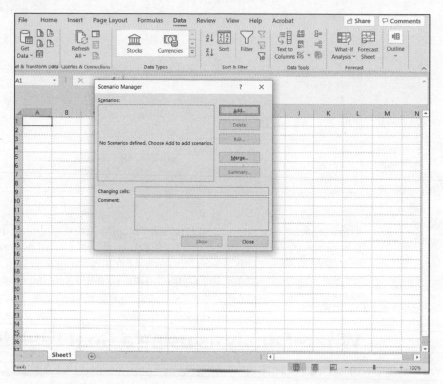

FIGURE 14-3:
The Excel
Scenario Manager
Wizard.

What-if analysis using a Data Tables feature

Data Tables is one of the three What-If Analysis tools built-in to Excel and available for Google Sheets as well. In this tool, you provide the scenario inputs, and it calculates the results. In Excel, you find it on the Ribbon's Data tab, on a pull-down menu under What-If Analysis. In Google Sheets, it's the WhatIf add-in that you need to download from Google Workspace Marketplace. (See Figure 14-4.)

To use Data Tables, change the values in some of the cells to reflect different scenarios and then wait and see how that action affects the results. This is a familiar and often used technique (although the tool that's used may vary) in data analysis.

WARNING

Do not guess at the values you input in Data Tables or Scenarios. This isn't a guessing game but rather a precise mathematical formula. You render all that precision useless if the values you enter aren't real and rooted in fact.

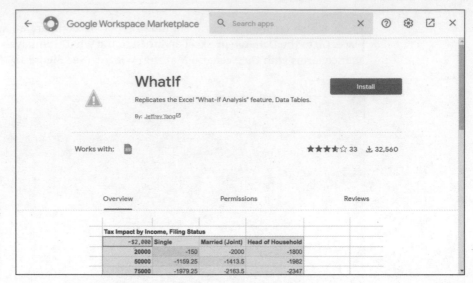

FIGURE 14-4:
The WhatIf
add-in, as shown
in Google
Workspace
Marketplace.

The Scenarios tool shows you possible outcomes for a single scenario unless you merge scenarios into one report. Data Tables shows you all potential outcomes in one table or sheet. This is possible because you're using only two variables — one for the row and one for the column. One scenario can have up to 32 different values.

What-if analysis using a Goal Seek feature

Of the three What-If Analysis tools built into Excel — Scenario, Goal Seek, and Data Tables — Goal Seek is more representative of a decision intelligence process in that you enter a result and it calculates backward to determine possible input values to produce that result.

Goal Seek is built-in to Excel and available for Google Sheets as well. In this tool, you provide the result(s) you want, and it calculates possible input values that can render that result, as shown in Figure 14-5. In Excel, you find Goal Seek on the Ribbon's Data tab, on a pull-down menu under What-If Analysis.

In Google Sheets, you need to get the WhatIf add-in from Google Workspace Marketplace to use Goal Seek. (See Figure 14-6.) To use Google Sheet's version of Goal Seek, enter the reference that contains the formula you want to resolve in the Set Cell box. Type the formula result you want in the To Value box. Enter the reference to the cell you want to adjust in the By Changing cell, and then click OK. Goal Seek provides you with the correct input values.

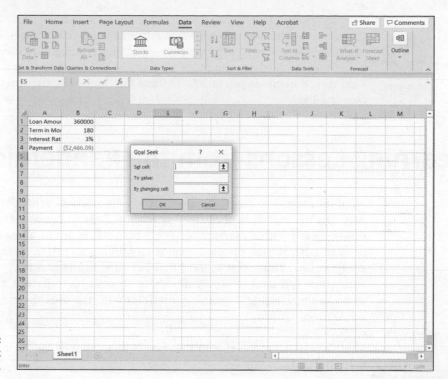

FIGURE 14-5:
Excel's Goal Seek feature.

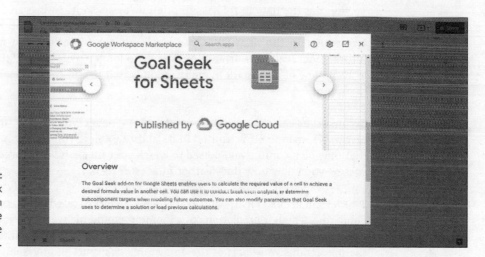

FIGURE 14-6:
The Goal Seek add-in, as shown in Google Workspace Marketplace.

For example, you may want to buy a commercial 3D printer for your manufacturing plant but also stay within the budget. Enter the loan amount you want to borrow to pay for the 3D printer, the term (number of months you want to take to repay the loan), and the monthly payment amount that fits the company budget. Goal Seek would then tell you which interest rate you need to negotiate with the lender to get the monthly payment and terms your company needs.

REMEMBER

If you see that the variable needed to achieve the results you seek is unrealistic or unobtainable, you need to adjust your expectations and enter different values. It's helpful to use Goal Seek to judge all possible options before you decide on one. That way, the actions you take from there to achieve this end will be both achievable and likely.

Learning Lessons from the Pandemic

What-if analysis, forecasting, and predictive analytics aren't panaceas. Though they can be invaluable in calculating what's likely to happen, those predictions center on one central assumption: Everything will continue along the path it's on now. In other words, the prediction is identifying an action at one point along a set trajectory. Think of it as tools that can quickly and accurately identify where your arrow will land — provided nothing changes its trajectory. No wind or rain or broken bow string — nothing interferes with nor aids the trajectory that the arrow is on.

There's just one problem with that assumption: change, and not stability, is the only constant.

To say that the flaw in this assumption imposes some impressive limits on predictive analytics and forecasting is a bit of an understatement. And here's the jawbreaker in the data lollipop: Data is always historical and never from the future. Even real-time streaming data is no longer real-time by the time you see it. It may be off the mark by mere seconds, but it still is technically historical at that point.

Because data can only chronicle what was and never what will be (at least not with certitude), data itself is limited in its ability to alert you to anything unexpected that may be incoming and poised to wreck your nice-and-tidy predictions. (Okay, so now you know how the weather forecaster feels.)

This lesson is most clearly and dramatically demonstrated by the recent COVID-19 pandemic. Though predictions of a looming pandemic were contained in the esoteric annals of epidemiologists and public health agencies, neither the data nor the predictions were part of the data stores or inputs in any analytics, predictive or otherwise, for most other organizations. All the data mining, analytics, and AI at work around the clock and across industries couldn't prevent just about every organization worldwide from being blindsided by one of nature's biggest and most destructive wrecking balls.

Not seeing the wrecking ball headed its way and then failing to find ways to recover from it was the double whammy that knocked the data-driven enterprise concept permanently off its pedestal. It's not that companies expect analytics and AI to be omniscient; indeed, that idea is widely feared. It's that organizations no longer believe data to be the bulletproof — or pandemic-proof — protection they once thought it to be.

Decision intelligence is catching on in a big way because people once again see the value of humans looking up from their analytics to see what else is happening in the real world that they may need to address. One tiny virus burned that point into the global business psyche.

REMEMBER

Data is no longer driving. Humans are steering again.

Refusing to make decisions in a vacuum

Tunnel vision is the reason so many organizations didn't see the pandemic coming and didn't anticipate the struggle to steer clear of it. That's the trouble with taking a data driven approach: No one's watching the other drivers on the high-stakes corporate highway. Instead, all gazes were locked on their data, which is like looking at reality in a rearview mirror. Worse, they were looking only at the pieces in that view that they believed pertinent to the road ahead on the company's current path. From that perspective, it was easy to miss an oncoming head-on collision.

Put another way, organizations were making decisions in a vacuum. They were operating primarily on the assumption that a myopic focus on business related data was their chief duty. It proved to be a near fatal error in judgment that many organizations don't plan to repeat — though some will surely do so.

REMEMBER

The key to avoiding making decisions in a vacuum lies not in adding more data and inputs to algorithms. Larger data sets don't necessarily carry more truths, and too many inputs in an algorithm can snarl the process like tangled fishing line. The answer, at least as it's defined in decision intelligence, is to widen the role for humans in making decisions and in so doing leveraging their strengths in wider perceptions, free associative reasoning, and leadership, among others.

In short, the way to stop making decisions in a vacuum is to ensure that people are looking up from their work to observe what else may be happening and consider more than just the data in front of them. This calls for diverse decision teams who have the time to reflect and wonder, to think and imagine, rather than overfill their days with repetitive work that is unlikely to broaden anyone's perspective. That way, the decision-making process can be built to provide a realistic path to a specified outcome most likely to truly benefit the organization.

Living with toilet paper shortages and supply chain woes

Real-life examples of the shortcomings in data-driven decision-making are plentiful. Many are even a bit painful. For example, few people made it through the COVID-19 pandemic without feeling some anxiety over the availability of staple supplies. One example was the shortage of toilet paper in the U.S. during the first several months of the pandemic. The oddest aspect of that shortage was that there really was no shortage.

To understand how a toilet paper shortage could happen despite plentiful supply, you need to consider the decisions made at the time and the consequences they produced.

To improve efficiencies, margins, and profits, most paper manufacturers and retailers relied on a just-in-time (JIT) supply chain system. The term *just-in-time* refers to moving raw materials to wherever it's needed just before it's needed. The material is delivered just in time so that it's neither too early (and needs to be stored) nor too late (and thereby interrupts production). This supply method substantially reduces warehousing and other overhead costs. But note that there's no room for error and little to no cushion if anything goes wrong.

In the premanufacturing supply chain, raw supplies are continuously delivered to the manufacturer almost immediately before the manufacturer feeds it into the process. After manufacturing, the supply chain delivers just enough finished goods to retailers and distributors to keep shelves fully stocked. In many cases, retailers and distributors are just a few handfuls of new customers away from running out of supply for the week.

Further, the raw goods in the first supply chain and the finished goods in the second supply chain are packaged in such a way as to increase efficiencies in material handling as well.

In the case of consumer rolls of toilet paper, the rolls of paper are smaller, shorter, and softer, and they have more plies (layers). The rolls are sealed in small packages that are then bundled for movement in store-size bulk. This means a retailer or distributor can handle the bundle in-store with hand trucks or other small equipment. Store stockers then need only to open the bundle to place the small packages directly on store shelves. Consumers can then easily pick up and carry the small packages to checkout counters and then home.

But in the case of commercial toilet paper for hospitals, office buildings, university campuses, and other public uses, rolls are much larger and longer, and the paper is harsher, thinner, and usually single ply. These rolls are put in larger packages and then bundled on commercial-size pallets. In this way, an organization can buy paper goods in bulk to save money but then redistribute it throughout their operations themselves. Generally, this requires warehouse distribution systems, including forklifts and other heavy equipment. It definitely isn't something you can drive in a grocery store, nor are the packages broken down into units that a consumer can pick up and carry home.

Both the commercial and the consumer supplies of toilet paper are precisely calculated to provide the exact amount needed without the need to store it or fear of running out. It's a perfect picture of efficiency until some unexpected force — like a pandemic — plows through it.

The COVID-19 pandemic caused a massive worker migration from workspace to homeplace as countries and cities strived to contain the spread of disease. When that happened, the demand for consumer toilet paper spiked well above the ready supply. Never in the history of automated analytics had consumer toilet paper been consumed in these extreme quantities.

Conversely, the demand for commercial toilet paper plunged because hardly anyone was at work, whether that was in an office, a restaurant, a public park, or anywhere else that has public toilets. The supply, however, began to pile up because the manufacturers were still producing on schedule. Production continued because everyone expected workers to return to their workplaces, shoppers to their shopping places, and kids to their school places soon. But that's not what happened.

As of this writing, the pandemic is 18 months in and counting. Most employees are still working from home. Demand for consumer grade toilet paper is still soaring. Demand for commercial grade toilet paper is still lagging. All the businesses involved in the production and distribution of toilet paper are still reeling, even if only a little.

Most people would view this problem as having an easy solution: Just reroute the commercial toilet paper to consumer retailers and distributors, right? If it were only that simple. And yes, it could have been that simple if a decision had been made earlier to facilitate cross-purposing and cross-distributions to build resilience into the supply chains.

Alas, this situation was data driven, not decision driven. The data said that cutting supplies close was cutting-edge smart. (It cut something, all right.)

Long story short, the very nature of just-in-time systems often requires that raw materials are sourced nearby to shorten travel times, and specialized manufacturing or assembly plants are strategically located to speed finished goods to key retailers or distributors. It meant that commercial toilet paper lived in one loop and consumer toilet paper in another and that the two neither crossed nor were compatible and therefore were not interchangeable.

Suddenly, an efficient system completely and utterly failed. Toilet paper manufacturers had no easy or fast way to retool to make more consumer grade goods in plants that specialized in commercial grade production. Nor was there a means to repackage commercial grade toilet paper so that stores could handle it without heavy equipment and consumers could fit it on home toilet paper dispensers.

In short, the entire debacle left everyone stranded.

Had the original decision been to increase resilience to ensure the continued profitability of the organization rather than on how to increase efficiencies to produce more immediate profits, the manufacturers, retailers, distributors, and the entire ecosystems of each and all supply chains would have prospered through the pandemic. And society would have fared better, too — because this scenario happened not just in paper goods but also across many supply industries.

And that, in a nutshell, is why you should move away from being a data driven enterprise and toward being a decision driven enterprise as fast as you possibly can.

Revamping businesses overnight

Lessons from the pandemic should be sufficient evidence that letting data drive the enterprise isn't such a hot idea. If you think the pandemic and the lessons learned from it to be too much of a fluke to cause your organization to change course, consider the high failure rates in current data and AI projects. By most accounts, about 80 percent of AI projects never make it to production. Of those that do, over half fail at delivering the objective. Failure rates that high are not only undesirable but are also generally deemed not worth pursuing.

Think about it: If you owned a car that broke down 80 percent of the time before you could drive it out of the garage and 50 percent of the time as soon as you made it to the end of the street, would you continue trying to drive it? Most people wouldn't.

But it's a mistake to throw out AI at this point. Make no mistake: Machine learning as we know it will likely be replaced by another form of AI that works better in the future. But for now, at least, ML works better in most use cases than anything else available. It's just that everyone is still figuring out how to perfect it now.

Decision intelligence can help put AI projects back on track in several ways.

First, it refines data selection. By first establishing the business impact you intend to create, you can better define which data to use (and which to exclude) from the training data set so that the AI model is better honed for its purpose and better educated on its mission.

But also, it's much easier to identify which data sets are pertinent to the decision intelligence process you're building when you know precisely where you're headed. In other words, it's easier to pick which hotels to spend the night in when you already know your destination and which hotels are between where you are now and where you're headed. The same is true in identifying and choosing data sets that will help you on your journey to the decision you already made.

REMEMBER

The point is to move away from being a data-driven organization and toward being a decision-driven organization.

The problem is, companies and organizations are impatient and seek to profit immediately from every action taken. That being the case, don't be surprised if decision-makers around you solemnly nod their heads and offer thoughtful comments as you painstakingly explain decision intelligence. Ten minutes after they leave the meeting, they'll be looking for results or they'll move back to the status quo.

That's not a criticism of decision-makers. Company leaders have to answer to a lot of people and keep the company on track as well. Much of their impatience is born from necessity — though, clearly, some of it isn't. But that's okay because you can quickly flip to the decision intelligence model. The key is to start small and with the automated decisions already in progress. You can look at your decision there and work backward to discover the ways in which you can improve how quickly, directly, and accurately you render that decision at scale. Or you change the decision itself to something that delivers a more favorable business impact.

For example, if you're a bank or a mortgage lender using AI to approve or decline mortgage applications, look closer at the machine decisioning at work there. How can you flip that model from its fixation on rating credit scores and income to a new decision, such as "Find any and all data that correlates with a strong tendency to pay on time," or something of a nature that expands your ability to automatically identify good mortgage applicants so that you can capture a larger market share.

In this case, your decision would be "to increase market share by identifying more qualified applicants beyond the standard scoring mechanisms," whereas your previous data driven approach was to "mark approved any clients that meet these criteria only."

At the time of this writing, the U.S. is experiencing a shortage of available housing, and buyers are struggling to outbid one another, even for subpar houses. Mortgage lenders are struggling to feast on more of the action. Given that interest rates are low, high volume matters more than usual for this industry. The tendency is to play a numbers game by being lax on the prequalification of mortgage applicants and betting that a significant percentage will pass the loan approval process so that the resulting waste won't hurt you. Or, to play a different numbers game, you'd work on prequalifying the obviously high-quality loan applicants and focus exclusively on servicing those accounts.

It's smarter to find a way to pull ahead of your competitors by identifying loan quality signals beyond the traditional standards so that you can produce more loans for a larger number of qualified applicants faster. Make your own special sauce, so to speak, with which to make a more profitable spread.

In the case of the pandemic induced toilet paper shortage problem (from a business perspective), the smarter decision would be to flip the "increase profits/ margins by increasing efficiencies" just-in-time model with a model that seeks "to find cushions and increase efficiencies to maximize profits *and* business resilience."

That's how disruptors work, by the way — they figure out what they can rip away or replace in standard models to create a new model capable of eating the competition. Uber, for example, stripped vehicle leasing and ownership, medallion rights models, payroll, and other costly assets and liabilities in the traditional taxi model to create a ride share company. What ride share companies actually do is distill the taxi industry to its most profitable essence by ditching everything else. There's an app for that precisely because someone reduced an industry model to a mobile application.

Not all these examples can be accomplished overnight — though some feel as if they were. But steps building up to those events can be taken immediately and with maximum leverage if the decision is known in advance.

REMEMBER

Impatience is not the enemy of decision intelligence. Inertia is.

Seeing how decisions impact more than the Land of Now

It's easy to fall for the seduction in AI's speeds at scale. Just remember two things before you're totally smitten:

>> AI usually crawls before it runs.

>> You need to think about more than what's happening in the Land of Now in judging AI's impact.

American businesses in particular, but companies based in other countries as well, tend to be hyperfocused on immediate profits and results. That's not a healthy approach to business in general, though it's perfectly understandable given the fast pace of change and the cacophony of stockholders, customers, and others wanting more, faster — not to mention the opposing forces of disruptors and competitors marching on your turf.

You don't have to lose sight of immediate benefits in decision intelligence, and it would probably be irresponsibly reckless to do so. However, it's equally or more reckless to not finish the calculation to include evaluating the impact in both the midterm and the long term.

Just as making a decision in a vacuum is a bad idea, so too is believing that an impact stops at some arbitrary point you designate. That isn't how any of this works. Indeed, that kind of thinking is where unintended consequences are spawned, and most of them are bad news for your business.

In most cases, looking further ahead will be easier with forecasting tools such as those embedded in Microsoft Excel or Google Sheets but that are plentiful in other tool categories as well, such as business intelligence (BI) apps.

Whatever tools you use, here are some areas you need to consider evaluating in terms of future impact:

>> The effect on resources

>> Opportunity and lost opportunity costs

>> Image and brand impact

>> Return on investment (ROI)

>> Expected value (EV)

>> Capital budgeting effects

>> Differential analysis

>> Relevant costs (those avoidable costs that are incurred only when making specific business decisions)

>> Qualitative factors (those decision outcomes that cannot be easily measured, such as impact on employee morale)

» Differential revenue (the difference in revenues or expenses between two alternatives)

» Avoidable versus unavoidable costs

» Diversification impacts, such as on your investment portfolio in terms of its diversification as a risk mitigation strategy and/or in terms of the impact on minority communities, customers, or employees

» Business expansion impacts

» Merger and acquisition impacts

» Product line impacts

» Other factors relevant to the action or impact

Another good tactic is to decide on a long-term impact you want to create for the company, build that process backward in the usual decision intelligence way, and use it as a benchmark for shorter-term decision intelligence projects. This way, you have something against which to measure short-term impacts to ensure that your long-term business goals are met as well.

Rebuilding at the Speed of Disruption

The COVID-19 pandemic has forever changed the world as we humans know it. The new rules aren't yet set, a new normal isn't yet defined, and most of the data that businesses have relied on for years is now almost worthless in terms of forecasting. There's little point in looking at historical data if you don't think you can mine some truth from it that applies today, let alone next year, five years, or ten years in the future.

Perhaps the most prudent path forward now is to rebuild rather than simply re-create or reuse your former data mining processes. The past is gone. You can't rebuild it and expect everything to return exactly as it was.

Instead, you need to rebuild your business into something capable of competing in a heightened state of flux. In other words, you need to rebuild the affected parts of your business at the speed of disruption. Ideally, you disrupt your own company over and over again because that is what it takes to emerge from this sea change to rule the market on the next patch of dry land.

REMEMBER

Decision intelligence is forward-looking. Data driven is looking back.

In decision intelligence, you look forward and decide on the business impact you want to create *in the future.* That future can be an hour from now, a hundred years from now, or somewhere in between. But it's still out front of wherever your business is now.

Conversely, a data-driven enterprise hopes to catch a glimpse of the future by looking back to see what happened before in similar circumstances. But similar circumstances no longer exist, courtesy of a small virus with a lethal aim and a long reach.

This situation calls for stronger business leadership. It also increases demand for employees and partners who are innovative, critical thinkers who can respond to change quickly and imagine new business scenarios in which the organization can clearly succeed.

In short, human talent is now the crux of business success as the source of constructive disruption.

The number one rule is that nothing about your business is sacred. Be willing to change your business model, its products and services, and how and where it operates. Now, absolutely anything about the business should be subject to change. Business leadership as well as the rank-and-file need to be okay with all of that.

The days of 100-year-old companies are coming to an end. Businesses that last for long periods will be those whose leaders are willing to make big changes as needed over time. That's the reality of the times we humans live in — the age of continuous disruption, where we are constantly evaluating and changing how business is done rather than simply buying technologies to do the same processes better. Though the definition appears simple, the reality isn't.

Continuous *innovation* is continuous improvement of the same product or process. Continuous *disruption* gives rise to completely different offerings, processes, and models. And it usually does so by breaking what came before and the industry that wrapped around it. It's a purposeful act and almost entirely decision based.

Embracing agility and flexibility to this degree calls for an entirely different mindset and a new breed of business leaders. While companies sort all that out, search for the new talent they need at every level, and wrap their minds around the difference in continuous innovation versus continuous disruption, your company can begin by simply starting out with a few decision intelligence projects. Pick a destination, decide on an outcome, and go for it.

Rather than ask "How can I do this better?" ask "Why am I doing this at all?" If you know the Why, you can more easily find a better How or a different route.

Redefining Industries

Industry convergence — the process whereby new connections are formed between companies with seemingly unrelated technology and business model focuses as they evolve — was already well under way before the pandemic came along and changed everything. A phone company, for example, evolves to also perform as an Internet service provider (ISP) and a cable television provider while a cable company extends its offerings to include phone service and Internet connections. Now the two companies are direct competitors who have converged from separate industry beginnings. Most consumers would find it difficult to label either of those companies as belonging to a single industry.

Industry convergence is a major force in innovation and continuous disruption. Some industries are dying or are already dead. Some industries are being swallowed up by other industries. And new industries are rising as well. As more organizations and industries go fully digital, the lines between them will continue to blur until none of the former well-defined industry labels will apply.

Add to that the upheavals of climate change and a pandemic and it's easy to see that this is no time to rest on your data laurels. The good news is that digital organizations are exceedingly flexible and well suited to surviving and thriving in the face of constant change, if they take advantage of the benefits that decision intelligence can offer.

Just like individual organizations will use decision intelligence to decide and achieve many of the future events they pursue, so too will industry associations, lobbyists, and other organized groups. Most of these groups will soon discover that rather than having lost their sense of purpose, they now have a new mission.

In any case, industries and organized groups have already been studying industry convergence and the forces of change on their horizons. This is nothing new to them. However, decision intelligence offers a strong methodology to aid their decisions on a way forward for their members and causes.

Beyond that scope lie the rising forces of companies using decision intelligence methods to deliver business impacts felt far beyond their purview. Individually and collectively, these will affect the industry from which they hail as well as any industry with which they interact, converge, or compete.

Chapter **15**

Trickle-Down and Streaming-Up Decisioning

Traditionally, major business decisions were thought to occur upstream — emanating from the C-suite and making their way down through the organization. Any decisions flowing back up from downstream, which is say decisions made by the rank and file, were considered to be not much more than tweaks to the command from the top.

The terms *upstream* and *downstream* carry a lot of connotations, which means that, in emotional terms, one term is perceived as superior and the other as inferior, one is in front and the other in the rear, or one is on top and the other on the bottom. It's just human nature to give everything in business a position and rank in the hierarchy.

But that's not the only way to view decision flows. Two-way, bidirectional decision flows also occur. Systems thinking, where a holistic view takes into consideration the totality of factors and interactions that can contribute to a possible outcome, further deviates from linear decision flows. It's not uncommon for both of these circular models to outperform one-directional dictates.

That's because strategic decision-making skills are needed at almost every level of business. If appropriate and logical decisions aren't happening throughout the organization, the company can fail in a variety of ways — "for want of a nail," as the proverb-turned-nursery-rhyme goes:

For Want of a Nail

For want of a nail the shoe was lost.

For want of a shoe the horse was lost.

For want of a horse the rider was lost.

For want of a rider the message was lost.

For want of a message the battle was lost.

For want of a battle the kingdom was lost.

And all for the want of a horseshoe nail.

People downstream need the authority and the means to decide that the proverbial nail is needed and then to go get the nail and apply it where and how it's needed. In so doing, the smallest decision creates a big effect.

Both upstream and downstream decisions are important, and the impacts of each can flow to the opposite position with equal punch. In other words, the impacts of business decisions can trickle down or stream up. The direction is of less importance than the impact on the business.

The bottom line is that every decision counts; therefore, every decision *must* be *either* strategic or directly related to a greater strategy. No decision occurs in a vacuum. Account for its impact from the beginning in order to direct the action and control the result.

Understanding the Who, What, Where, and Why of Decision-Making

Upstream decisions are generally defined as decisions made before the requirements are settled and the execution begins. By this definition, all decisions in decision intelligence are upstream because you make the decision first and work backward to determine the processes, tools, and teams necessary to bring the decision to bear.

But in practice, decision intelligence can be used for upstream, downstream, and systems decision-making.

Admittedly, downstream isn't usually thought of in terms of decision-making, but rather as where the decision is executed or delivers impacts. Thus, decisions made downstream are more likely to be change decisions — changes made to an existing upstream decision in order to improve results or to stay the course.

For example, consider product management decisions. Given that product releases and availability are highly subject to market conditions, downstream product management involves reinforcing and protecting the sales of primary and secondary products accordingly. This means that making any changes to the upstream decision from somewhere downstream may be necessary in order to give declining products some additional oomph, drop failing products from the lineup, provide alternatives for sold-out items, or resurrect tried-and-true products to improve any sales slippage, among other activities necessary when forced to adapt to market forces and customer demands.

The same is true in the AI process, wherein a data scientist or an AI scientist makes an upstream decision and then sets the AI to autonomously and continually improve the decisioning model downstream. In this case, it's the machine that is making change decisions down the line. Those changes are made within the parameters of the upstream decision but require testing to ensure that their impacts are acceptable.

Given this state of affairs, it's self-defeating to consider only upstream decisions as strategic or important. All decisions have value and impact. In light of this fact, you may need to rethink how decisions are managed. You may also find that shifting from up- and downstream thinking to systems thinking works better in some use cases.

REMEMBER

Systems thinking takes a holistic view of the totality of factors and interactions that can contribute to a possible outcome.

Decision intelligence works well with systems thinking, which can give you a powerful advantage in decision-making. However, upstream and downstream linear flows will still have a place in many use cases, and decision intelligence works well in those types of decisions as well.

Look at who actually makes upstream decisions. Typically, they're made at a relatively high level in an organization, whether by a chief in the C-suite, the lead AI scientist, a topline software developer, or a line manager. For example, in marketing, the conceptualizing of a product, price, and competitive positioning takes place in upstream decision-making. The same type of activities occurs upstream for new product management and in research and development (R&D). Ditto in software development. AI scientists or researchers and data scientists work upstream conceptualizing, developing, and setting the business rules for AI models, automation, or advanced analytics. Finally, the CEO and the board of directors are focused on making high-level strategic decisions to steer the entire organization forward.

In short, upstream decisions tend to be long on concept and short on minutiae. It's up to the people downstream to find the best way to implement the decision within their purview.

REMEMBER

Sometimes, the person making the upstream decision is also making the downstream decision. Such is often the case where there are limited AI or IT staff, in small- and medium-size businesses, or when a single person is deciding and executing on their own.

In short, there are as many ways to make decisions as there are decisions to make. The point in decision intelligence is to ensure that the business decisions you make are logical, based firmly in reality, and executed with a specific outcome in mind.

Trickling Down Your Upstream Decisions

As I mention at the beginning of this chapter, upstream decisions are typically high-level, strategic determinations made before the requirements are set and the execution begins. By contrast, downstream decisions consist mostly of *change decisions* — changes to an existing upstream decision. Change decisions are made in response to market conditions, test results for automated outcomes, weather changes, supply chain issues, or other contributing factors.

Though decision intelligence works well in decision-making in an upstream as well as a downstream context, it also works well with systems thinking, which takes into account the totality of factors and interactions that can contribute to a possible outcome. Both downstream decisions and systems thinking decisions are addressed in later sections. In this section, only upstream decisions are addressed.

Upstream decisions are most often made by people in leadership positions such as board directors, C-suite members, line managers, project managers, AI and data scientists, and lead software developers.

The strategies behind upstream decisions can vary wildly in importance, logic, style, and purpose. So can their outcomes. In other words, just using the DI methodology alone won't make your decisions sound. A DI approach may well help keep you on track when it comes to realizing the outcome or impact you have targeted, but it's entirely up to you to ensure that the outcome you're targeting is appropriate, obtainable, and effective for your cause or mission.

For example, in industries like the oil and gas sector, where companies tend to adopt new technologies quicker than they do new business models, upstream decisions tend to focus on improving efficiencies. In other words, the intent is on keeping the existing business model and most of the business processes intact while focusing on squeezing more efficiency out of said model and processes.

AI is a general-purpose tool that is highly capable in improving efficiencies, which makes it the tool of choice among the efficiency hunters. Beyond the appeal of harvesting the gains in added efficiencies, this group also benefits from AI's consistency in decision-making, especially with regard to compliance and governance.

This approach also works well for companies or industries that are late to the full-out digitalization party and want to hurry to make up for lost time.

Gains can be secured in the efficiency approach, but only to a point. If a business process is considered sacrosanct — meaning that it can never be changed — then there's a limit to how much efficiency you can wring from it. It will eventually become as good as it can get.

The same is true of business models. If models are never changed, they eventually succumb to market forces. Consider how the world's best horse buggy manufacturer failed after the horseless carriage came along and ran over it, so to speak. The world is filled with business models that similarly won't survive a disruption. Yet upstream business decisions are made every day under the assumption that the business is eternal.

At the other end of the spectrum are the native cloud companies — highly agile companies capable of disrupting established businesses and industries. This group is born all-digital and is brazen enough to ditch a traditional business model without so much as a "see ya, wouldn't want to be ya" salute. Upstream decisions for this group are all about innovation and disruption. These are the Ubers and the Amazons of the world that fearlessly strip away many formerly considered necessities to reveal a purer, leaner, and often industry-destructive model.

This group tends to focus on identifying the parts of a traditional business that are actually making bank — delivering revenue, in other words. They have no trouble labeling parts of the business model as excess flotsam — useless stuff that plays no part in generating revenue. They also have no trouble unceremoniously discarding the stuff they consider useless. This is how an app driven, ride sharing company successfully and profitably ditched the taxis in the taxi industry.

Most companies across industries are somewhere on the spectrum between the extremes of the efficiency mongers and the system disruptors. Many are just trying to figure out where to start and what to focus their strategies on. Most have made big strides in becoming a data driven enterprise, only to discover that most of their data mining projects delivered precious little gains. The question in their minds is where to go from here.

These companies are tired of wasting precious resources and are now testing new technologies like AI to harvest measurable and bankable gains. Unfortunately, many of those projects never make it to production. Most that do make it simply fail later. This group is among the primary drivers behind the shift from data driven to decision driven enterprise models. This pent-up demand became the impetus behind the development of decision intelligence.

Another group that consists of extreme outliers also exists. They're heavily focused on manipulating outcomes. These are the cult leaders, the misinformation spreaders, the propagandists, conspiracy theory groups, and other malcontents who make decisions for personal gain. The lesson to be learned from this group is that no matter their intelligence, ideology, or intent, if the human decision maker isn't logical, the outcome likely isn't beneficial to more than a privileged few and the processes may not be, either.

Unfortunately, illogical or malevolent decisions aren't incompatible with decision intelligence. If the decision is world dominance and the decision maker is intelligent and lucid, the methodology can aid in the assembling of processes and tools to achieve that outcome.

This is why companies must be diligent in choosing the individuals and teams who are charged with upstream or high-level decision-making, whether or not they're using decision intelligence methods.

Looking at Streaming Decision-Making Models

Four structured decision-making models (using the principles of management) apply to upstream decision-making for humans: They're rational, bounded rationality, intuitive, and creative. They differ substantially, as Table 15-1 makes clear, but they all require experienced and rational mindsets.

TABLE 15-1: ## The Four Structured Decision-Making Models

Decision-Making Model	Overview
Rational	The decision is classified as important.
	Alternative options are identified.
	Information is gathered and quantified.
	The aim is to render the best possible decision.
	Rational critical thinking is required.
Bounded rationality	Time or money to invest in this decision is short.
	Minimum criteria or expectations are clear.
	The goal is a speedy decision rather than a maximized outcome.
	It aims to render a "good enough" decision.
Intuitive	Intuition is typically a trigger to explore options.
	Time or competitive pressures exist.
	You have extensive experience in the topic or with the problem.
	A gut decision is in reality a highly evolved, subconscious process.
	It calls for pattern discovery in the situation and comparisons to similar experiences, followed by rapid evaluations of alternatives in sequence.
Creative	A problem exists but may be unclear or changing.
	Solutions do not exist or are unsatisfactory.
	New and highly original approaches or solutions are needed.
	Openness to change exists.
	You have experience, plus creative problem-solving and critical thinking skills.

By contrast, upstream structured decision–making models for machines are designed using business rules established by leaders in the business and built into models by programmers, developers, and AI specialists.

On the flip side, the importance of upstream decision makers delivering targeted outcomes is why cybersecurity professionals must be cognizant of the traits and intents of decision makers on the opposing side. To understand the decision makers leading these nefarious groups is to have the upper hand in how the situation plays out and what defense measures are required.

The thing to remember is that all decisions in decision intelligence are upstream decisions, if you think about it: You make the decision first and work backward to determine the processes, tools, and teams necessary to bring the decision to bear. Just keep in mind that decision intelligence methodology is both agile and flexible. It's capable of mapping out both offensive and defensive business plays with targeted outcomes. It's also highly capable when it comes to downstream and systems thinking decisioning.

Making Downstream Decisions

Professionals downstream execute the plan received from upstream decision makers. The function of the professionals working downstream is to manage the details and bring the decision to fruition. This often entails making change decisions that are designed to realign with the targeted outcome.

For example, downstream software developers can find bugs in a single project or cross-project bugs in multiple projects with interdependencies. Upon finding such critters, they typically make fast and useful work-arounds. They then notify upstream decision-makers of the bug and continue to address it with work-arounds until a permanent fix for the bug is made upstream, which then flows back downstream.

The same scenario is true for AI projects. Upstream AI scientists, researchers, and data scientists work with AI models, automation, or advanced analytics to solve problems or create new advantages for the company. Sometimes they do the downstream work as well, but often it's the automated platforms or other professionals who take care of the decision implementations downstream.

For example, AI may engage in automated continuous improvement of its own model. If it does so, it's working under the auspices of the business rules that are set upstream. If later testing finds that the AI model has drifted too far from the data or has decayed or the outcome is less than satisfactory, the professionals upstream generally create a replacement project that corrects these issues — corrections that may or may not require a change in the governing business rules. In some cases, downstream professionals or automated platforms may create work-arounds or improvements to keep the project on course.

Though change decisions like these are the norm, strategic decisions can be made downstream as well. Typically, downstream strategic decision-making comes from people who possess institutional memory, which is a combination of personal memories and experiences on the job. These personal insights on professional matters provide a unique understanding of the company history and culture involved in decision-making and process building. Unfortunately, far too many companies have lost this vital resource by way of layoffs, retirements, job changes, or other types of attrition.

That's unfortunate because it's exceptionally difficult to replace this resource. Institutional memory consists mainly of undocumented insights, experience, personalized and institutionally honed skills, and a knowledge base built over time. In other words, it exists in forms that are difficult to capture digitally. Humans pass the knowledge among themselves in natural encounters, ranging from meetings and training sessions to chats around the proverbial water cooler.

Replenishing institutional memory as a source of knowledge in digital form has met with limited results. Tracking and mining customer and employee experiences doesn't render the same view, nor does tracking the history of documented decision rules or process evolutions.

The best digital alternative to retaining institutional memory appears to be central knowledge libraries with tools like content management systems and notes programs like Evernote, Microsoft OneNote, and Coda, where employees can easily contribute their memories of events. Think of these as a collective diary of sorts.

REMEMBER

Where institutional memory exists, strategic decisions tend to arise almost effortlessly on cue. If necessity is the mother of invention, then institutional memory is the father of timely actions.

From whatever downstream source, the gist of the importance of strategic decisions at this level is defined by the timeliness and appropriateness of the actions taken. Some decisions will be the equivalent of finding and replacing the lost nail in the horseshoe that cost the kingdom the war in the old nursery rhyme. Others will be intuitive and creative solutions spurred by perspectives not available in the high view of upstream decision makers.

In any case, decision-making isn't the linear flow of events most people expect. Rather, it's a circular path wherein a top decision is made upstream and flows downstream where other decisions are made and flow upstream.

WARNING

Bad, fatally flawed, or incorrect decisions made upstream cannot be corrected, saved, or reversed downstream. Make sure your upstream decisions are rock solid before you send them downstream for implementation. If you discover your initial decision to be flawed, kill it before implementation and build a new decision intelligence project on a different decision.

Learn to recognize the options and importance throughout this circular flow and leverage it wisely, both in making the initial decision in decision intelligence and in the decisions that will follow as you work backward to assemble the tools and processes necessary to manifest the original decision.

Thinking in Systems

Though upstream and downstream decision-making will continue to be used, and rightly so in many cases, systems thinking can reveal important insights that are not readily available from those two perspectives. *Systems thinking,* for those not acquainted with the term, is a method in organizational design that considers the differences in contexts among the different parts of a system and the impact of changes made in one part on other parts.

For example, using systems thinking in marketing might mean decisions would be evaluated based in part on how they impact different players in the ecosystem. In the case of marketing, that ecosystem might include all the entities involved throughout the process of creating and implementing a digital or in-store advertising campaign. The reason for considering your decision's impact on the other players in your ecosystem isn't driven by empathy necessarily, but to get a true and more conclusive read of the total impact on the organization.

Similarly, systems thinking in technology would require close consideration of software interdependencies before any change is made that may disrupt the connections and balance throughout the system.

REMEMBER

A *system* is any grouping of interdependent but separate elements or entities. It's a group defined by the relationships between members. Any organization is a system, as is any person's body or life. On the individual level, a decision may be great for increasing financial security — such as accepting a new job — but truly awful for another part of the subject's life system — such as unwanted intrusions on family time.

In decision intelligence projects, make a point to use some systems thinking to better manage impacts that are not generally foreseeable in more linear upstream-downstream contexts. One recent example of that would be the product shortages that began occurring during the pandemic. Much of that has been caused by just-in-time production models that left no options available to respond to a widespread catastrophe. Had companies stored more raw materials or products, they would have had more options in changing their production and distribution models to fit pandemic-induced requirements.

The transportation of materials and goods was also disrupted because of a chip shortage that delayed trucking repairs and replacement, further disrupting supply chains. Most long and short haul trucking companies have few or no trucks or parts in reserve for such an emergency, nor a contingency plan to ensure business resilience. The thing is, had manufacturers, retailers, and trucking companies actually taken any of these necessary steps before the pandemic, profits would have likely dipped, prices may have increased, and stockholders may have been angered long before the pandemic happened.

Even so, the wiser course is to think of entire systems such as supply chains, production, and distribution in order to build a hybrid solution across the system that is capable of balancing costs and adding resilience for all. Cooperative systems thinking in decision-making isn't the norm at present, however.

Taking Advantage of Systems Tools

When you're using systems thinking in decision-making, it involves these four objectives:

>> Mapping all parts and dependencies in the system

>> Understanding the system's dynamics

>> Understanding a system's hierarchy

>> Developing and testing solutions for various points of impact in the system before deployment

Systems can be quite large, such as galaxies, the collection of things affected by climate change, or smart cities. They can also be quite small, such as gut microbiomes or an electrical system in a smartwatch. Systems thinking, however, has only four patterns for making decisions for any type or size of system: distinctions, systems, relationships, and perspectives. (Put them together and you have DSRP.)

Systems thinking tools are also sorted in four broad categories: brainstorming, dynamic thinking, structural thinking, and computer modeling/simulation. Most of these tools are available in free and/or premium versions. Some brainstorming tools, for example, are IdeaBoardz, Coggle, WiseMapping, FreePlane, and Mindomo. Figure 15-1 illustrates how the Coggle brainstorming tool works.

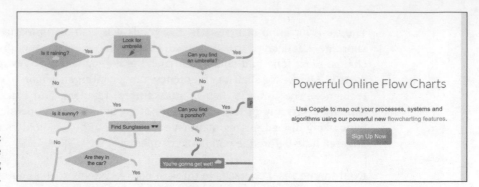

FIGURE 15-1:
The Coggle
brainstorming
tool.

Dynamic thinking tools can include past, current, and future behaviors. Essentially, they map cause-and-effect and help you discover which processes magnify change and which neutralize or balance change. Examples of these tools for systems thinking include behavior over time (BOT), causal loop diagrams (CLD), and system archetypes (SA). Figure 15-2 illustrates how Brainpartner's causal loop diagrams work.

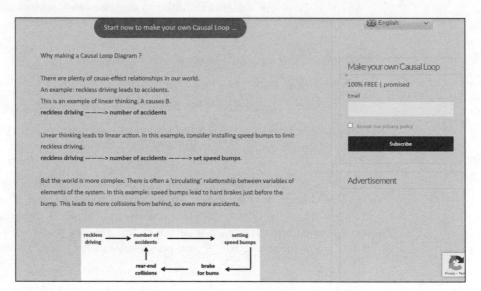

FIGURE 15-2:
Brainpartner's
causal loop tool.

Structural thinking tools depict how one variable affects another over a full range of relevant values. It's particularly useful in clarifying nonlinear relationships between variables. In short, these tools help you generate, gather, and organize information about a system, no matter how complex the system.

Examples of structural thinking tools are Visme, Miro, LucidChart, and Smart-Draw. Figure 15-3 gives you a peek at Visme's structural thinking tool.

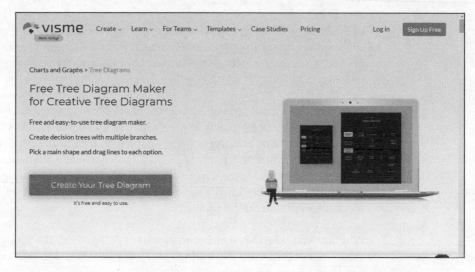

A wide variety of disparate computer modeling and simulation tools are available, most of which are tailored to specific subjects, industries, or systems. Examples include two prominent categories: computer aided design (CAD) modeling, and computer aided engineering (CAE) simulations.

Examples in CAD options are SolidWorks, KeyShot, CAD Civil 3D, and SkyCiv Structural 3D.

Examples in CAE are MATLAB, Fusion 360, Solid Edge, Simulink, SimScale, GNU Octave, Altair OptiStruct, and MoldFlow.

REMEMBER

Your goal in decision intelligence projects is to aim and hit a specific target: the business impact you want to produce. Make sure you test that impact before you implement the DI process, to ensure that you know as best as can be known what that impact will be in the real world and what else it may affect. Systems thinking is a great way to gain a broader perspective of the proposed impact and any repercussions or unintended consequences.

Conforming and Creating at the Same Time

In business as in life, no one is forcing you to make decisions one at a time. Indeed, it's standard operating procedure for many people within an organization to make decisions simultaneously, sometimes separately and sometimes jointly, in parallel or serially.

It's therefore not only possible but often desirable to put two different or opposing decision intelligence projects in play where one seeks to create a business impact that conforms with existing boundaries such as traditional processes, AI models, and business rules and another project that decidedly does not. The opposing exercises can reveal some surprising insights, depending on whether one project is essentially playing devil's advocate or simply coloring outside the lines for a more creative take on the problem.

Whether you take this contrarian approach or another, the point is that there is value in continuously disrupting your own business by constantly seeking to innovate.

Companies that successfully engage in continuous disruption practices typically create networks and platforms from which a series of unique offerings arise to the delight of customers and the dismay of industries. In doing so, they typically align themselves with one of the four main types of purposeful disruption:

>> **Offensive:** Create your own disruption — a product, a process, a service or a model.

>> **Defensive:** Counteract a competitor's disruptive act or product.

>> **Chance:** You just happened upon a timely, innovative idea.

>> **Self-disruptive:** Make your previous product or service of less value by introducing an innovation that displaces it.

Think of it all as acing the F. Scott Fitzgerald test. Fitzgerald famously said that the ability to hold two opposing ideas in one's head and still function is the ultimate test of a first-rate intelligence. In other words, he advocated the use of many models to be considered simultaneously over trying to create one perfect model of the world. Though Fitzgerald offered that opinion back in 1936, it's still a smart approach to making informed and solid decisions today.

As you go about choosing which decisions to create a decision intelligence project from, look to see whether you can also create another opposing or incongruent project to expand your grasp of possibilities.

Directing Your Business Impacts to a Common Goal

In decision intelligence, you make the decision first, which equates to a specific business impact you seek to bring about. But before you begin to map the processes and tools you need in order to get to that impact, make sure you have also checked the direction it will take.

You probably know by now that decisions often impact more than one target, whether or not you had multiple targets in your sights. But what you may not have yet discovered is that these targets can lie in a multitude of different directions. In other words, they exist in different spaces.

REMEMBER

When checking for unintended consequences, collateral damages, or other negative outcomes that can diminish the impact you're seeking, be sure to look for potential effects in multiple directions.

The systems thinking tools mentioned earlier in this chapter can help you identify and visualize reverberations of your decision throughout an internal or external system. External systems may include supply chains, product ecosystems, manufacturing, and distribution systems. Internal systems may include purchasing, warehousing, product picking, shipping, returns, payment systems, and social media/app rating systems.

TIP

System spread isn't the only place you should be looking for potential side effects to your decision. Look also downstream and upstream. For example, in the downstream direction, some workers may experience disruptions or delays in their workflows. This in turn can cause them to seek work-arounds, which can result in the formation of shadow IT — the unapproved use of technologies and company data — which can then lead to inadequate or no security or compliance controls or other responses that prove problematic to the business. Delays and frustrations in their workflows can lead to dramatic drops in talent recruitment and retention efforts as well.

Conversely, in the upstream direction, an impact can embarrass leadership by causing public backlash or by delivering an impact that doesn't conform with the company's mission. Or, you could be delivering an impact that, if someone in the C-suite had had sufficient notice, could have been leveraged to additional positive effect for the business but now exists only as a lost opportunity.

WARNING

Beware of analysis paralysis, where overthinking alternatives leads to a decision freeze. The point here isn't to overthink the decision, but rather to actively seek to leverage it while mitigating risks in as many ways as you can. This makes decision intelligence projects, which are by nature highly targeted, even more effective for the organization.

One obvious direction that commonly requires a check for decision impacts is company or department budgets. Make sure you aren't guessing at these impacts by ensuring that estimates are accurate and are quickly replaced by actual costs. (In fact, it's best to monitor costs in real time, if at all possible.) Check to see whether your project progress assessments are realistic and accurate and that sensitivity analysis — commonly known as a what-if analysis — and predictive models are consistently tracking with real events.

TIP

Don't just repeat decisions with refreshed models. Be aware that change is the only constant. Look for what else you might want or need to add as considerations in the decision. One example is data privacy and ethical AI governance, which may be needed to comply either with changes in regulations or for moral reasons, such as the need to keep from inadvertently causing harm to employees, customers, or the public.

A less obvious direction to check for incoming impacts is community impact. Look for things like potential infringements on the local economy or the environment or on public school and daycare burdens if you move more employees to an area than can be accommodated. Impact studies on community and environmental concerns may need to be a part of your considerations in determining the consequences of your business decisions.

REMEMBER

Be concise, but be thorough. Make few assumptions, and when you do make them, check them often for relevance and usefulness. Look to see what and whom your decision may collide with and whether the outcome is positive, negative, or neutral for your organization and affected parties.

Dealing with Decision Singularities

Decisions are actions. Without a committed action, there's no decision. Yet making no decision is also an action. In decision intelligence, as is the case with any verdict, decisions distill to one choice: the decision to act or not to act — although the decision to act can also have several choices in the type of action to be taken.

When an organization is stuck in one mindset or so enamored with its business model that it resists changes and instead solely focuses on improving efficiencies, it has already made a master decision not to act in any other way. Any other decision taken by or within the organization preserves the status quo. Dedication to the status quo creates a decision singularity — a single master decision that takes priority over all else — so strongly defended that no subsequent decision can override it.

In less flowery language, this stubbornness is evidence of confirmation bias on an organization-wide scale. All decisions are made on the central assumption that nothing about the business is to change and, further, that there is no need for change to the business — ever.

In such scenarios, internal disruption, also known as *innovation*, cannot happen to any appreciable degree. Legacy trumps change, and risk tolerance is generally very low. If the organization isn't careful, it won't survive emerging market challenges often wrought by disruptive competitors.

When companies possess such single-minded adherence to a single decision (decision singularity) and find that they must make at least a token change to remain competitive, they usually do it via acquisition. In this context, this is yet another form of deciding not to act because the company has merely tacked on another company that does something different but has not in any way changed itself.

The age when companies 100 years old and counting reigned supreme has come and gone. Experience in antiquated ways of doing things amounts to naught. Today, a company is only as profitable and secure as its ability to innovate, disrupt, change, and make the hard but correct decisions.

Agility and fluidity in the business model is now a requirement. The market landscape has been reset by disruptors ranging from a pandemic to companies that play by very different rules. These are not what were once referred to as fly-by-night companies, meaning those with ever-changing but always disreputable business models. These new disruptors, skilled as they are at rapid adaptations to market forces, more closely resemble seasoned sailors at sea who skillfully capture changing winds to arrive at their preferred destination.

To avoid becoming trapped in a decision singularity, don't regard anything about your organization to be sacred, except perhaps its mission (but even that should be interrogated.). Go into decision intelligence projects with purpose and intent, but not devotion to a product, service, or business model. Understand that you cannot protect the business from change but must instead find ways it can embrace it.

Decisions bring change, either by improving the organization's circumstances through wise action or by succumbing to external forces by way of either inaction or bad decisions.

Decisions are actions that bring change. Decision intelligence is intelligent change brought to bear by way of intentional action with a defined purpose.

Revisiting the Inverted V

Using decision intelligence moves your organization from being data driven to being decision driven. In essence, this means that you're no longer fishing for actionable insights in data using analytics — rather, you're taking aim at an action that is supported by data and analytics.

It doesn't matter whether the data sets used are humongous volumes of digital information or a series of facts stored in your head. Neither does it matter whether you're running the analytics on advanced algorithms in software or in the miraculous processes used by the human mind. The point is that analyzing information can be mesmerizing, entertaining, amusing, alarming, and sometimes useful. Unfortunately, there's too much waste, delay, and distraction in that method for businesses to harvest measurable business gains reliably and consistently.

To eliminate the waste and distraction and ensure that the business gains something from every decision, you need to focus on the decision and the outcome it renders. This is why decision intelligence begins at the end and ends at the start.

The best way to visualize this methodology is to think of an inverted V. This is the shape that results from working your way up from the query to the output from the analysis and then working your way back down again. Typically, you take a different and more direct path once the destination is settled, than you do if you're starting with information and trying to learn the destination. Decision intelligence is a methodology and not an exact process, so the steps are flexible and customizable to fit each decision.

In any case, you will soon realize that it's more important to keep the decision fixed than the queries or the path. It's this newfound flexibility in the path that gives you room to discover and deploy more pointed and efficient efforts that consistently deliver a predetermined business value.

REMEMBER

Decision intelligence is a multidisciplinary approach. Among the varied resources you can use are inputs and direction from business leaders or department heads, as well as the decision sciences.

The inverted V works in determining better paths to your decision, even when digital data isn't used in the calculation. If you're making a decision on the back of a cocktail napkin, you can compare how you would normally arrive at a decision and then work backward from the decision to check for a better way to get there.

Another way to think of this is to map a route from your home to any other location. Then ignore that, and from that location, map a route back home. Odds are good that the two will differ at least at a few points. You may have witnessed this phenomenon when using a GPS system that maps one way to your destination, but another way back home.

This phenomenon happens in this scenario in part because you're familiar with the lay of the land close to home and configure your route to accommodate its features. But when you begin mapping your way back home from the destination, you're considering a different set of factors pertaining to that location and thus your two routes differ significantly.

Decision intelligence allows room to insert creativity and other influencing factors into the decisioning process. Each step will thus be taken in context and within the parameters of the end decision. Just beware of pitfalls along the way. Your natural tendency will be to build on knowledge you already have, including the outputs from earlier data queries. Those outputs, even (and maybe especially) those billed as actionable insights, aren't actually decisions and often aren't actions either, unless they're tied to automation. So, this wasn't where you were trying to go anyway. You shouldn't be looking to validate or re-create earlier data insights, nor should you be using those outputs as your launch point. If you are, stop. Your mission is to look for a better way to reach the right decision, not a new way to re-create a previous decision.

Another pitfall lies in discounting or failing to incorporate the decision sciences in addition to (or even in the absence of) data and data science. Data isn't a panacea, and analytics aren't omnipotent. Respect and use them as tools and not as the final word in answers.

The decision sciences include a mix of disciplines such as psychology, economics, philosophy, statistics, and management science. Decision theory, a set of quantitative methods in statistics for making optimal decisions, can be a great help as well. Each of the disciplines commonly grouped as the decision sciences present quantitative methods to optimize decisions.

I don't want to leave you with the notion that the inverted V is some kind of magic bullet. Failures will occur, even after the most studious application of the inverted V approach. I could cite multiple causes, but the most common ones include these:

>> Either the desired business impact or the decision itself is too broad or vague.

>> You're mirroring traditional data mining outcomes (confirmation bias).

>> You're assuming that data matters more than anything else in the process.

>> You botch implementations.

>> You're working with guesses rather than accurate estimates.

>> Company will or leadership commitment is lacking.

>> You're suffering from decision singularity (a decision to maintain the status quo).

Revisit the inverted V model to ensure that your processes aren't wandering from your goal or that any of these common problems aren't plaguing your efforts.

IN THIS CHAPTER

» **Looking at DI career moves**

» **Seeing why adding your take matters**

» **Engaging your DI superpowers**

» **Finding your sidekicks**

» **Dealing with risk**

» **Making sure hyperautomation doesn't make you hyperventilate**

Chapter **16**

Career Makers and Deal-Breakers

The move to data driven enterprises provided some assurances and some cover for decision makers. It's difficult to make the case that the decision maker is responsible for a bad call when the call was based on actionable insights produced by analytics that proved to be insufficient or incorrect.

Though decision intelligence (DI) removes that cover and restores full responsibility to human decision makers, it is nevertheless welcomed by business leaders who are looking to make a bigger mark in their organizations, industries, and careers. If you listen closely, surely you can hear the quiet chorus of private exclamations of "Yes!" in C-suites and elsewhere (perhaps accompanied by a bit of a fist pump?).

Switching from data driven to decision driven puts control back in the hands of business leaders. However, they still use data and analytics to augment their thinking. Data and analytics thus become their sidekicks rather than their overlords.

Expect *AI assistants* — those predictive chatbots and digital assistants such as Alexa, Google Assistant, Siri, and their enterprise-level counterparts — to embrace this new role in enterprise as well as in personal settings. Not only are their respective AIs constantly learning, but their makers are also adding features that loosely follow DI methods. One day soon, they'll get right to the point of what you want in the moment rather than present just the facts from which you decide.

For example, Alexa might suggest a different beach than the one you usually go to based on your preferences in crowd numbers, ease of access, and availability of specific beach services. Rather than present you with a list of "Beaches near you," the assistant will recommend a specific beach and ask whether you want to reserve beach chairs and order beachside food and drinks ahead of your arrival.

Yes, AI is an impressive sidekick that is becoming more so with every passing iteration. And, just like your beach-lovin' Alexa, data analytics apps will feed information directly to decision makers as they enter meetings or consult on key decisions.

For now, decision makers will likely make their mark by deciding what data and tools they'll use to ensure that a decision results in a specific business impact. This is why decision intelligence is the key: Every decision must produce a business benefit. The best way to do that is to keep your eye on the ball — in this case, keep your eye on the outcome of your decision.

AI will also continue to play a significant role as it automates decisions. It's an excellent tool for implementing and continuously improving decisions at scale. Almost no organization of significant size can operate without this valuable machine-assist.

As to the human decision makers, their business acumen, critical thinking and creative problem-solving are now back in vogue. It's time to strike the pose and get on with it.

Taking the Machine's Advice

If you're unsure of what to do when AI or analytics gives you a recommendation, you're not alone. Trust me, though: You can figure this out. Simply follow the adage "Trust but verify." You verify by testing the algortihmns' outputs regularly. Do your homework first so that you know how to correctly complete your project.

But, generally speaking, when all is said and done, take the machine's advice.

Hesitancy is understandable but not particularly helpful. Industry analysts estimate that 85 percent of all AI projects fail. A high failure rate is expected to continue through the end of 2022 — and possibly beyond. Then there's all the talk about whether AI can be trusted. It's enough to make any sane businessperson question whether they should bet the business on decisions based on or implemented by AI.

Companies that see the high failure rates may take the numbers to mean that the technology is flawed. That, however, would be a mistake. As is common with new technologies, the fault lies almost solely with the operator.

But if you know where the pitfalls are, it becomes easier to avoid them. Here's the shortlist of what you should look out for:

>> **The data isn't ML-ready.** Cleaning the data for machine learning purposes doesn't mean just removing inconsistencies and making all the fields conform. For example, if you want all date fields to be consistent, then all dates must be recorded the same way (such as day/month year, month/day/year, in text or numbers, or a mix). It also means providing truly representative data and checking for data corruptions that can warp those data sets. For example, do you know what data your 24/7 sensors are picking up right now? Well, do you? It might be something that appears innocuous but throws your representative data into disrepute.

>> **The data doesn't "step up and represent."** Data has to be representative for machine learning to work. That means you need to avoid using too little data or data that's too narrow or too lopsided to present the machine with a full view of the problem or situation. For example, providing only data from helicopter crashes may cause the AI to erroneously assume that all helicopters crash or that all conditions present in crashed helicopters contributed to the crash.

>> **Your shiny new system can't sync succesfully with legacy systems.** Legacy systems are old and clunky, but if they're still the bedrock of your company, make sure your ML projects can play nice with these systems when they reach production. If not, that ML project may become just a pretty toy that ends up on the trash heap when it won't work in the business.

>> **New is not always better.** New AI feels a little like owning a Porsche for the first time: You're proud and thrilled and immediately jumping behind the wheel with no real destination in mind. Though that can be a fun experience in a Porsche, it's likely to be more of a train wreck in AI. The bottom line here is that AI isn't good at everything. I know — you've heard differently. Excited buzz aside, AI totally stinks at doing certain tasks and completely rocks at others. Some projects are better handled by traditional analytics than by AI. Choose projects that AI is good at and that have a return on investment (ROI) that can be realized and measured.

>> **You fall victim to the Superman complex.** AI is democratized by virtue of its being embedded in almost all software these days. But further, AI tools are becoming easier to use and more people are now using them to build AI of their own. Unfortunately, many of these people believe that the arrival of user friendly tools means they can succeed in new AI projects on their own or with a minimal team. Nah, bad idea — don't sideline the pros. This is *not* a job for Superman. It's a full-on operations project that requires a whole team of diversified experts to score any wins.

>> **Zombie projects <ahem> take over.** Zombie ML projects are projects that are outdated but still lumbering around the business. There are lots of causes of decaying AI projects that refuse to die — model drift, for example, or shifting user demand or difficulties in updating ML projects or changes in business needs. The temptation is to leave the zombies as they are, but you should always remember: Though automation is good, driving ML on autopilot usually leads to bad results. Kill your zombies.

>> **You lack executive buy-in.** If company leaders have no will, you have no way to succeed. Gain and retain support for the project from day one or else your project will die long before you try to take it live.

More traditional analytics have also fallen short on their promise. Many products that are billed to deliver actionable insights actually render facts that companies have yet to figure out how to leverage.

That's one reason Dr. Antony Fauci, as chief medical advisor to the president of the United States, could tell the nation what was happening during the early days of the COVID-19 pandemic but not necessarily what people should do about it. This situation led to confusion on issues like masks for the vaccinated and whether it was safe to reopen schools.

Here, too, the fails are more often caused by the operators than by problems with the technologies.

This list describes a few common pitfalls to avoid in analytics projects:

>> **Second-guessing the results:** Humans tend to trust their impressions over the data. But the truth is, human impressions are rarely accurate reads on the situation. (Human memory is also problematic.) Almost always, the data turns out to be right and the human is wrong. Even so, this lack of trust persists. Test or cross-check your outputs against other data outputs rather than against a user's opinion or your own. Remember that there's a reason courts value data over eyewitness accounts — and you should, too.

- >> **Garbage detail:** The old adage "garbage in, garbage out" still applies. The list of possible data issues is long, but they all require your diligent attention. By most accounts, data scientists spend about 80 percent of their time cleaning data. That number should give you an idea of how important — and how big of a time sink — this task is.

- >> **Tracking the wrong data:** Even if you ask the right question of data, you are certain to receive a wrong answer if the data you use is irrelevant, poorly managed, incorrect, out of date, or out of sync. Think hard about what you track, why you track it, and how you manage it, because this information is crucial to producing the outcomes you need.

- >> **Label laments:** Language matters more in data usuability than most people realize. Words are often ambigious, making searching, querying, and other functions prone to error. The problem lies not just in words with multiple meanings (for example, the word *lemon* can refer to a fruit or a color) but also in inconsistencies in how data is labeled. Much of data science amounts to the labeling of items, and rightly so. Without proper identifiers, your analytics can't help but make you stumble.

- >> **Tool angst:** Your organization has invested in the latest tools, but no one knows how to use them. Or, you have old tools and no one enjoys using them. Either way, you're not getting what you need from your data using these tools. Fix these untenable tool challenges by ponying up for training classes or buying new tools — or both.

If you have successfully avoided these pitfalls and pursued your work with diligence, AI and analytics performance won't let you down. Most of all, trust the outputs because, by doing so, what you're really doing is trusting your work or the work of your team. The machine only did what it was told or trained to do.

REMEMBER

Your career rests on making the right moves. Using analytics and/or AI is the right move.

Adding Your Own Take

Getting the analytics or the AI right in decision intelligence is only part of your career success story. The other part boils down to your talent, business acumen, critical thinking skills, creative problem-solving skills, and empathy — in other words, all the soft skills that are hard to automate and thus the very characteristics that protect your job from being taken over by the machines. My advice to you? Get *good* at using your soft skills.

In decision intelligence, you begin with a decision. Use all the wisdom and math available to you in the decision sciences to guide you in making a decision that will deliver a desirable business impact with a meaningful and significant return on investment (ROI). And, you should certainly bring all that to bear, at least in making important decisions — if not in making *all* decisions.

But even so, know that the decision ultimately rests on your shoulders, and that it will be the application of your soft skills that tips the scales between mundane and exceptional, interesting and useful, and job-saving and career-making. In that sense, DI is a form of fortune telling, similar in many ways to the fortune telling capabilities of predictive analytics.

As similar as they are, they still have some important differences. In predictive analytics, historical (past) data is mined and a trajectory of events is plotted based on the direction the path is now on. It's an accurate prediction of the future if — and only if — nothing happens to change the course of that path. Decision intelligence, on the other hand, predicts the future by creating it. You start with a decision about the impact you want to bring about, and then you work to make that event happen. As you work backward from the decision you're deliberately focused on making all the necessary moves to create this impact. If you succeed, you shape the future (or at least a small piece of it) into what you want it to be.

REMEMBER

With the DI method, you can use data and all its trappings — or not use any digitalized data sets. Data, data tools, and data science are but a few of many elements at your disposal.

What isn't optional is *you*. You aren't limited by the data you have. You're limited only by your own mind. Your success at this strategy will help your company realize its goals but will also propel your career to new heights. You see, it is these very skills that you add to the DI process that companies most seek in both employees and leaders. Everything else, employers can simply automate.

Decision intelligence joins human skills with machine capabilities to form more intelligenct conclusions. It's also a method to guide human-only decisions so that they result in desirable outcomes. In either case, your contributions matter significantly.

WARNING

Not everything you can contibute is of equal value. Make your input count rather than distract from the DI process. Adding noise to appear to be a contributor will likely lead to your downfall.

Mastering your decision intelligence superpowers

Being an excellent decision maker is as much an art as it is a science. Business and political leaders who excel at achieving this delicate balance tend to leave a distiguished mark on history or in their fields. To some degree, DI mimics the processes that past top achievers likely used intuitively.

Put simply, decision intelligence is a formula for developing a superpower that is uniquely your own.

Because your innate talent positions you to make decisions augmented by data, several sciences, mathmatical equations, and impressive new technologies, it's magnified to the level of a superpower. Because it's *your* acumen, skills, and talent that are being maginfied, this superpower is as unique as you are.

In short, decision intelligence is a career-making tool if you have it within you to push its capabilities in your favor — and your company's favor.

But DI isn't a formula in the truest sense of the word, because it isn't a methodology populated by myraid wash-rinse-repeat steps. Working your way backward from the decision will require the fashioning of a unique composition of steps using a custom selection of tools and data sets. For those decision makers well versed in any or many of those actions, the process will seem easier, though not necessarily easy. For those who are developing and honing their skills, the process may feel like a harder challenge bedeviled by numerous obstacles. But that's generally how donning and using a superpower goes, isn't it?

The good news is that you don't have to be a hero all by yourself. You can assemble and lead a team of heroes and sidekicks that will render results worthy of all.

REMEMBER

The DI process can be difficult. It can be easy as well — sometimes. But when done right, it's always worth it because the impact is as sure and true as anything can be in business. And who doesn't want a recurring record of success if such achievements end up on their résumé?

Ensuring that you have great data sidekicks

Most DI projects will incorporate or center on *digitial decisioning*, which means they'll incorporate AI (which, in all honesty, is just automated decisions.) But not all DI projects will be centered on AI or analytics. Some will involve other decision sciences and other tools and types of data. Whatever the focus, many DI projects will require a team of professionals to design, implement, and manage the project to fruition.

Which types of professionals you need to add to your team depends on the nature of your project. But whatever you do, don't try to run with fewer team members than you need. Remember always that skills trump titles, so be sure you have a clear understanding of the skill levels of all your team members. For example, researchers and decision makers learned during the pandemic that AI wasn't up to the task of discovering treatments and vaccines for the virus. The technology that did deliver when it came to vaccine and treatment development was *bioinformatics,* an interdisciplinary field and set of specialized technologies designed to collect and analyze complex biological data. Bioinformatics teams differ from AI teams in the mix of specialists in their respective interdisciplinary blends.

If you were to take on a DI project aimed at curing a disease, you may want to use the pandemic bioinformatics teams as a kind of template. Be sure to customize any template or team example you choose to emulate, though, to fit supporting the decision you're after in your DI project.

But beyond considering individual pandemic projects, you may also want to look at the systems thinking in related projects. This can give you valuable insights into the dynamics and makeup of cross-project efforts.

For example, the Transformational Bioinformatics Group published new software in support of researchers struggling with choosing the right COVID strain for pre-clinical models and vaccine testing. The work incorporated in the software was led by CSIRO's senior principal research consultant, S.S. Vasan, and funded by the Coalition for Epidemic Preparedness Innovations (CEPI). It's part of the newly created Australian Centre for Disease Preparedness (ACDP), which is a critical player in Australia's detection-and-preparedness efforts for future biosecurity threats. CSIRO stands for the Commonwealth Scientific and Industrial Research Organisation, which is the Australian government agency responsible for scientific research.

By making the software widely available to the world's COVID defense ecosystem, all projects can benefit from CSIRO's work and accelerate their objectives. Understanding the importance of any success in the world to Australia's objective to save its people led to a more intelligent approach to realizing that impact.

Though sole AI projects failed at adequately addressing the COVID-19 threat, machine learning did play a pivotal back-room role in speeding vaccine development. A mere six months after the cornovirus that caused the disease was identified, vaccines were already in clinical trials.

The work of several key virologists and immuniologists used computational immunology to identify vaccine targets and develop potential vaccines in mere hours. Machine learning took the lead in making sense of massive amounts of rapidly changing patient and lab data to support that cause. The contributions made via AI were results from the analysis of huge quantities of patient data which added to the incredible speeds in moving from determining the genetic sequence of the virus to developing vaccine candidates to adminstering the final vaccines in human arms.

But make no mistake, the specialists involved in these computations and the development of the computational tools were equally vital, and it's the summation of decades of work in their fields that made this mad sprint both possible and successful.

The mathematical models they used began as ordinary differential equations that described and predicted how systems changed over time and space. They were developed further by immunologists dedicated to defeating diseases, even though early on they had trouble finding support and funding for their ideas for specialized computing. (It's a good thing they pressed on!)

Immunologists, virologists, epidemiologists, public health professionals, geneticists, and other experts from a variety of disciplines may not be considered sidekicks by the comic-book definition. But their willingness to play the part of hero sometimes (and sidekick sometimes) led to some of humankind's most stellar achievements. Each and every one of them made the decision to switch positions as necessary to bring about the impact they sought — in this case, COVID vaccines.

Whatever decision you take and then build your DI process from, be sure to add to your team the necessary number of sidekicks who can also step up and lead as heroes when needed. The stronger your team, the more laser focused your processes; and the more defined your decision, the better and faster your outcome.

REMEMBER

Algorithms and data are good at telling you what can be observed from the data, but they aren't good at telling you which decision needs to happen. Decide first which decision needs to be made, and then lean on algorithms and data to provide support through what was previously known or predicted to be.

The New Influencers: Decision Masters

The world will always need data scientists and other data science professionals. It's fortunate for them, and for the rest of us, that much of the work is now automated. But the entirety of their work hasn't been automated — and likely won't be in the forseeable future. After all, computers are bad at many of even the most basic decisions, such as nuanced intrepretation using context when necessary to dicipher whether, for example, the word *lemon* in a cell on a spreadsheet refers to a fruit or a color. Computers are also bad at telling people which decisions to take.

Data scientists may not be able to tell you what decision to make either, but they're good at making other decisions, such as determining what data is relevant and what data isn't in regards to a given business problem, and what queries make sense to meet business goals. Data scientists are also good at setting business rules to keep AI on track and keep the business out of regulatory hot water.

Data scientists and data science professionals have lost none of their shine and importance. But that doesn't mean there's no need for new types of talent to make great business decisions.

Enter the decision masters. This evolving field of professionals is skilled at making decisions using tools, methods, mathematical formulas, and tactics from several of the decision science fields. Typically, these folks aren't strong in the practice of data science, but they are intimately aware of the usefulness and capabilities of analytics and machine learning.

Though their offical title has yet to be standardized, the positions of decision scientist or decision master are rising in much the same way as the role of chief data officer (CDO) once did. Parallels between the positions are striking. Chief data officer became an official position when leaders of organizations came to understand that data is a valuable asset and needs to be managed as such. The official job description goes something like this:

> The *chief data officer* is a corporate officer responsible for the governance, use, and protection of data across the enterprise. The CDO oversees a range of data related functions to ensure that the organization is fully leveraging and capitalizing on one of its most valuable assests: data.

As AI has matured, analytics and automation have become even more advanced. And, as more businesses turn to DI to ensure that projects consistently deliver business value, the need for decision masters will increasingly become apparent.

Again, the final title may be different, but for the purposes of this chapter, I call this new position *decision master.* The job responsibilities will likely include overseeing DI "recipes," managing AI models and features as assets, and managing decisions as assets.

REMEMBER

As is the case with AI models, many decisions (and their related processes) are repeatable and sharable, which prevents various decisioning efforts and new DI processes from reinventing the wheel or repeating a decision that has already been exhausted.

Given that speed and innovation are and will continue be the two top necessities for businesses to remain competitive, no time can be wasted on worn-out or out-dated ideas or in starting every project from scratch. Managing decisions will be the best way to ensure that decisions are made, shared, and leveraged to the organization's best advantage, just as the CDO manages data in much the same way.

Thus the roles of chief data officer and decision master will complement rather than replace one another, and the successes of each will define the level of competitiveness and success the enterprise has reached.

In another likely parallel development, decisions decay over time as AI models do and drift from the data they're built on. In other words, as the data and business circumstances change, decisions lose relevance and impact. Platforms will likely rise to assist in managing hundreds of thousands (if not more) decisions in a single enterprise. Further, because DI projects may span entire systems, the management of these decisions must likewise span across projects and entities in the system.

Decision masters who truly excel will become the major influencers of their time. That's because they will be highly effective nurturers of disruptors and idea incubators within their own companies, in their industry, and across entire systems. Their status will rise as decisions start to be considered valuable intellectual property and company assets.

It remains to be seen whether decision master will be a C-suite position from the start or will begin as a position closer to AI scientist or AI developer positions in the hierarchy. That, too, is a strategic decision for each company to make. Most companies won't address this issue until DI adoption reaches the tipping point internally.

Defining the skill sets that decision masters need will be a challenge as well. These skill sets are likely to be different than or go beyond the skills that AI researchers or data scientists possess, simply because the focus of each is different. The focus of decision masters will be on the recipes in decision-making rather than on the digital mechanics.

REMEMBER

Companies like Google have already appointed people as chief decision scientist or chief decision officer, so, clearly, these positions are not predicted occurrences in the future but rather actual positions that exist *now*. Furthermore, decision sciences and decision theory and related skills are already being taught in many universities and online courses. Those seeking the next hot job role would be wise to add or hone these skills now.

Preventing Wrong Influences from Affecting Decisions

Decisions can be negatively influenced by several factors. Be aware of some of these pitfalls so that you avoid making the wrong decision, chasing the wrong business impact, or falling prey to a manipulative scheme.

Bad influences in AI and analytics

AI and analytics are important and useful tools, but they aren't foolproof. Anyone who has worked with data and statistics is aware of the many traps and snafus that can warp models and deliver bad results. Some of those same issues transfer to AI and analytics.

Statisical errors include Type 1 (false-positive), Type 2 (false-negative), standard errors, and sampling errors. Further, biases can be an issue, including sampling bias, nonresponse bias, response bias, and order bias. The following list describes the major characteristics of these biases:

>> **Sampling bias** occurs when the method of sample collection, by its nature, excludes some demographics or groups from responding and thus over represents other groups. For example, completing an online survey may capture a disportionate amount of computer savvy people and exclude people who have limited or no access to computing devices and services.

>> **Nonresponse bias** refers to the people who are unwilling or unable to respond to a survey who differ significantly from the responders in some way. This makes the study biased toward the responders. For example, if a mailed survey were sent to voters and one party responded in large numbers but other parties were disinterested and didn't respond, the survey would be biased in favor of the party that responded.

>> **Response bias** comes from distractions or pressures on the respondent during the survey causing the respondent to give a false or incorrect answer. For example, asking about sexual history or reproductive healthcare choices in the presence of a spouse or parent, or conducting the survey in a noisy or busy area.

>> **Order bias** is created when the order of questions in a survey influences the respondent to perceive some responses as better than others.

Any of these errors and biases can also transfer to analytics software if steps aren't taken to guard against them. Why? Because these are human errors, and humans program software, so human errors creep in there as well.

Data errors can run the gamut from failing to be representative to recording and labeling errors and from corruption to decay. Here are some problems that cause data or other errors in analytics:

>> Insufficient data amounts

>> Irrelevant data

>> Out-of-date data

>> Corrupted real time data (sensor malfunction or misreads)

>> Poor-quality data

>> Inaccesible data (*siloed* data)

>> Skill shortages

>> Scalabilty issues (the inability to handle large sizes of data or huge numbers of automated responses, for example)

>> Budget shortages

>> Lack of support for projects

>> Pressure to reach a preferred conclusion

>> Lack of understanding of statistics

But beyond these issues are several others that can badly influence decisions, not only in DI but also in every related implementation or cross-project. These include a completely different set of biases. Biased decisions of this kind can be immoral or not, but — either way — they are detrimental and costly to the organization, including

>> Information bias (key variables are measured or classified incorrectly)

>> Selection bias (an error in selecting participants that results in a failure to randomize the sample)

>> Confounding bias (points to an association which is true but misleading in a particular use or context)

>> Confirmation bias (searching for and using only information that conforms or supports a specific opinion, belief, or value)

>> Loss aversion (a fear of loss that can make a person make a bad decision in an effort to avoid a loss or chance of loss)

>> Gambler's fallacy (the incorrect belief that a future event is probable or improbable based on a past event when actually both events are independent of one another)

>> Availability cascade (a self-reinforcing process that adds plausibility to an untruth: "repeat something long enough and people will accept it as truth")

>> Framing effect (the way the information is presented — "framed," in othere words — affects the decision for better or worse, and usually for the worst)

>> Bandwagon effect (the tendency to adopt a belief or opinion because others hold it as truth)

>> Dunning-Kruger effect (a cognitive bias where incompetant people greatly overestimate their knowledge or skill)

My list, however, is far from exhaustive; you might encounter literally hundreds of other biases. The point is that flawed thinking or research methods can badly skew results or render them entirely useless.

Perhaps the biggest elephant in the room is misinformation — the intentional spread of untruths. Misinformation about COVID-19 is now costing human lives in many different countries, as conspiracy theories discourage people from taking any of the available life-saving vaccines or trusting medical personnel to treat them once ill. Despite the diligent efforts of government, public health, and private healthcare providers to counter misinformation, the number of post-vaccine pandemic deaths soared past early, prevaccine COVID deaths.

Disinformation — purposely falsified information, in other words — presents another grave danger in decision-making. In terms of data, disinformation can amount to feeding wrong data into an organization's data stores or manipulating data within it. This can lead to a myriad of real-world dangers, such as potential assassination by incorrect prescription dosages sent digitally to a pharmacy, dams that open based on false data triggers and drown towns downstream, and electric grids that run too hot and create a blackout, for example.

REMEMBER

Misinformation and disinformation can badly influence AI and analytics if it exists in the data, or throw a decision maker widely off the mark if misinformtion or disinformation influences the decision maker's beliefs, opinions, or research methods. Many a career in other fields has been ruined by misinformation and disinformation. Take steps to ensure that you aren't operating under false assumptions and that any data you use hasn't been corrupted.

The blame game

Scapegoating, or shifting the blame onto someone else, is an old tactic used in both defensive and offensive moves in business. In decision-making, shifting blame seeks to distance the person responsible from any negative reprecussions. It can also be a decision made as part of a long-term strategy to bring about the fall or ruin of a business opponent or competitor in the constant jockeying for positions of power.

So the blame game can be a defensive move after a decision goes bad, or an offensive play as a decision to remove a person seen as an obstacle to the decision maker's rise to power.

Either way, it's not a good development. Check for the following warning signs that this behavior may be affecting your DI projects:

>> **Exclusion:** A deliberate effort to exclude one or more persons on the team from participating in the work or key discussions. Whoever is being excluded (it can be more than one person) is likely the targeted scapegoat. But it is more often the case that team members are excluded due to poor planning, an invitation oversight, or the false belief that the team leader or another team member knows everything the excluded person(s) would know.

>> **Finger pointing:** Fault finding is often a regular occurrence — usually, with one or more people on the team doing most or all of the finger pointing, at least initially. However, fault finding can spread throughout the team if all members become wary and feel threatened.

>> **Plausible deniability schemes:** This involves efforts to create believable distance from crucial processes, key decisions, and impact fallout so as to escape blame later. This is more typical on decision projects where the impact is already known to be negative in nature.

To ensure that your DI project doesn't fall prey to the blame game, consider following these guidelines:

>> Assign responsibility for each action to a specific role.

>> Introduce accountability measures.

>> Make an audit trail for the project and ensure that all changes and tasks are documented and trackable. This concept is fundamental to both quality improvement and DI, but remember that in both cases the focus is on auditing the process and not affixing blame to any one person.

>> Openly value and encourage emotional intelligence and empathy.

>> Create an atmosphere of openess and insist on transparency.

>> Replace any team members who create a toxic environment for others.

Ugly politics and happy influencers

Politics exist in layers. Outside the organization are layers of geopolitics, national politics, and then state and local politics. Inside an organization are layers of politics as well, generally and collectively referred to as organizational politics, office politics, or workplace politics.

According to a study by Harvard University, *organizational politics* refers to any number of activities aimed at creating or increasing influence to improve either personal or organizational interests. These are soft skills, brilliantly played to move other people and factors in alignment with goals that may not be obvious to those who are affected.

Politics aren't inherently bad — only dysfunctional politics are. But even functional politics can affect decisions in ways that seem dysfunctional to casual observers. If, for example, functional politics are seeming to negatively affect downstream decisions, there may not actually be a problem, because the results feed into a larger strategy with a desired impact requiring a decision further down the line to take an otherwise unexpected turn.

Politics can be used to better situations for the organization and its members. This requires a good understanding of political capital and the political terrain. Political terrain is traditionally described by metaphors representing four domains: the weeds, the rocks, the high ground, and the woods. Each domain has two dimensions: the individual and the organizational levels. The following list gives the details:

>> **The Weeds section in organizational politics** forms almost organically via personal influence and informal rules. This area can be a source of resistance to change in an organization. Look for influencers here that are typically working in whisper campaigns, social media memes, and other means to bring the opinions of others in alignment with their own. Of course, influencers in this domain can instead influence people in positive, low-pressure ways, but that is far less common. It just depends on which people are the main players here and what they aim to achieve.

» **The Rocks** section is populated by formal authorities, hard rules, and sufficient political capital to sway movement among others. This area can serve as a stabilizing force for the organization because it's often ruled by leaders and managers who are typically pro-organization. However, it can also be the place that can wreck your decisions and plans if you haven't obtained their support and buy-in.

» **The High Ground** combines formal authority with the heft of organizational systems such as rules, policies, procedures, processes, and formal guidelines. These people serve as the guardrails for authority figures within the organization that may go rogue. However, they can be idea and innovation killers, too, in their zeal to protect the status quo. Yes, this is another pocket that is likely to resist change, but they also have an impressive arsenal with which to shoot down a change initiative completely.

» **The Woods** domain is where everything unspoken but heavily enforced resides: the culture, norms, hidden assumptions, unspoken routines and pecking orders. This is also a political place where heavy divisions in leadership can lurk unseen. Politically speaking, it's wise to develop an understanding of the hidden and the nuanced so that your decisions don't inadvertently run afoul of them. If you intentionally take decisions that run afoul of these threads in the organization, it's best to do it knowing what to expect and, hopefully, with allies in place to support your decision.

There are ways to use office politics in forming your decision or in implementing it. Here are a few to consider:

» **Map the political terrain to the organization chart.** You're looking for the influencers who circumvent the formal structure yet exert considerable power over it.

» **Track your organization's informal network:** You want to find out which influence flows you can leverage, which hotheads and bullies you need to avoid, and which interpersonal relationships might prove advantageous to your cause.

» **Build connections to help you learn and navigate the political terrain.** If you're an outsider to the informal network that already exists, you can easily confuse cues and miss nuanced signals. Building connections with people who know the network well will provide the guidance you need to overcome these shortcomings.

Decision intelligence is quite helpful in such efforts because it can help organizations map out whom (individually and in groups) to influence and in which direction to sway them to create the impact the organization needs in order to succeed. Just keep in mind that in politics, as in all phases of business, timing is everything. Therefore, incorporating both the order of influence and the time frames in which actions must occur will likely be an integral part of your DI process.

REMEMBER

If dysfunctional politics are influencing decisions, the organization might be on a collision course. Corrective actions, however, may be nearly impossible to take. In these cases, no matter how well a DI project is planned and executed, it will fail if it cannot overcome or circumvent hostile political actions or dictates.

Risk Factors in Decision Intelligence

Decision intelligence is most often used to improve the commercial application of AI in driving profit and growth. But it can also be used, and is used, to make other types of decisions, with or without the aid of AI or data, depending on the scope of the decision and the skills and preferences of the decision maker.

In all its applications, the goal in decision intelligence is to make the decision first so that the rest of the effort is highly targeted to produce an impact of certain business value. As sound as that process might be, that doesn't mean that the process eliminates risk.

Some of the risks, quite naturally, are shared with the use of AI in general because AI is used in some DI projects, including

>> Jobs lost to automation

>> Privacy violations

>> Algorithmic bias

>> Market volatility

>> AI data manipulation of other AI

>> Inequality exacerbations

The United Nations raised the alarm on human rights issues associated with AI and recently encouraged a moratorium on the sale of AI until some safety measures can be developed and installed. The human rights issues they named include these:

>> Surveillance of persons by nation states and private concerns

>> Invasion of privacy

>> Biometric data exposures

>> Escalated discrimination

>> Human tracking for oppression purposes

REMEMBER

Check your DI projects for tools like AI that may cross these and other boundaries, which can create legal troubles, public backlash, and other penalties and repercussions for actions you never intended to be part of your process. You must be certain that any AI use meets strict ethical requirements.

It's a simple remix of the golden rule: If you wouldn't want someone, another organization, or a government to use AI this way on you, don't do it to others.

REMEMBER

No decision a company can make is so important that it warrants risking human lives.

Other risks exist for a variety of DI projects with or without an AI component. These can track closely with the domain within the decision or on which it is based. For example, a financial decision will incur the normal risks associated with similar financial decisions. Typically, these risks belong to one of these four categories:

>> **Market risk:** The risk of loss due to overall market conditions. For example, a drop in a company's stock value because of investor concerns over the future of the industry to which it belongs. Or, a rise in value of a particular shoe brand because it suddenly became very popular among teenagers.

>> **Credit risk:** The possibilty of loss due to a borrower's failure or inability to repay.

>> **Liquidity risk:** The risk incurred when an individual, business, or financial institution cannot meet its short-term debt commitments.

>> **Operational risk:** The risks incurred during a business' daily operations.

The same is true of any decision that resembles decisions made in other domains — product development or marketing, for example. The risks associated with a domain are risks as well for the DI projects coming out of those domains.

Certain organizational risks, as listed here, also track with the same types of decisions made by other processes:

>> Reputational damage

>> Communications failures

>> Supply chain breakage

>> Compliance issues

>> Security vulnerabilities

Though it's wise to be cognizant of risks, it's important to understand that the DI methodology generally contains no more risks than the same decisions made by other processes. It can also reduce risks by ensuring that decisions result in business value rather than incur a loss in resources or expense.

DI and Hyperautomation

Hyperautomation is the act of rapidly automating at scale as many business and IT processes as possible. It's a framework that involves the use of several advanced technologies, including robotic process automation (RPA), machine learning, and AI. It is sometimes called intelligent process automation or the next phase of digital transformation or digital process automation. But by any name, it means more machines doing more stuff.

Some of the things machines are doing more of are a bit unexpected to the uninitiated, such as AI creating more AI all by itself or the act of automation being automated as well.

Here are some tools commonly used in these efforts:

>> Process mining tools

>> Task mining tools

>> Robotic process automation

>> No-code/low-code development tools

>> AI feature stores

>> Integration — Platform as a Service (iPaaS)

>> Workload automation tools

>> Business process management

>> Decision management

>> Business rules management

>> Natural language processing (NLP)

- » Optical character recognition

- » Machine vision

- » Virtual agents

- » Chatbots

- » AI/ML

Hyperautomation is a prime area for the use of DI to ensure that all automated decisions meet company requirements and company goals. In other words, though more machines are doing more things, DI ensures that they're doing so in a profitable manner — every time and in every way.

Some of the decisions are pointed at increasing efficiencies in existing processes or developing new ones to replace the old. Other decisions are made to add revenue streams, detect and react to opportunities for additional profits, and find areas in the business that are ripe for expansion and growth.

The latest in these efforts is the advent of digital worker analytics (DWA). This class of analytics seeks to discover and rank automation opportunities. The theory goes that the more processes that can be automated, the better human workers can be augmented. The better workers are augmented, the higher their performance becomes.

Yes, we're back to valuing the soft skills that humans are good at and that are almost impossible to automate — hence the need to combine the two by augmenting human workers with machine capabilities. That's true in decision intelligence and true in hyperautomation and digital decisioning.

Enter digital workers — virtual employees, in other words. They are software robots that stitch together various processes that are difficult to integrate and thus mimic how a human works with things manually. That's why they're called *digital* workers — they work using user interfaces like human workers as well. That's kind of awesome when they do the tedious stuff necessary to work with legacy systems or go sort out errors and fix them, move data from here to there, and generally do all the things that human workers dislike doing.

Yes, that's Robotic Process Automation (RPA) automating tasks that can't be handled in typical API integrations. That's because RPA is surface level automation software (a software robot) — meaning it uses other software like a human would, from the user interface. An Application Programming Interface (API) is a line of one-size-fits-all computer code, meaning it is standardized so that applications can connect to interact. RPAs make human workers more productive because they can spend more time using their talent instead of wasting it on mundane issues.

Digital workers are commonly found in finance and IT workloads doing work like back-office finance or procurement processes. But they're rapidly beginning to spread to other departments and other functions as well.

Meanwhile, digital worker analytics are busy finding new ways that digital workers can do more stuff.

Though DI is a smart approach to deploying these technologies in meaningful ways, there's a flipside you need to consider as well. If you're unaware of technological advances and emerging use cases like these, your DI projects may be obsolete before you even get started.

Remember that one of the prime benefits humans bring to the decision table is the ability to observe changes in the business environment and adapt quickly to them. Additionally, the mark of genius lies in connecting dots that weren't connected before — in other words, being able to quickly discern patterns among unrelated items and discover how to use them.

Look up and out often. Form diverse and interdisciplinary teams. Look for decision masters who possess skills unique to finding solutions to questions that exist and those that have yet to be asked.

Make decisions on, about, and for technology. Make decisions for your own life and the success of your organization.

This new age requires new thinking and better methods of getting things done. Decision intelligence is an important framework to help you achieve all of that.

One more (vital) note: You need to stay relevant and far enough ahead of the machines to remain employed or in business. That was, after all, the impact you most want to see your decisions create, was it not?

5

The Part of Tens

Chapter **17**

Ten Steps to Setting Up a Smart Decision

Decision intelligence is a flexible framework that keeps AI and decision implementations on track in producing business value by keeping the work aimed squarely at the target. Intended to help resolve high failure rates in AI and data-mining and analytics-based projects, decision intelligence also applies to any business decision, whether large data sets are part of the process or not.

The bottom line here is that decision intelligence flips the enterprise model from data driven to decision driven.

Your mileage may vary, depending on how well your decision intelligence process is designed and deployed. In this chapter, I show you ten actions you can take to help ensure that your decision intelligence process is successful.

Check Your Data Source

Accurate and dependable data is essential to any decision-making process. Check to make sure the data comes from a reliable source.

If the source is a person, group, or organization, ask from what sources they collected the data. You're looking for reliability indicators such as a source's commitment to ethics, willingness to provide transparency, and a history and industry reputation for providing quality data.

If your source is a machine (typically, a sensor), don't assume that the source is reliable. Data corruption can occur via simple means, such as leaving a sensor on but with a lens covered, a worm crawling across a sensor mic or thermometer, or simply a malfunction. About 40 percent of sensor data is useless anyway because it's meaningless, but more data can be corrupted by false reads and damaged or dirty sensors.

Track Your Data Lineage

Data lineage tracks data from its origin, what happens to it afterward, and where it moves to over time. Make sure the tracking methods you use are fully automated and provide an audit trail. It's the only way to be sure that the data you're using is trustworthy.

With data lineage tools, you can track a data error to its cause, trace a data change back to the person who made it, and determine who has had access to the data over its lifespan. Such tools are also invaluable when it comes to data governance and compliance efforts.

Most modern business intelligence (BI) applications come with embedded data lineage tools, but you can find other tools outside of BI apps as well. Most of these non–BI tools use one of three techniques to establish and track lineage:

>> **Pattern-based tracking:** This approach in establishing data lineage looks for patterns in the metadata across tables, columns, and business reports. The pluses to using this method include its focus on the data and not the technologies it sits on so that makes things a bit simpler, its usefulness in identifying manual data flows and for data where it is impossible to read the logic in the code which is typical with proprietary computer codes. Minuses include missing details in transformation logic (points when and where data is modified), and it ignores the application (and thereby the context and use of the data).

>> **Data tagging:** This approach determines data lineage by tracking the tag given it by a tool made for this purpose. The tag is then tracked by the same tool from the beginning to the end of the data's lifecycle. One disadvantage of this approach is that its use is limited to data tagged by the tool and thus cannot track the lineage of data not tagged by that same tool.

>> **Self-contained data lineage tracking:** This tactic tracks every data movement and transformation within a self-sustained environment — including data processing logic, master data management, and other elements — to uncover the details in the data's full lifecycle. No external tools are needed to track the data lineage. Pluses here come from the fact that you can find and track errors in data processes, lower the risk in implementing process changes, migrate systems without data loss, and create a data mapping framework. The biggest drawback is similar to that of data tagging in that you can't track the lineage of any data that exists outside of this isolated environment.

>> **Lineage by parsing:** The most advanced tactic in data lineage tracking. lineage by parsing involves automated reads of the logic used in data processing. Think of it as a type of reverse engineering. Pluses are its accuracy and speed. Minuses include its complexity and subsequent difficulties.

Here are several examples of tools that will handle data lineage for you:

>> Ovaledge: www.ovaledge.com

>> Octopai: www.octopai.com

>> Collibra: www.collibra.com

>> CloverDX: www.cloverdx.com

>> Datameer: www.datameer.com

>> Trifacta: www.trifacta.com

>> Atlan: https://atlan.com

Most of these products offer free trials, so you can try them and see which best fits your needs. In any case, make sure you know where your data has been. Otherwise, major trouble is headed your way.

Though data lineage work is performed throughout the pipeline, it primarily occurs at data ingestion, during data processing, in the query history, and in tracking user access to objects and fields in data lakes.

Know Your Tools

The key to using information to make decisions — and to sorting through alternatives — is to use the right tool for the tasks in your chosen process. Which specific tools you need depends on the process you have built within the decision intelligence framework. A list of all possibilities would be far too long to include here.

Though most vendors try to make tools truly intuitive, users tend to favor one over another because it fits their way of thinking. Feel free to do the same.

Take the time to learn your tools, at least from the high-level view. Then choose tools based on how well they do the job and how easy they are for you to use.

Use Automated Visualizations

Unless you're a statistician or a whiz at the intracacies of building visualizations, skip the selection menus and templates and go with the business intelligence (BI) app or visualization app's recommendation on the visualization instead.

The various visualization types are designed to convey specific types of information, and, if you end up choosing the wrong one, you may interpret the data incorrectly — which can lead to a failed decision. If you're curious about which visualization fits which purpose, the following list can serve as a simple starter guide to the various types (just keep in mind that there are literally hundreds, if not thousands, of visualizations, so this is no comprehensive overview):

>> **Comparision visualizations:** Bar and column charts, tables, and population pyramids

>> **Pattern visualizations:** Line graphs, scatter plots, and density plots

>> **Price change visualizations:** Candlestick charts, Kagi charts, and point and figure charts

>> **Relationships and connections visualizations:** Heat maps, Venn diagrams, SWOT tables, and tree diagrams

>> **Proportions visualizations:** Bubble charts, pie charts, and progress bars

>> **Ranges visualizations:** Bullet graphs, Gantt charts, and span charts

>> **Geographical visualizations:** Transit maps, dot maps, and choropleth maps

>> **Concept visulations:** Flowcharts, brain maps, and funnel illustrations

>> **Events over time visulizations:** Calendars, timelines, and spiral plots

Even if you're a visualization master, you can save time using the automated version. If you're new to visualizations, let the automated feature or the AI guide you through the maze of charts, graphs, and other artistic-looking squiggles because it isn't as much about the aesthetics as it is about consuming information correctly.

Impact = Decision

Sometimes it's a struggle to decide on a decision, and you end up with some vague notion or general direction you want to pursue. Perhaps the decision at the top of your decision intelligence process now looks something like "Sell more!" Well, that's a lofty-sounding goal, but it isn't one that can guide you to a specific action that will enable you to do that very thing.

Instead, think of your decision as a specific business impact. That will help you craft a decision that has specificity and sensitivity sufficient to defining the specific steps that will lead to the precise action that creates the impact you desire.

So, rather than mistake a goal for a decision, you're now thinking in terms of a specific action and then you decide to do take that action.

For example, if you're a bank and you want to increase the number of mortgages you close, you don't make that goal your decision, because it could lead to increased risk, poor performance, and little to no actual value to the business. Just lowering the bar so that more mortgage applications are approved is unlikely to improve your business's market share of quality loans.

Instead, look for an impact that has business value. In this scenario, it might be adding other qualifiers as inputs in your algorithm or as new business rules. You're looking for qualifiers outside of traditional formulas that can help you identify high-quality borrowers who may be just under the radar. Now you have a less-competitive route to secure more high-quality mortgage deals without increasing the risk for your business. Impact equals the decision; they are two sides of the same thing.

If you need help making your decision crystal clear, let a data scientist guide you. It's harder to do than you may think so it's smart to get help.

Do Reality Checks

Every sales manager everywhere has high hopes and routinely jacks up sales goals for each sales rep under their command. Unfortunately, the hike may be based on nothing more than a PFA number. (PFA stands for *plucked from air*, because it has no basis in fact or reality.)

The same is true in making business rules for automated decisions (namely, AI) wherein the rules aren't grounded in business realities. Examples of such include leftovers from a former time that no longer carry any meaning or rules that sounded good to whoever put them in place at the time.

Using guesses instead of calculated estimates is also a risky approach.

Build in a number of reality checks throughout your decision intelligence process to make sure you're headed for impact and not just playing with pipe dreams.

Limit Your Assumptions

You can't eliminate all assumptions from a decision. That's because holding on to a few assumptions can prevent a decision from getting too chaotic to be functional.

For example, the model of a rational decision assumes that the decision maker has complete and accurate information about the various alternatives and possesses the intelligence, skills, time, and resources to make a rational decision.

Would you really want to skip assumptions like that and have to prove to yourself that you're rational before even beginning to consider a decision? You might feel a little stressed or nutty occasionally, like everyone else on the planet, but, usually, making the assumption that you're capable of making a rational decision is your best plan.

The goal isn't to remove all assumptions, but rather to limit them to the most useful that are also anchored to reality. If a person isn't rational or lacks the necessary skills and cognitive ability, you should not put them on your decision team. In other words, don't broadly use assumptions — instead, use assumptions that apply to the specific decision or decision maker.

Think Like a Science Teacher

You may not know all the science and math used in making a given decision, but that's okay because software does that part for you. One thing you do need to know how to do is describe the decision, processes, data, and tools you used to support it and explain how you challenged assumptions and tested results and why you're creating the business impact you're targeting.

You also need to be able to do all that in language that is perfectly understandable to other people who may not share your level of expertise or understanding of the problem.

To do that, think like a science teacher. Learn to communicate complex ideas in terms anyone can understand. You're not dumbing down anything — you're sharing knowledge and generating interest in your project and its outcome.

This is the key to many tasks you have to accomplish — from making a business case to securing funding in budgets or donations. Act like a science teacher and encourage people to support your effort, share your passion for the project, and build enthusiasm to increase adoption rates of the decision intelligence framework as well as the outcome of your DI project.

Communication is essential, and good science teachers are terrific at it.

REMEMBER

A common reason that AI projects never make it to production is the lack of executive buy-in — that, too, is often a communication failure. Work on making your DI project transparent from beginning to end and explain it well to those who need to understand or support it. But be forewarned that if the company leaders lack the will to see a given decision made or taken, there's no way for you or your team to do it.

TIP

Missteps in decisions are common when the decision maker is operating unaware of changes in direction at the top of the organization. Checking in with key business leaders (formal and informal) early on will help you gain important new insights and retain early support.

Don't rest on your laurels, though. Actively fan the flames of support while they're hot. If you don't, you're unlikely to stir lukewarm support from the ashes later.

Solve for Missing Data

Decision intelligence requires a keen focus on delivering business value from every decision. Quite often, the process involves data and analytics, and the assumption is that, when it does, the decision is all but failsafe. But is that really true?

Partial versus incomplete data

Data will always be incomplete, and for numerous reasons. Some pieces of information will be lost to time and space. Other bits were never recorded or aren't yet digitalized. Still other information is difficult to capture accurately or in proper context. Storage mediums decay or become obsolete, rendering them unreadable by newer technologies. And so it goes.

For whatever reason, the data you have is at best representative, but will never be complete, because no data set will include complete data on every member or element in any given universe.

Other missing data issues stem from incomplete data such as lost values, entry inconsistencies, missing answers to questions, and variables without observations and the like in tables, surveys, spreadsheets, and other kinds of data sets.

Because these data perils persist, even the dreaded AI singularity, should it ever become possible, would be more than a few zillion data points short of a full data set. It may need to employ a digital worker, an automated worker that works like a human would, to clean up its singularity.

Clues and missing answers

It's a given then that all projects are likely subject to missing data, so why operate on the mistaken assumption that the machine knows more than we humans do? We're better able to address the issues, and, as long as proper steps are taken, we can then rely on the analyses. For example, we know to clean data before using it for any analysis, and we know how to carefully prepare it for machine learning before we use it in those types of applications.

REMEMBER

Data prep is such an important step in data analysis that data scientists spend roughly 80 percent of their time just working on getting the data in shape.

As for data missing from the rest of the universe being analyzed, that can be generally handled via inference. To *infer* is to reach a conclusion based on evidence and reason. Let your mantra be infer, infer, infer!

Take Two Perspectives and Call Me in the Morning

The tendency will be to step back and admire your own work in arriving at a decision to pursue a decision intelligence project. Before you let your pride and enthusiasm carry you away, however, add at least one other perspective to your reality checks. This will quickly reveal any oversights, points likely to create resistance, errors in judgment, and other issues that may not be visible from your perspective.

Once you've secured another perspective, sleep on the decision and revisit it later. By freshening your view, you can likely see places in your thinking that need tweaking, facts or data you may have overlooked, and risks in a more discerning light.

These tips can help you stay the course and produce true business value for every decision. As you work more with the decision intelligence framework, you'll improve at it, because practice does do that for a person. Along the way, you'll likely devise your own list of tips and shortcuts to teach others how to do it, too.

Chapter 18

Bias In, Bias Out (and Other Pitfalls)

hough decision intelligence is a multiuse decision methodology, it is most often used to gain more value from AI. Though not responsible for errors in AI, the two share some common pitfalls.

Given that AI is automated decisions and that decision intelligence is a framework for making decisions, it should come as no surprise that these two elements also share common problems with decisions made using other methods.

A Pitfalls Overview

Shared pitfalls include, but are not limited to:

» Biases

» Wrong or flawed assumptions

» Guessing rather than accurately estimating

» Defaulting to consensus

- » Failing to consider alternatives

- » Losing sight of purpose

- » Suffering from tunnel vision

- » Truncating debate

- » Relying on too little (or too narrow) information/data

All of this is to say that there is no foolproof way to make a sound decision.

The wiser course is to be diligent and to always be on guard for common flaws and pitfalls in order to prevent or eliminate them from your decision-making. Failing to do so will inevitably lead you astray, no matter which framework, mathematical formula, method, or technology you use.

The next few sections look at some real-life examples of how AI decisioning pitfalls can result in real harm.

Relying on Racist Algorithms

A healthcare algorithm used by hospitals across the U.S. to predict which of some 200 million people were likely to require additional medical care turned out to be biased in favor of white people. Interestingly, race wasn't one of its variables. But a variable that correlated with race was all it took to skew the results. That variable was healthcare cost history. Other variables that correlate with race, such as income or addresses, could cause a racial bias as well, but those weren't variables in this case.

At first glance, you might assume that healthcare cost history would be bias free, but comparing base, average, or total healthcare costs for the period lacks nuance and context. For several reasons — including lack of trust, transportation, and access — people of color incurred lower healthcare costs than white people for the same health conditions. The algorithm predicted people of color to be healthier than they were, and white people to be sicker, so that more healthcare resources went to the white group.

Though this unintentional but egregious error was made by an algorithm, it could just have easily been made on a standard spreadsheet. Check your work to make sure events like these don't warp your outcomes.

Following a Flawed Model for Repeat Offenders

Meet an AI called COMPAS, which stands for Correctional Offender Management Profiling for Alternative Sanctions, used by U.S. court systems. COMPAS predicted which offenders were likely to offend again. The AI rendered twice as many false positives on black offenders as white.

Risk assessments are a primary use case for AI, and the court systems were simply trying to follow a prudent path in managing risks — in this case, recidivism. Researchers found flaws in the COMPAS data, model, and process behind making the algorithm. One significant problem was in the survey of prisoners, a population containing a higher concentration of black offenders. But here again, race wasn't a variable. The problem here was a sampling bias because the survey wasn't representative of all offenders.

Using A Sexist Hiring Algorithm

In 2015, Amazon discovered that its hiring algorithm was biased against women. That AI had been trained on data consisting of résumés submitted to Amazon by job applicants over the previous ten years.

It turned out that the majority of those résumés happened to be submitted by men. The AI "learned" to favor terms used in men's résumés and to discredit female-oriented keywords such as *women's* or the name of female-only universities. Amazon caught the problem and made repeated attempts to correct it before more or less abandoning the project.

Redlining Loans

Redlining is a practice that determines risk by neighborhood based on race alone. Politicians and civil servants responsible for local, state, and federal housing policies, in partnership with financial lenders that issue loans for a variety of needs, have historically used maps made by the government to draw a redline around "undesirable" and "high risk" neighborhoods based on the concentration of non-white residents.

Though many public and private lenders are trying to eliminate the practice, AI-based loan approval systems have picked up the practice merely by being trained on loan applications from years past.

Not all decision intelligence projects involve AI. But that doesn't mean that they're problem free. Even if you're making a relatively simple decision or using simpler tools like spreadsheets and SWOT tables, you need to watch for obstacles that can lead you to the wrong conclusion.

The next few sections look at some common pitfalls in any type of decision.

Leaning on Irrelevant Information

Having more variables and more data isn't always a good thing. Make sure the data you're weighing in your decision-making process is directly relevant to the problem — and discard anything else.

Falling Victim to Framing Foibles

How you frame the problem, question, or scenario you're trying to make a decision about heavily influences your approach and interpretations. Make sure that fear of loss, desire for gain, or emotional involvement in the project doesn't shape how you frame the decision to be made or lead you to defend the indefensible. Constantly reevaluate decisions as time and events progress, and stay emotionally neutral.

Being Overconfident

Being overconfident is a trap for confirmation bias. Most people over value what they know and discount what they don't know. To back up both assumptions, they look for anything in the decision-making process to confirm their stance. Check ego and overconfidence at the door. This exercise isn't a test of what you know, but rather a map through a sea of uncertainties. If you go off-road chasing something else, you've defeated the purpose of using decision intelligence.

Lulled by Percentages

Most humans will take more risks when the risks are presented in terms of percentages. That's because too many folks fail to do the math. What seems like a little can be a lot: 1 percent might mean 10 million people or five bags of corn. It's relative, in other words. Finish the math to get a better grasp on what's at stake before you make a decision.

Dismissing with Prejudice

The human tendency is to discount things that sound extreme even when they're not. Guard against dismissing information that you feel is too extreme or doesn't meet your firsthand (but badly outdated) experiences and knowledge of the situation. Don't dismiss information without rechecking your own biases and memories first. Remember always that facts change. You need to be operating with (and not dismissing) new facts.

It helps to have a team working on making decisions for the enterprise to help guard against these issues. Further, you need to put a policy in place so that everyone in your organization knows what steps to take to ensure better decisions going forward.

Index

D

D3.js, 112

Dark Web, 128

DARPA (Defense Advanced Research Projects Agency), 142–143, 172

data
  augmented, 49–50
  big, 26, 127
  clean, 33
  following, 27
  incomplete, 282
  as information, 26–31
  missing, 282–283
  open, 128
  partial, 282
  partial versus incomplete, 282
  stolen, 128
  synthetic, 49–50
  virtual, 49–50
  wrong, tracking, 255

data analysts, 124

data analytics
  actionable outcomes, 32
  anomaly detection, 14
  autonomous systems, 16
  chatbots, 15–16
  classification and categorization systems, 15
  common use cases for, 14–16
  conversational systems, 15–16
  versus decision intelligence, 21
  identifying patterns in, 48–52
  and math, 43
  pattern recognition, 15
  personalization systems, 15
  pointers, 13
  predictive modeling, 15
  recommendation engines, 15
  ruts and roams of, 29–30
  sentiment and behavioral analysis, 15

Database as a Service (DBaaS), 107

data-centric systems, 70

data collection specialist, 125

data corruption, 276

data democratization, 13–14, 90

data drift, 160

data-driven model, 17, 47, 83, 107, 126, 225

data engineers, 14, 119, 124

data lineage tracking
  data tagging, 276
  lineage by parsing, 277
  pattern-based tracking, 276–277
  self-contained, 277
  tools, 277

Datameer, 112, 277

data mining
  boxed-in thinking in, 29–32
  goal of, 26
  job roles in, 14
  and machine learning, 29
  overview, 25
  pointers, 27–28
  and querying, 29
  traditional processes in, 30

data mining engineers, 14

Data Mining for Dummies (Brown), 28, 31, 85

data mining specialists, 14

data platforms, 23, 112

data science
  versus decision intelligence, 28
  versus decision science, 75–77
  overview, 12
  role in decision intelligence, 157–163

data science leader, 119

data scientists
  as bad question-makers, 46–47
  job role in AI, 14
  leveraging current roles, 120–121
  overview, 117–118
  roles of, 126, 260
  upstream decision-making, 234

data sidekicks, 257–259

data singularity, 48, 82

data sources
  checking, 275–276
  expanding notion of, 161–163

data strategists
  demand for, 124
  hiring, 125–126
  roles, 118
  talent and skills, 126

feature stores, 135, 160

Federal Trade Commission (FTC), 141

FICO Decision Management Platform, 22

financial key performance indicators, 189–190

finger pointing, 265

Fitzgerald, F. Scott, 244

FlexRule Decision Automation Platform, 193

fluidity, in business models, 247

follow the leader, 136–137

formulary, 125

framing, 77–78, 264, 288

Frankenstein data, 139

FreePlane, 241

F. Scott Fitzgerald test, 244

FTC (Federal Trade Commission), 141

Fusion 360, 243

FusionCharts, 23, 113

G

gambler's fallacy, 264

garbage details, 255

general business, 76

General Data Protection Regulation (GDPR), 15, 97, 141

geneticists, 259

geographical visualizations, 279

GLBA (Gramm-Leach-Bliley Act), 97

GNU Octave, 243

goals, 245–246

Goal Seek feature, 218–219

Google

  Analytics, 106

  Assistant, 16, 19, 252

  AutoML, 111

  Big Query, 107

  Charts, 23, 113

  Cloud AI platform, 23

  Flu Trends, 169

  Sheets, 186, 190, 217–218

  Workspace Marketplace, 218–219

Grafana, 113

Gramm-Leach-Bliley Act (GLBA), 97

gross profit margin, 189

group thinking, 92

growth share matrix, 191

gut instincts

and decision theory, 153–154

mistaking for decision science, 64–65

H

Hadoop, 39, 53, 57, 73, 127

Hanning, Uwe, 12, 28

HCD (human centered design), 155

healthcare, 76

healthcare algorithms, bias in, 287

healthcare records, 128–129

Health Insurance Portability and Accountability Act (HIPAA), 97

helicopter crashes, 49

heuristics, 75, 78–79, 89, 137

high ground domain, in organizational politics, 267

Hinton, Geofrey, 145

HIPAA (Health Insurance Portability and Accountability Act), 97

hiring algorithms, sexist, 287

human centered design (HCD), 155

human decisions

  adding, 88–90

  and decision theory, 151–152

  and ego, 137–138

  gut instincts, 153–154

  intuition in, 154

  versus machine decisions, 51–52

  and management science, 155

  mental errors in, 136–137

  overview, 151

  single individuals, 163–164

  social sciences in, 155–156

  teams, 163–164

human expertise, 35–36

human integrators, 211

human relationship management, 211

human rights, 268–269

hyperautomation, 270–272

I

IBM, 111

iBuying, 165

icons, in this book, 6

Ideaboardz, 241

working capital requirements (WCR), 189
World Economic Forum, 93
wrong data, tracking, 255
W.W. Norton & Company Inc., 52

X

XAI (explainable artificial intelligence), 107, 143–144, 172
Xnor.ai, 107

Y

Yahoo, 39

Z

Zillow, 165–166
zombie projects, 254

About the Book Author

Pam Baker is a veteran industry analyst and freelance journalist. Her work is published in many leading publications including, but not limited to, *Institutional Investor*, *Ars Technica*, *CIO*, *CISO*, *InformationWeek*, *PC magazine*, *The Economist Intelligence Unit*, *The Linux Foundation*, *TechTarget*, *Dark Reading*, and many others. She's the author of several previous books and a popular speaker at science, healthcare, and technology conferences. Her speech on mobile health data and analytics has been published in the *Annals of the New York Academy of Sciences*. Former analyst engagements include research and reporting for ABI Research, VisionGain, and Evans Research. She is a member of the National Press Club (NPC), the Society of Professional Journalists (SPJ), and the Internet Press Guild (IPG).

For LinkedIn bio, references, and clips, check out https://www.linkedin.com/in/pambaker/.

Dedication

To Nana Duffey, Stephanie Baker Forston, and Donald "Ben" Baker. I love you all dearly. Thanks for always being my inspiration and support team through this and other writing marathons. To you three and the rest of our bountiful family, you are my world and the reason I do everything that I do. Thanks to all for rocking my world.

Author's Acknowledgments

In the best of times, producing a book is a huge undertaking requiring many highly skilled and creative people to manifest it in the real world. I offer my deep gratitude to the many people who made this book possible and made it far better than I could have done alone.

However, this book project was plagued with obstacles on my end, including several family members catching COVID-19 (but fortunately surviving it), my own surgery, and a looming trial for the DUI driver who killed my brother. Through it all, the Wiley editorial and production team never blinked and together we finished the book on time. There are simply no words for such empathy, compassion, and dedication. I offer my profound but woefully inadequate thanks to each of you for going above and beyond without a single word of disgruntlement. My life is better for having known and worked with you.

I extend a huge thanks to all the people who've helped me produce this book. Thanks so much to Meta S. Brown, for your technical edits. Also, I extend a huge thanks to Elizabeth Stilwell, Paul Levesque, Becky Whitney, and the rest of the editorial and production staff at Wiley. Many thanks also to Steven Hayes for making this book possible.

Publisher's Acknowledgments

Acquisitions Editor: Steven Hayes
Senior Project Editor: Paul Levesque
Copy Editor: Becky Whitney
Tech Editor: Meta S. Brown

Production Editor: Mohammed Zafar Ali
Cover Image: © Gorodenkoff/Adobe Stock Photos